IMAGES
of America

The Arizona State Fair

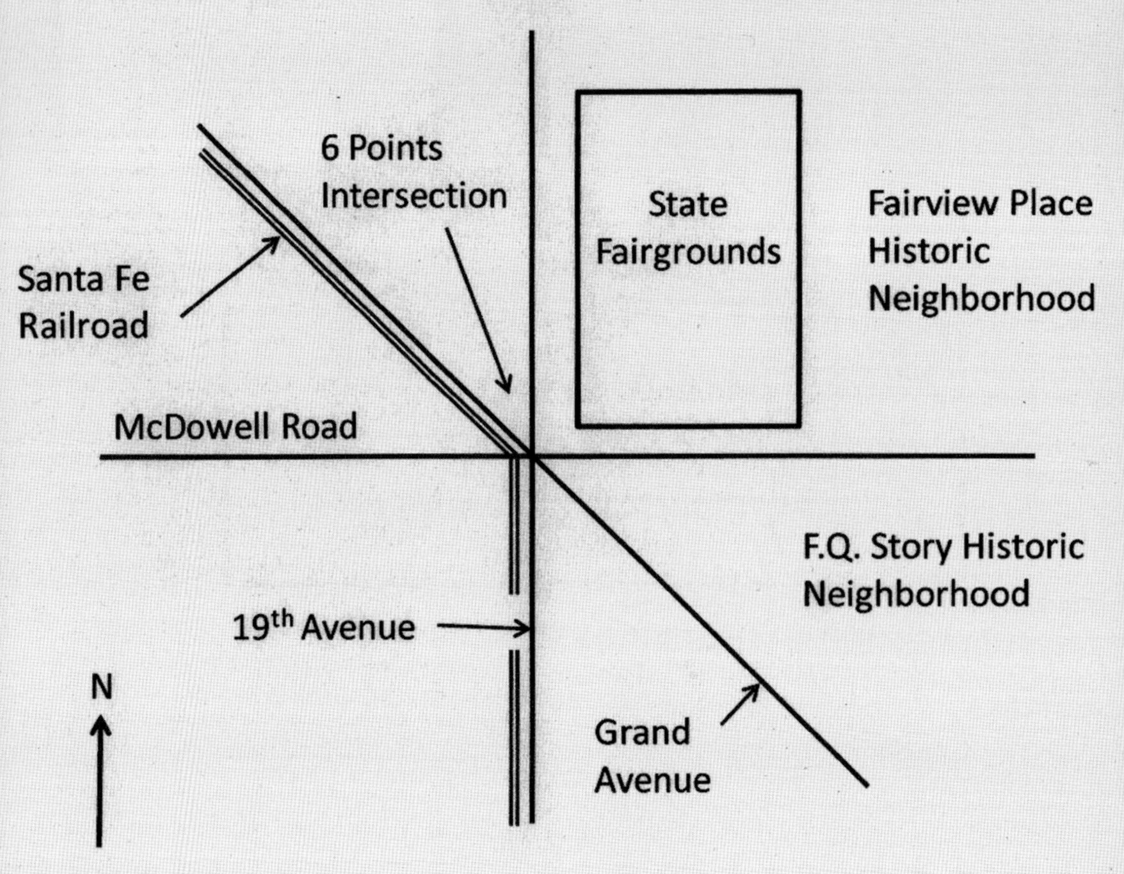

The location of the Arizona State Fairgrounds is at Six Points. The intersection is comprised of Grand Avenue, West McDowell Road, and North Nineteenth Avenue. Grand Avenue was known in territorial days as the Lower Fort McDowell–Wickenburg Wagon Road. Vintage homes in F.Q. Story, Fairview Place, Villa Verde, Del Norte, Encanto-Palmcroft, and Willo surround the historic fairgrounds. (Courtesy of Derek Horn.)

On the Cover: The beautifully buffed and groomed white-faced Herefords are ready to be judged in the show ring. The Arizona National Livestock Show began in the late 1940s to stimulate interest and pride in Arizona's agricultural heritage. The livestock show is held annually at the end of December on the Arizona State Fairgrounds. (Courtesy of the Arizona National Livestock Show.)

IMAGES
of America

The Arizona State Fair

G.G. George

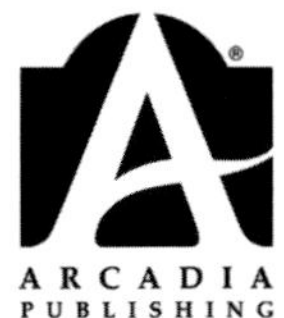

ISBN 978-1-4671-2520-8

Published by Arcadia Publishing
Charleston, South Carolina

Printed in the United States of America

Library of Congress Control Number: 2016952598

For all general information, please contact Arcadia Publishing:
Telephone 843-853-2070
Fax 843-853-0044
E-mail sales@arcadiapublishing.com
For customer service and orders:
Toll-Free 1-888-313-2665

Visit us on the Internet at www.arcadiapublishing.com

Contents

Acknowledgments

Many people assisted me with this book, and to each of the following, I extend my profound gratitude: Alyssa Jones, Matt Todd, and Liz Gurley, Arcadia editors; Edward Jensen; Derek Horn; John Jacquemart; Patrick Neary; Paul R. Jones; Allan Starr, Brian Bucher, Bill Kinnerup, Mel Martin, and the Phoenix Jaycees; Karen Womack Vold; Terry Johnston; Wanell Costello, Jack Bell, and Meg Anema, Arizona State Fair; Ann Woosley, Rebekah Tabah Percival, and Linda A. Whitaker, Arizona Historical Society; Rob Spindler and Elizabeth Dunham, Arizona State University Libraries and Special Collections; Jared Smith, Tempe History Museum; David Rock, Arizona Science Center; Ed Lebow, Inger Erickson, Michelle Dodds, and Kevin Weight, City of Phoenix; Jean Barry, Arizona Room, Phoenix Public Library; Wendi Goen, Arizona State Library Archives and Public Records; Col. Joseph E. Abodeely (US Army, retired), director of Arizona Military Museum; Rochell Planty and Dean Fish, president, Arizona National Livestock Show; Rebecca Heller, Western Spirit: Scottsdale's Museum of the West; Deborah Spotts, director of development, Phoenix College; the Encanto Citizens Association; the Arizona State Fairgrounds Stakeholders Group; and the many friends who shared stories and photographs from their personal collections.

INTRODUCTION

The Arizona State Fair has been a popular event for well over a century. The eagerly awaited annual tradition has consistently drawn large crowds with a range of attractions, including top-name stars, bands, rodeos, food booths, carnival games, farm animal displays and competitions, home arts exhibits, and rare experiences, such as elephant and camel rides. The arena events have included the Ice Follies, tractor pulls, and professional sports.

As you explore this history, you can imagine what it was like to listen to barkers along the midway, remember all-star rodeos, and appreciate the skills of hobbyists. You could see famous early racehorses and the record-breaking airplane *City of Yuma*. The fair typifies the romance of the frontier and the still vivid glamour of the cowboy way of life.

The modern fair had its origins when Phoenix was a much smaller town. In November 1884, the first territorial fair, known as the "Arizona Industrial Exposition," was held beside the sometimes dry, sometimes wildly flowing Salt River. Local businessmen promoted their home territory by showcasing what marvelous things could be accomplished in the arid desert environment.

Had you been there, you could have seen pony, horse, and mule races, along with handsome beef cattle and prize dairy specimens. Agricultural exhibitions included fruits and vegetables that grew large and glorious, thanks to widespread desert irrigation provided by a network of prehistoric canals, a legacy of the vanished Hohokam people. Jack Swilling, a townsite founder, recognized the potential and expanded the canals. Expositions were held annually until 1891, when the raging Salt River overflowed its banks, destroyed buildings, and eliminated the event for the next 15 years.

The Arizona Territory proved alluring to newcomers, attracting Eastern and Midwestern entrepreneurs. Three of these individuals, F.Q. Story, Gen. M.H. Sherman, and John C. Adams, created the Six Points area, which was to become the home of the fair.

The neighborhood known today as the F.Q. Story Historic District was mapped in 1867–1868. The area was bounded on the west by the Lower Fort McDowell–Wickenburg Wagon Road. In 1887, F.Q. Story purchased the acreage and partnered with General Sherman in the design and construction of the diagonal Grand Avenue thoroughfare. Referring to the 1888 improvements, a headline in the *Phoenix Daily Herald* read, "Straight as a line, level as a floor." By 1889, the Grand Avenue streetcar line extended to Six Points, and by 1893, the line was electrified. The rail line along Grand Avenue was completed in 1895, connecting Phoenix to Prescott and the rest of the world via the Santa Fe Railroad.

Attorney John C. Adams arrived from Chicago in 1894 and quickly became a community leader, being elected mayor in 1897 and 1905. He saw the potential and accessibility of the Six Points location (see page 2). Interested in demonstrating the prowess of his Arizona-bred racehorses, he decided another territorial fair was in order after a hiatus of 15 years. Being mayor, as well as owner of the grand Hotel Adams, he had the influence and the means to create his dream. Adams organized a syndicate that purchased 80 acres at Six Points in 1905, stretching from McDowell Road to Encanto Boulevard and from Nineteenth Avenue to Seventeenth Avenue, which became the fairgrounds.

The early development of the property included two racetracks, a grandstand, and several elegant brick buildings, all of which were in place by the opening of the Arizona Territorial Fair in 1905. The Arizona Territorial Fair transitioned into the Arizona State Fair in 1912 when Arizona achieved statehood.

Fairs flourished until 1918, when the fair was canceled because of the Spanish influenza epidemic. Again, in 1921, the cotton crop failure halted the fair for one year. In 1933 and 1934, the state did not fund a fair. However, the tradition was continued with an "Ag Show," hosted by the Arizona Farm Bureau Federation, in 1933. The National Guard hosted an industrial exposition in 1934 and provided an incentive for fair revival. However, six years would pass before another fair took place.

The Great Depression affected everyone, and on October 2, 1933, the *Prescott Courier* reported, "Arizona's first federal camp for transient men and boys was officially opened today at the state fairgrounds." The fairgrounds became the site of various New Deal programs during that era as buildings were constructed that exist today. Those programs provided money to reconstruct the 1905 grandstand, which burned and was rebuilt in 1936–1937, as well as two immense cattle barns in 1937. The Works Progress Administration (WPA) erected the Civic Building as Arizona's headquarters on the grounds in 1938.

Fairs resumed in 1940 but were discontinued from 1942 through 1945 because of World War II. The 81st Infantry Wildcat Division bivouacked on the fairgrounds. The grounds were used for military vehicle repair and the Ordnance Service Command Shop. As the railroad was nearby, the cattle barns sheltered troops overnight.

Diverse events have attracted crowds to the fairgrounds over the years. They included the Phoenix Jaycees Rodeo of Rodeos; book sales by the Volunteer Nonprofit Service Association; the annual Junior League Rummage Sale; the Arizona National Livestock Show; huge circuses; superstar concerts, including an early Elvis Presley after his Army stint; car shows and swap meets; home, garden, antique, and gun shows; school graduations; and the Maricopa County Fair.

The Veterans Memorial Coliseum hosted the Phoenix Suns Basketball team for 34 years; the Phoenix Roadrunners hockey team; Pope John Paul II; Mother Teresa; former president George W. Bush; and presidential candidate Barack Obama.

The state fairgrounds, which began as an event space, has proven to be much more over the last century. Possibly the most unusual event in its history occurred in the aftermath of Hurricane Katrina in 2005. The executive staff of the Arizona State Fair was called into former governor Janet Napolitano's office and directed to prepare shelter in the Veterans Memorial Coliseum for thousands of evacuees fleeing the devastated areas. The evacuees had no idea what awaited them as they boarded planes in New Orleans for Phoenix. The gigantic coliseum was effectively turned into a mini-city. Professionals and volunteers coordinated everything from food, clothing, and temporary shelter, to medical care for humans and animals, job assistance, and housing.

Arizona residents were honored to help by contributing to the relief effort. A great many lined up at the fairgrounds entrance on McDowell Road, waving welcome signs as busloads of people arrived from the airport. There was such an outpouring of support from Arizonans wanting to help that well-wishers were finally asked to participate by way of organized relief efforts rather than just showing up at the gate.

Throughout its life, the Arizona State Fairgrounds has been many things to many people. From the best place to show off Arizona's bounty to a place of refuge for victims of natural disasters, this small piece of ground has been a gift of nature and man.

One

From Territory to Statehood

Visualize the dusty, arid streets of the original Phoenix townsite: cowboys in town for supplies or a haircut with their horses hitched to a rail on Washington Street and one or two women shopping for necessities. Streets were sparsely populated. Imagine seeing Native Americans, Mexicans, and even a glimpse of the infamous Baron of Arizona, James Addison Reavis-Peralta.

Desirous of creating an educated society, citizens organized the Phoenix Elementary School District in 1871. Churches, newspapers, and merchants helped the territory evolve. Phoenix incorporated in 1881, and the small town came to life.

Residents in the wild territory wanted an event in which everyone could participate, and in 1884 the first Arizona Territorial Exposition was held. The exposition occurred annually on the banks of the river at Central Avenue until 1891, when all was washed away by the raging Salt River. No more fairs were held on that site.

Visionary early citizens were banding together for eventual statehood. In preparing for the grandeur to come, the territory had mounted exhibits and sent representation to the 1876 Centennial International Celebration in Philadelphia, the Chicago Columbian Exposition of 1893, and the Louisiana Purchase Exposition of 1904 in St. Louis.

In 1905, John C. Adams, owner of the Hotel Adams and mayor of Phoenix, organized a banquet and invited leading businessmen without divulging the intent. During dinner, Adams spoke about the advantages of a fair and his grand plan. It would have the best racetrack in the country with other modern accoutrements, like a grandstand and brick buildings. The plan was foolproof. Adams announced that the legislature had passed a bill appropriating money for buildings and maintenance the previous year. That evening, a new Arizona Territorial Fair Association was organized, and Adams became president. The association purchased land at Six Points for the fairgrounds, the fair site today. The territorial fairs resumed in the fall of 1905, transforming into the state fair in 1912.

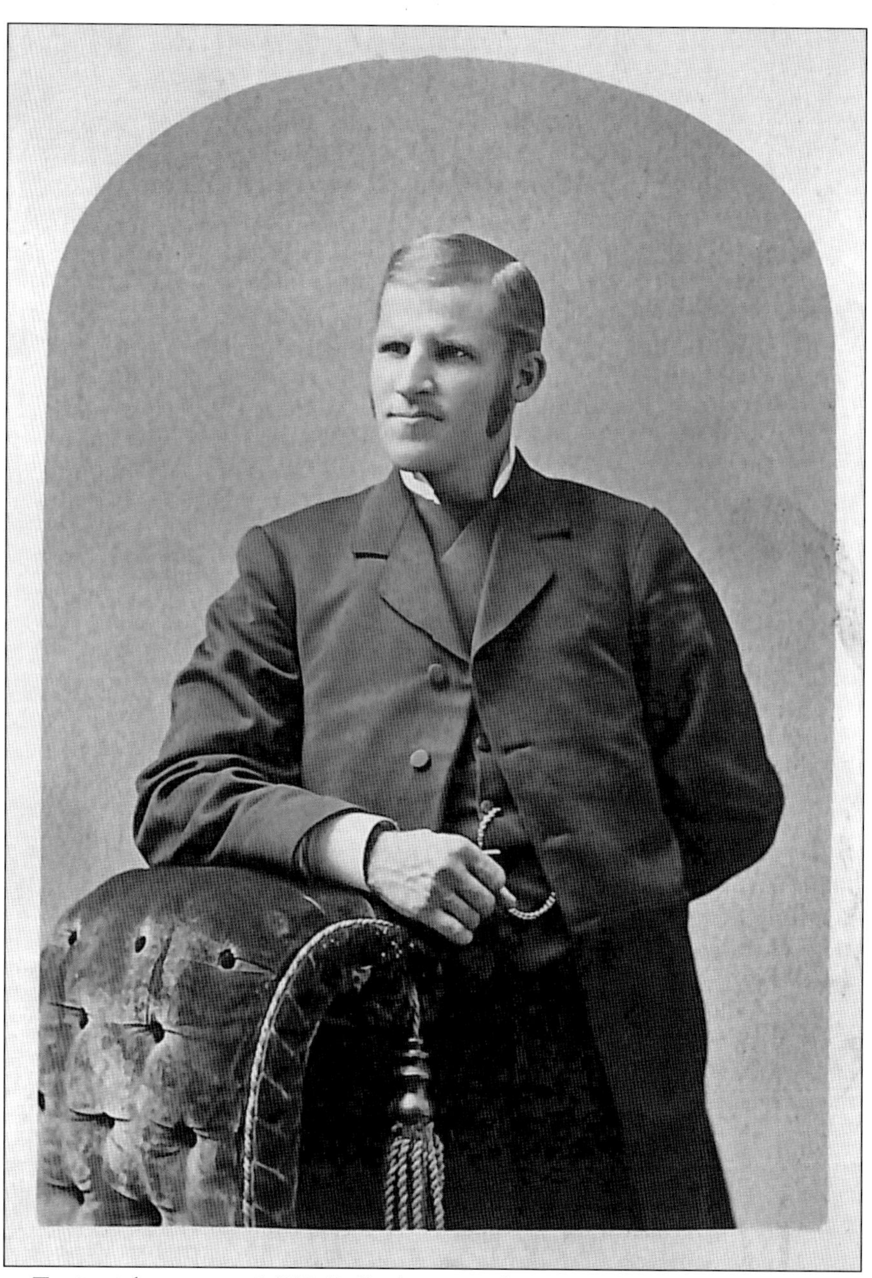

Arizona Territorial governor A.P.K. Safford recruited 20-year-old Moses Hazeltine Sherman to teach school in Prescott in 1873. By 1876, Prescott had built a new school with Sherman as principal. That same year, he represented Arizona at the Centennial International Exhibition in Philadelphia, above. Sherman was named Arizona adjutant general in 1883, and thereafter, he was referred to as General Sherman. Ever entrepreneurial, he eventually moved his operations to the valley and cofounded the Valley Bank with W.J. Christy. By 1887, Sherman headed the Valley Street Railway Company with its horse-drawn cars. The company expanded and was electrified by 1893, which was the better for taking crowds to Six Points, the area that would become the fairgrounds. Sherman, F.Q. Story, and John C. Adams were pivotal business pioneers who created the environment in which the territorial fair could flourish. (Courtesy of the Sherman Library.)

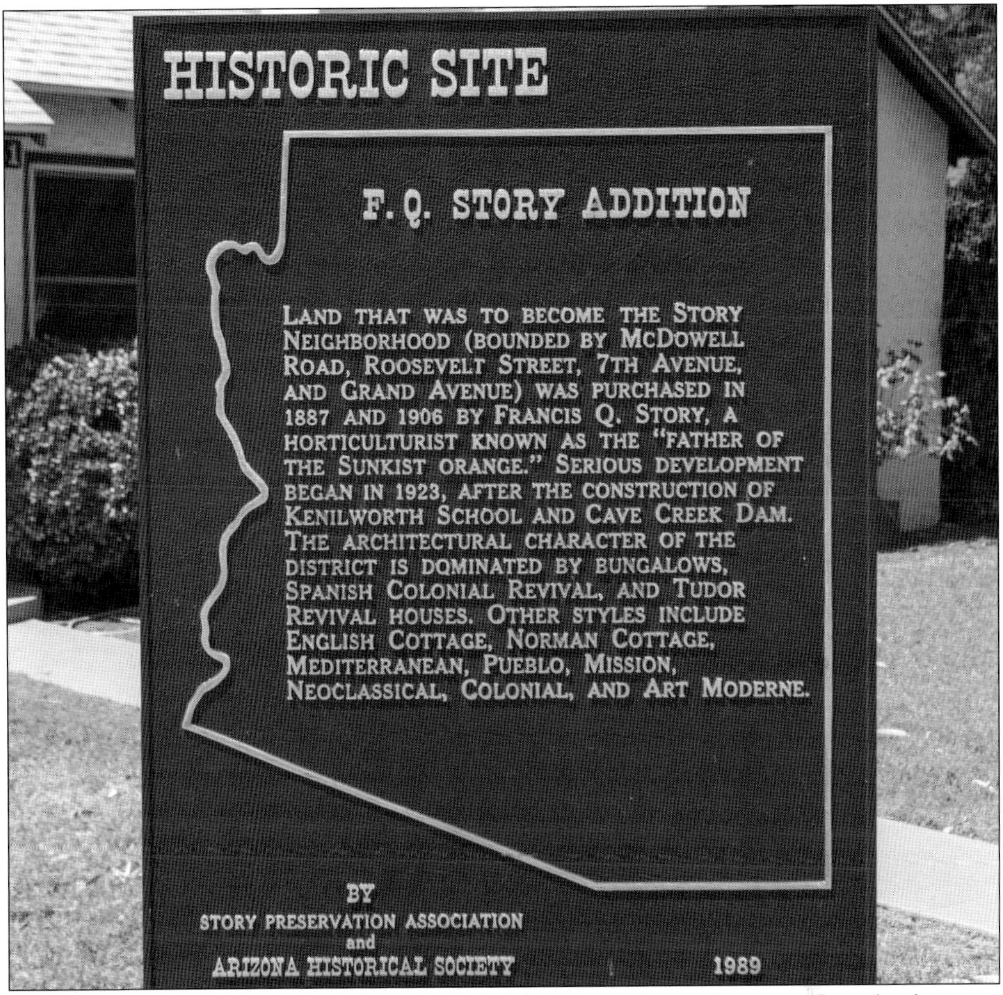

Francis Quarles Story recognized the potential of Arizona and owned property here, but he never made his home in Arizona. A wool merchant from the East, Story had originally traveled to California for health reasons. He became an important leader in the California citrus industry and is credited with being the father of the Sunkist Orange advertisements. He recognized the potential for citrus in Arizona. Story purchased acreage in 1887 that became the area known today as the F.Q. Story Historic District, above. He was involved with M.H. Sherman in the development of Grand Avenue in 1888, and the streetcar line that ran along the western edge of Story's land holdings. The restored Franklin Police and Fire High School, below, is on a portion of Story's original holdings. (Above, courtesy of Edward Jensen; below, courtesy of Encanto Citizens Association.)

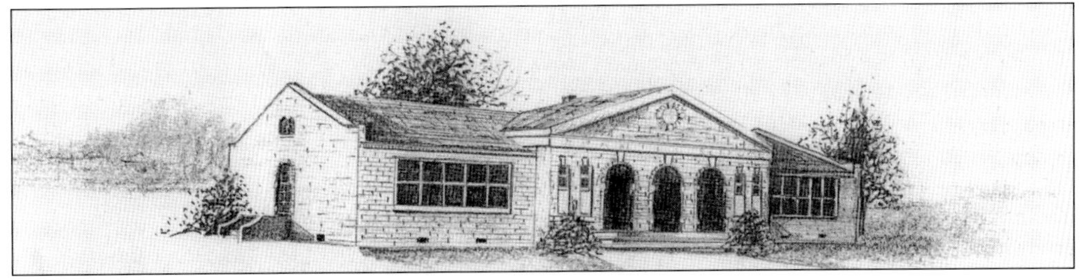

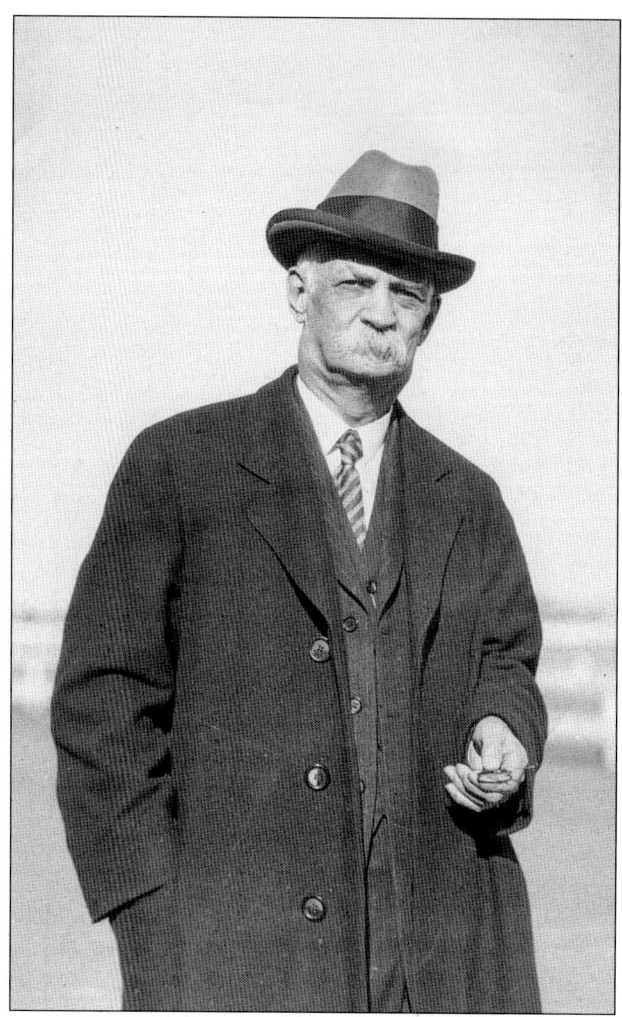

Arizona Territory proved a magnet at the end of the 19th century for progressive thinkers. Chicago lawyer John C. Adams, left, had seen the Arizona exhibit at the Chicago Columbian Exposition of 1893. He arrived in Phoenix in 1894 and was elected mayor in 1897 and 1905, taking office at city hall (pictured below). He owned the elegant Hotel Adams (see page 36) and became the vital force in the creation of the new fairgrounds. Adams had cultivated contacts in the territorial legislature to revitalize the concept of the fair. In 1905, he hosted a sumptuous dinner for potential backers at his hotel to unveil his ideas. Attendees enthusiastically supported the idea and formed a syndicate, and the fair was reborn. In 1905, the territorial fair opened at Six Points with brick buildings and the finest racetracks west of the Mississippi River. (Left, courtesy of McClintock Collection, Arizona Room, Phoenix Public Library; below, courtesy of Picture the Past Antiques.)

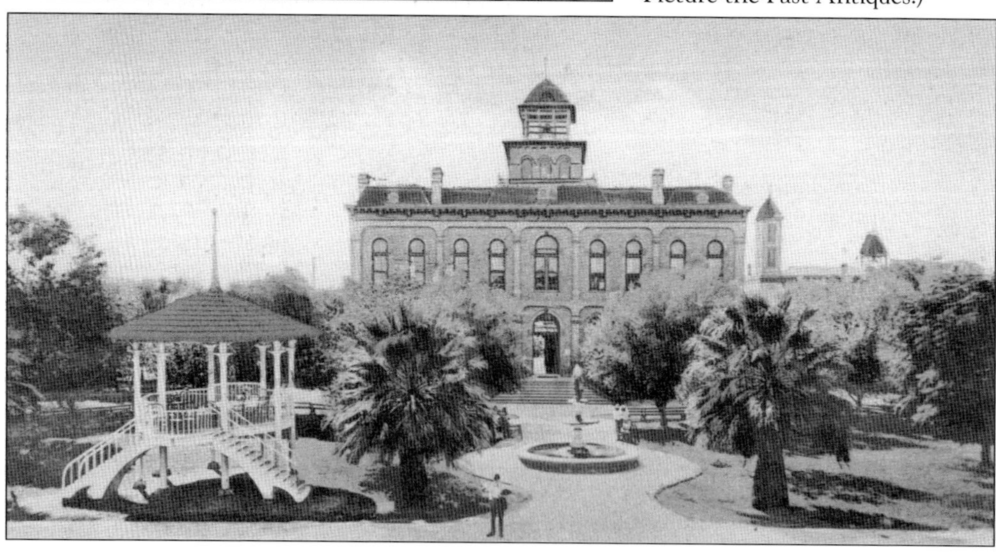

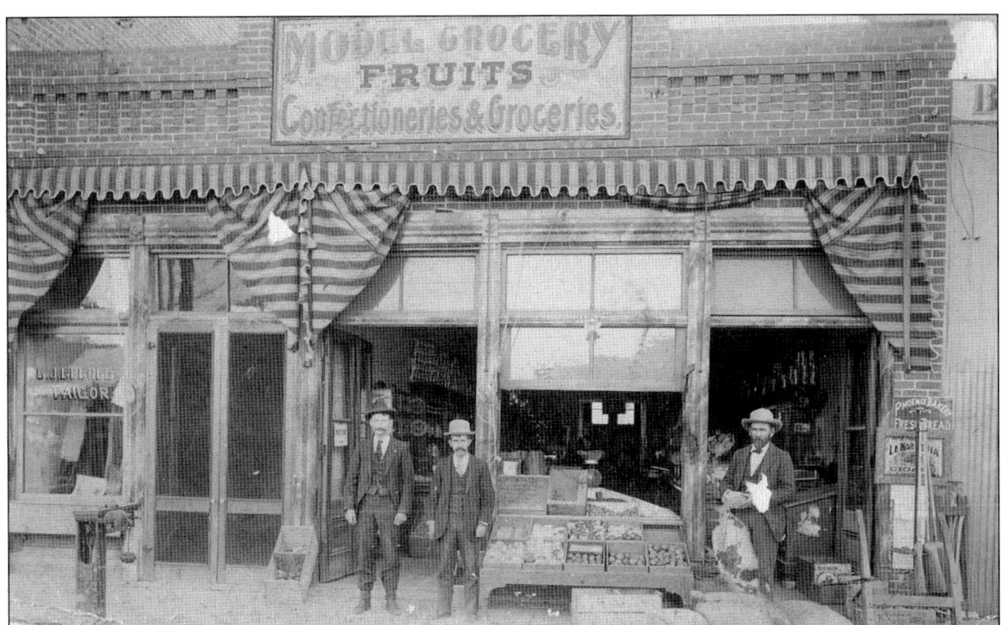

Immigrant Charles Donofrio arrived in Phoenix with $10 in 1887. He was one of the new arrivals who would help build Phoenix. He made a deal with a Washington Street merchant to sell oranges in front of his establishment in exchange for sweeping the store. After a return trip to Italy, Donofrio returned in 1891, opening the Model Grocery at 39 East Washington Street, above. Donofrio moved into the fruit business on a grand scale in 1896 by purchasing the entire Salt River Valley strawberry crop of 750,000 boxes. He invented Cactus Candy, sold at the fair. Donofrio is shown third from left, below, at one of his establishments. (Both, courtesy of Kim Koldoff Kasper.)

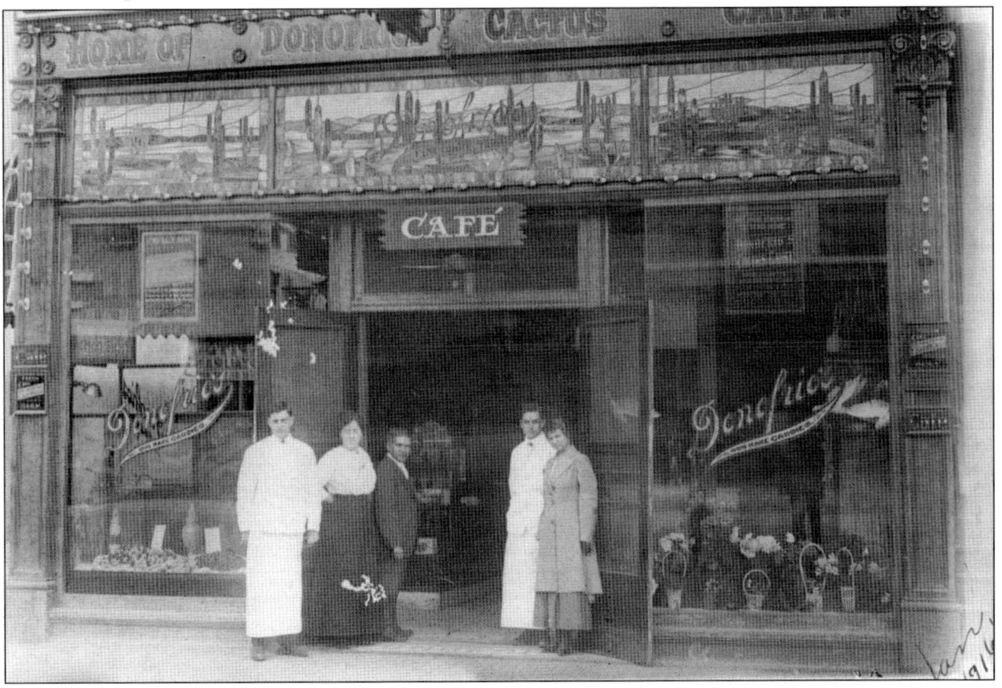

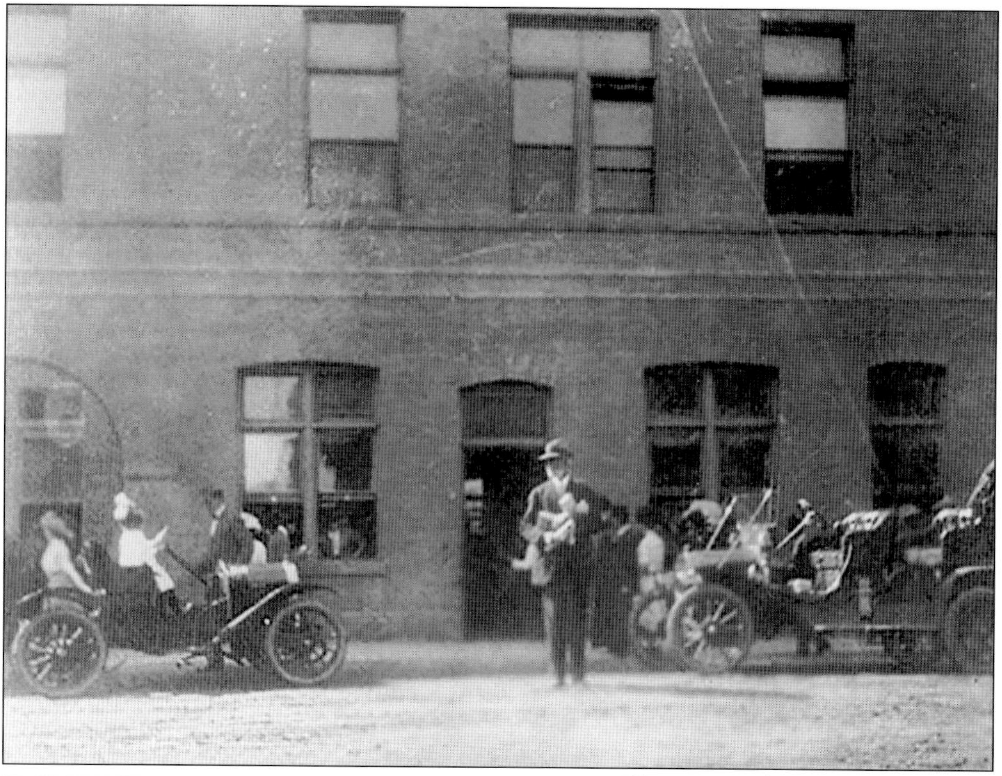

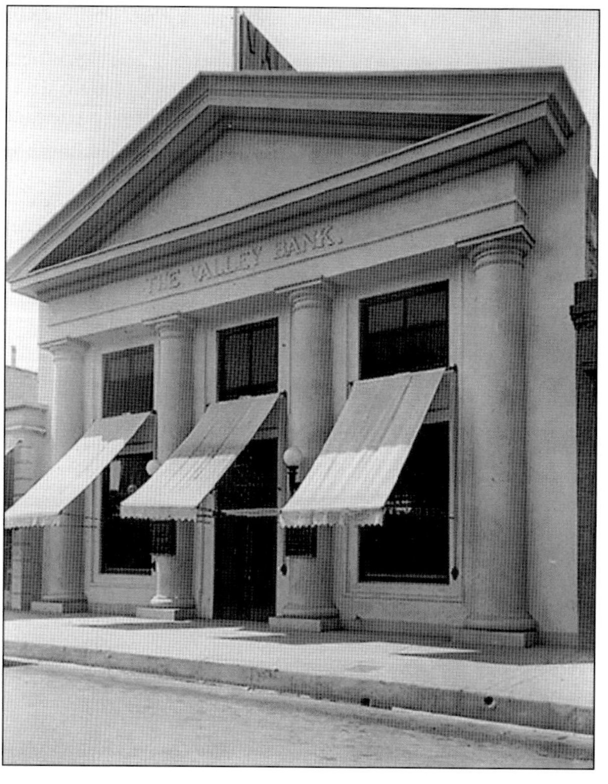

Phoenix was becoming sophisticated by the turn of the 20th century, and many wooden or adobe structures were giving way to bricks and mortar. The first post office opened in 1869 with Postmaster J.W. Swilling, the discoverer of the ancient canal watering system. This building, above, was the newer Territory of Arizona Post Office, photographed in 1904. The first cars had arrived in Phoenix in 1900. The Valley Bank, at left, was founded by entrepreneurs M.H. Sherman and W.J. Christy. This Greek Revival building showcases the elegance Phoenix leaders aspired to for their town, which was fast growing into a city. (Both, courtesy of the McClintock Collection, Arizona Room, Phoenix Public Library.)

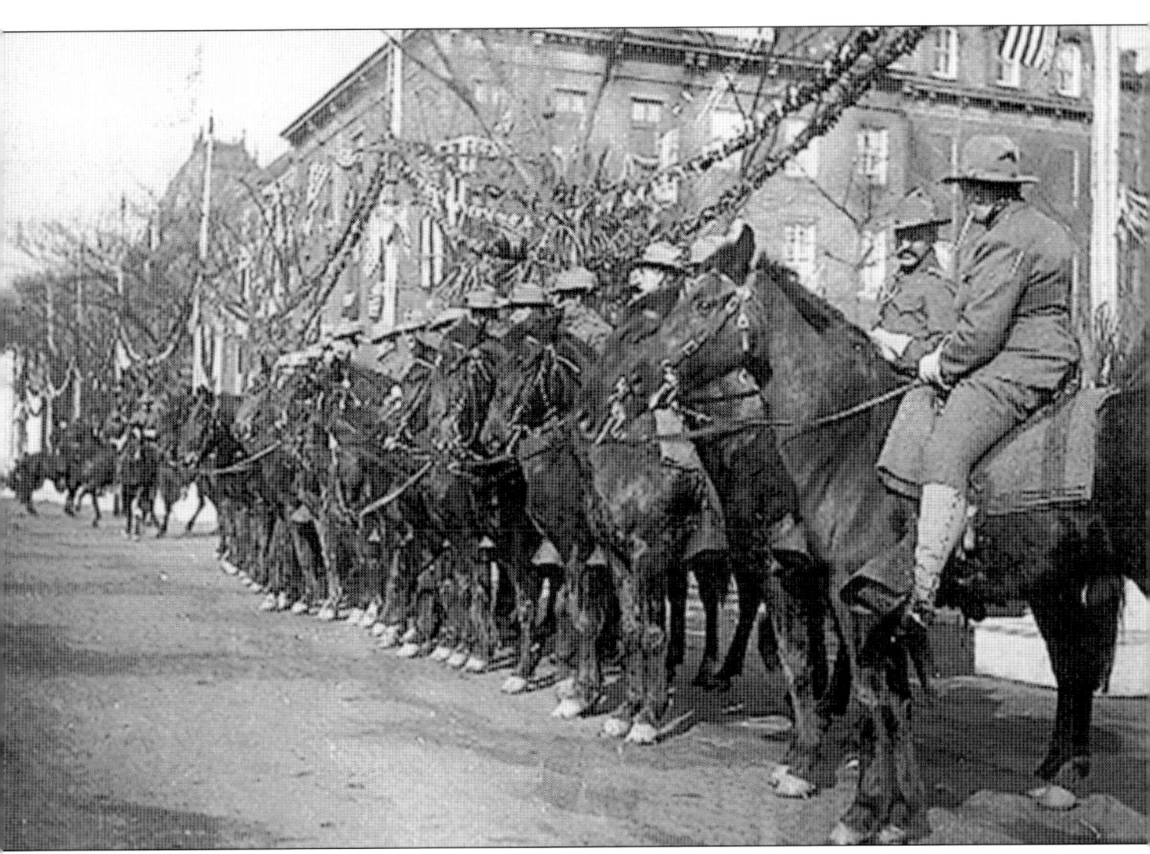

The Rough Riders, above, provided the escort at Theodore Roosevelt's first presidential inauguration on March 4, 1905. Roosevelt had assumed the presidency after President McKinley's assassination in 1901, serving the next three years. An avid outdoorsman, Roosevelt was familiar with the fact that Western states had been prone to either too much or too little water. The Federal Reclamation Act, passed in 1902, allowed for the construction of irrigation works for the reclamation of arid land. In 1906, construction began on Roosevelt Dam to control the Salt River, which had washed away the original fairgrounds. Roosevelt had warm memories of Arizona, as he noted several times on his visits to the state, most notably at the dedication of Roosevelt Dam in 1911. Dwight Heard purchased the *Arizona Republican* newspaper to advocate for Roosevelt's presidential campaign in 1912. (Courtesy of the McClintock Collection, Arizona Room, Phoenix Public Library.)

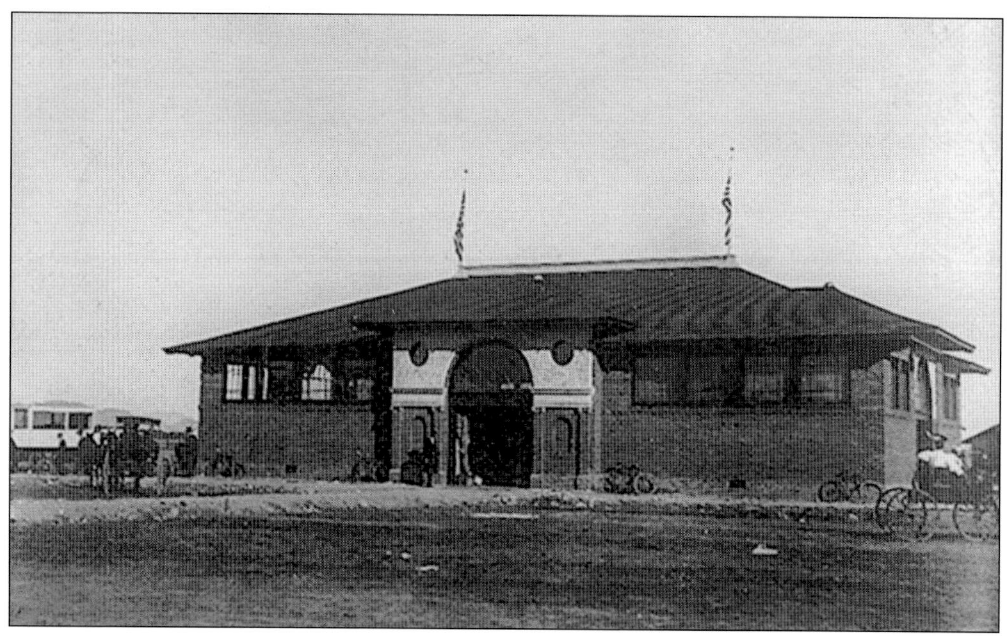

The 1905 territorial fair opened to great enthusiasm in Maricopa County but exhibited the richness of all Arizona counties. Originally set for early December, the opening had to be postponed to the last week of the year due to a severe rainstorm. The newly constructed main exhibit building on the grounds was referred to as the Women's Building, shown above, as it displayed the needle arts, education, and agricultural bounty. Several new buildings at the Six Points Fairgrounds argued for a bright future for a territory aiming for statehood. The sturdy Mining Building, pictured below, showcased the riches of copper mines and other minerals in Arizona. (Above, courtesy of the McClintock Collection, Arizona Room, Phoenix Public Library; below, courtesy of Jack Bell, Arizona State Fair.)

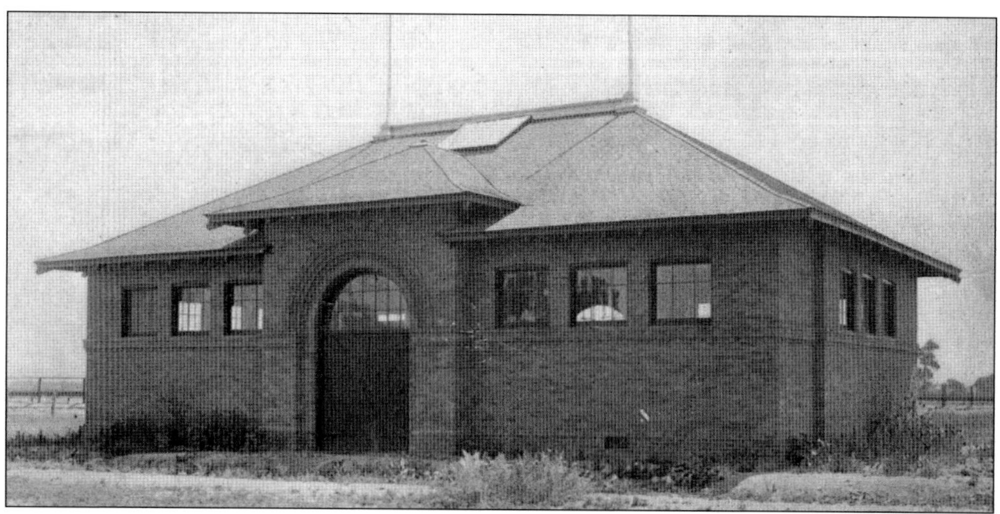

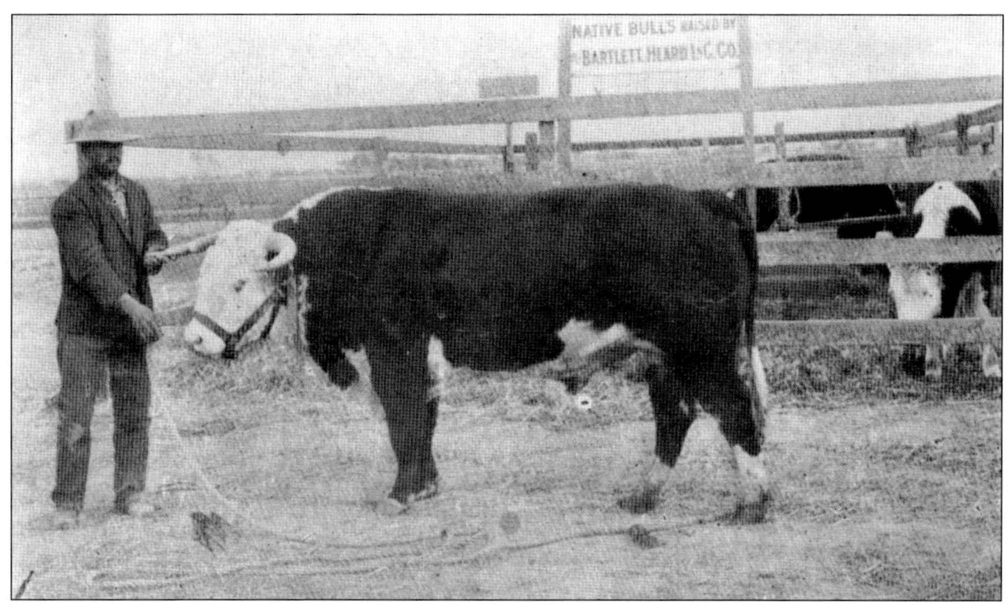

The sign above this magnificent Hereford bull shown at the 1905 fair reads, "Native Bulls Raised by Bartlett-Heard Land and Cattle Company." Dwight B. and Maie Bartlett Heard had arrived in Phoenix in 1895, from Chicago, and quickly became leaders in the community. Dwight Heard was the third president of the Arizona Cattle Growers' Association. Showcasing the majestic racehorses and cattle developed in Arizona was a prime reason for staging the fairs. Pictured below, extensive wooden cattle barns and stables, located on what had formerly been an alfalfa field, were in place for the resumption of the territorial fairs in 1905. (Both, courtesy of Derek Horn.)

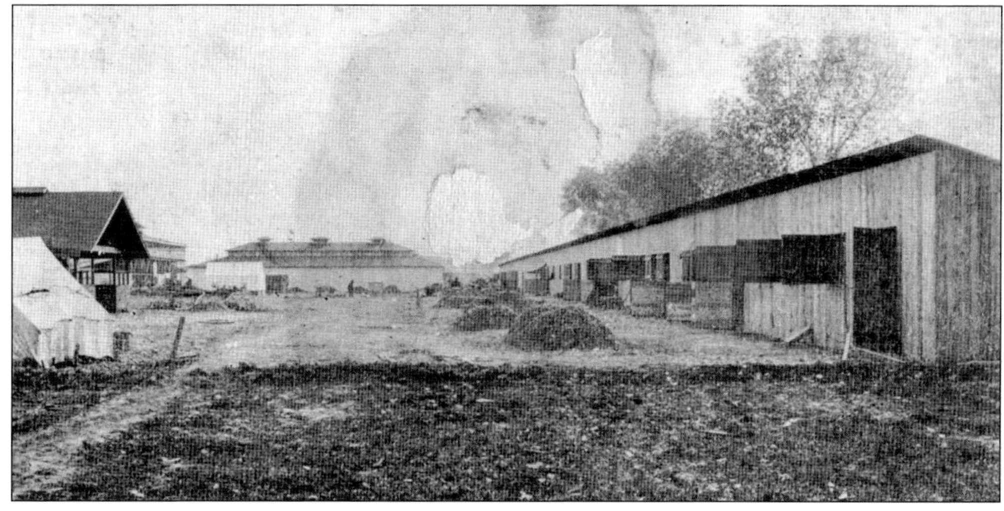

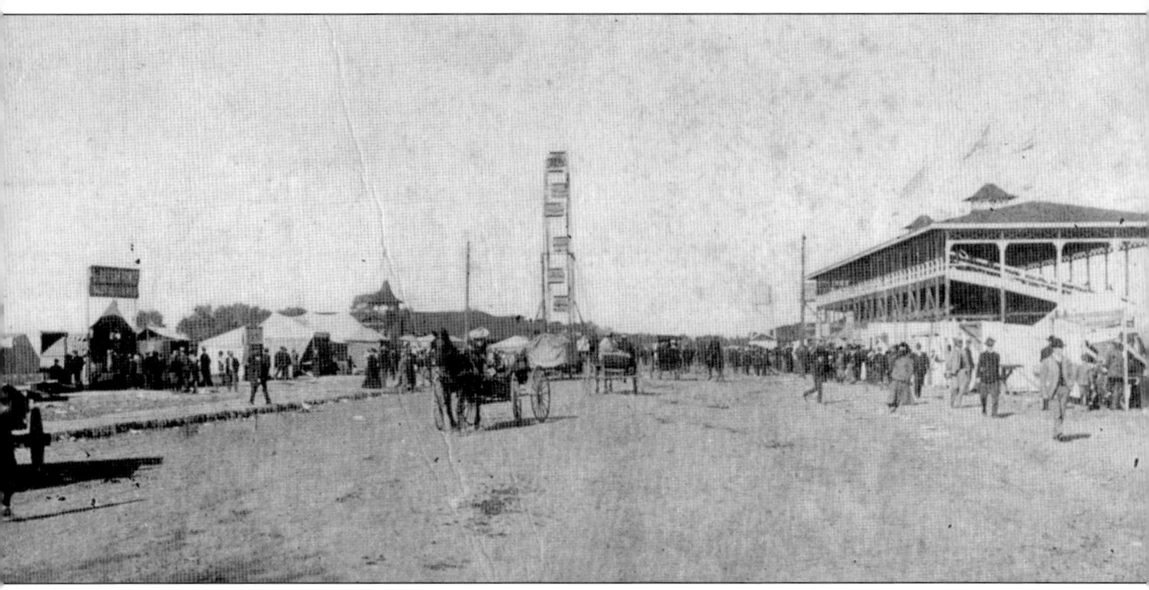

The Hassayamp, pictured above, was the name given the midway at the fair. The midway had food vendors and games of chance. The legend of the Hassayampa River foretells that, once an individual drinks from its waters, one does not speak the truth again. Andrew Downing came to Arizona in 1902 and was named poet laureate in 1915. His poem about the Hassayampa begins, "There's a legend centuries old / By the early Spaniards told / Of a sparkling stream that 'lies' / Under the Arizona skies / Hassayampa is its name/ And the title of its fame / Is a wondrous quality / Known today from sea to sea / Those who drink its waters bright / Red man, white man, boor, or Knight / girls, or women, boys or men / Never tell the truth again!" (Courtesy of Derek Horn.)

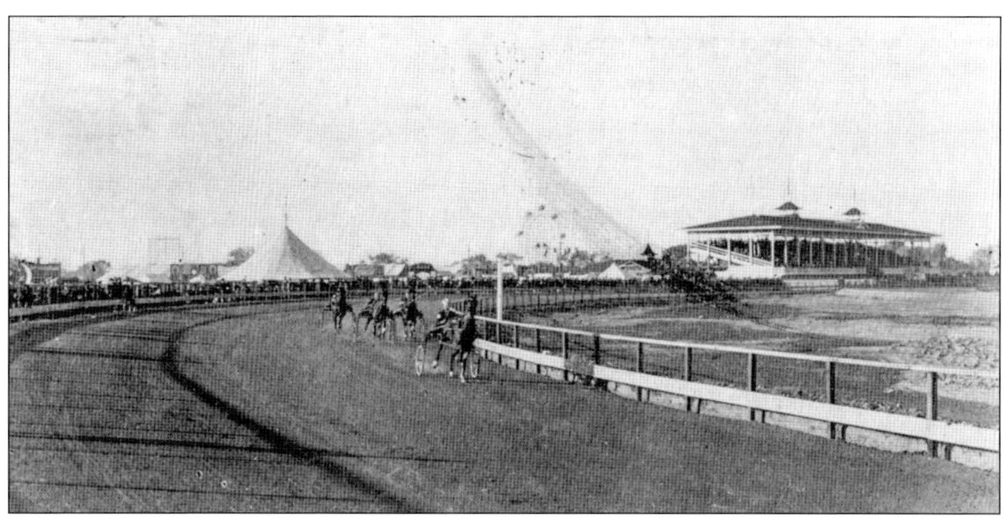

Hazel Patch, a famous trotter, is shown leading at the quarter at the initial fair; the horse set the track record of 2:05. Hazel was the daughter of the most famous stallion in the world at the turn of the 20th century, the champion harness racing horse, Dan Patch. Note the wooden grandstand, Ferris wheel, and large tent on the grounds, which added to the glamour of the setting. The judges are pictured in the elevated judge's station, below. The time clock that depicted Hazel's winning time is clearly shown. Arizonans wanted to make this a world-class fair and succeeded by attracting top names and attractions. (Both, courtesy of Derek Horn.)

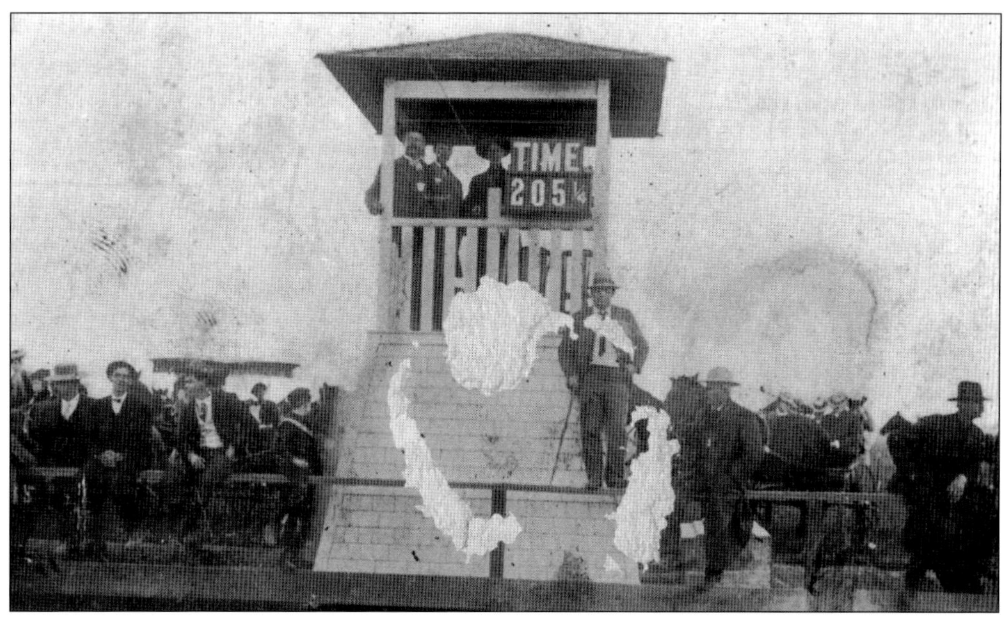

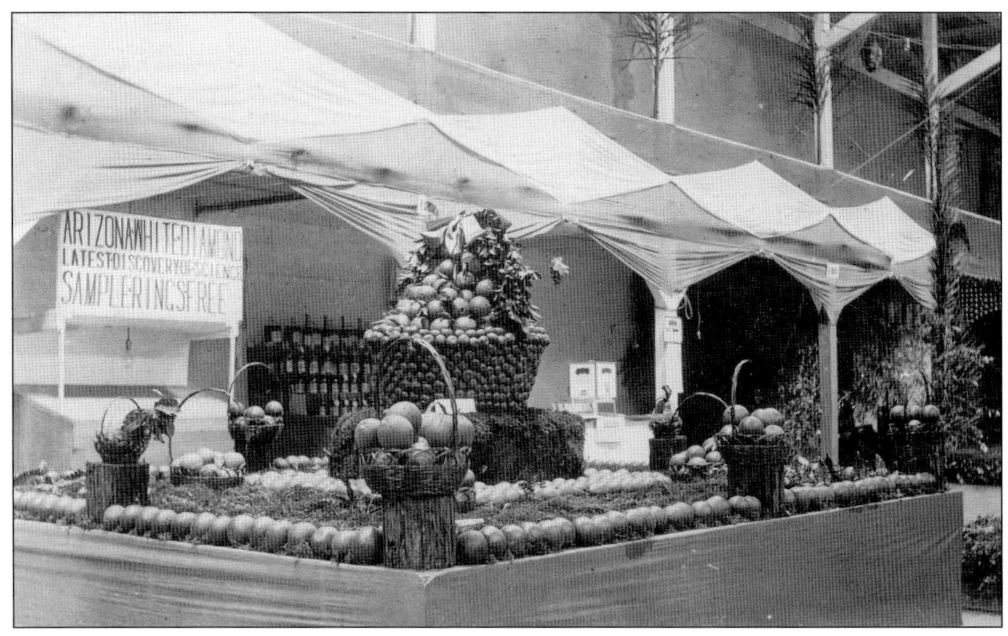

The revitalized system of prehistoric canals produced luxurious and desirable produce around Phoenix. The fruit stand, above, advertises Arizona White Diamond grapefruit as the latest discovery of science. The proud grower offered "Sampler Rings Free" as an enticement to try this innovation. The Lily Milk Special Delivery, shown below, which appeared in 1907 at the territorial fair, featured a milk cow that had been specially trained to pull a wagon. Milk was normally delivered by horse-drawn wagons. That exhibit had garnered first prize at the California State Fair and a banner at the Pasadena Tournament of Roses that year. (Above, courtesy of Jack Bell, Arizona State Fair; below, courtesy of the Arizona State Library, Archives and Public Records, History and Archives Division, Phoenix.)

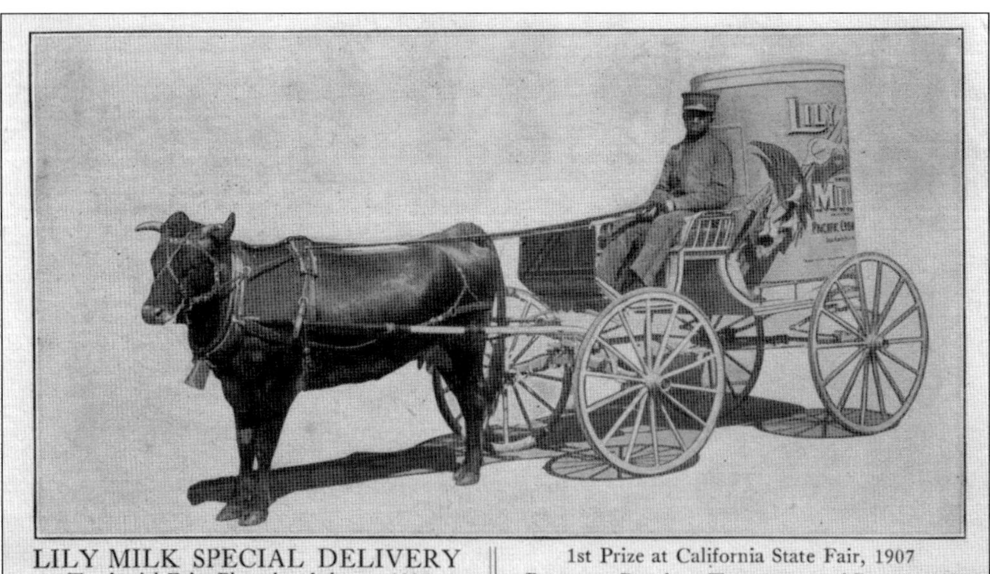

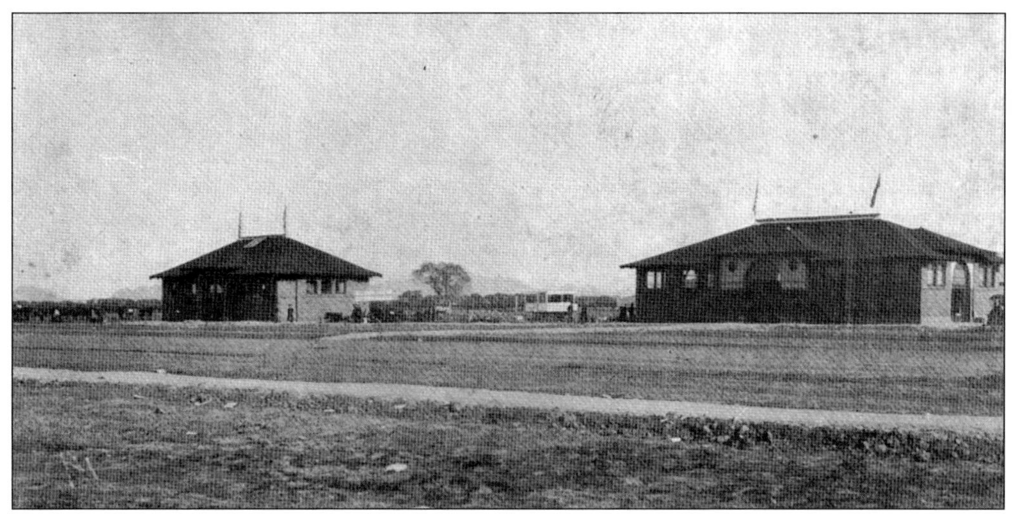

The juxtaposition of the original Mining Building and the Main Exhibit Building is shown above. Fair promoters spared no expense to showcase the Arizona Territory to citizens across the United States, thus attracting famous horses, car racing enthusiasts, and early airplane flights to the grounds. Dan Patch, shown below, was the most famous horse of his time in America. Known as "the Wonder" or "the Miracle Horse," Dan was a natural pacer. Ditties were written about the champion whose record of 1 minute and 55 seconds endured for 32 years. People flocked to see him trot at the fair from 1907 through 1909. (Above, courtesy of Derek Horn; below, courtesy of Tempe History Museum.)

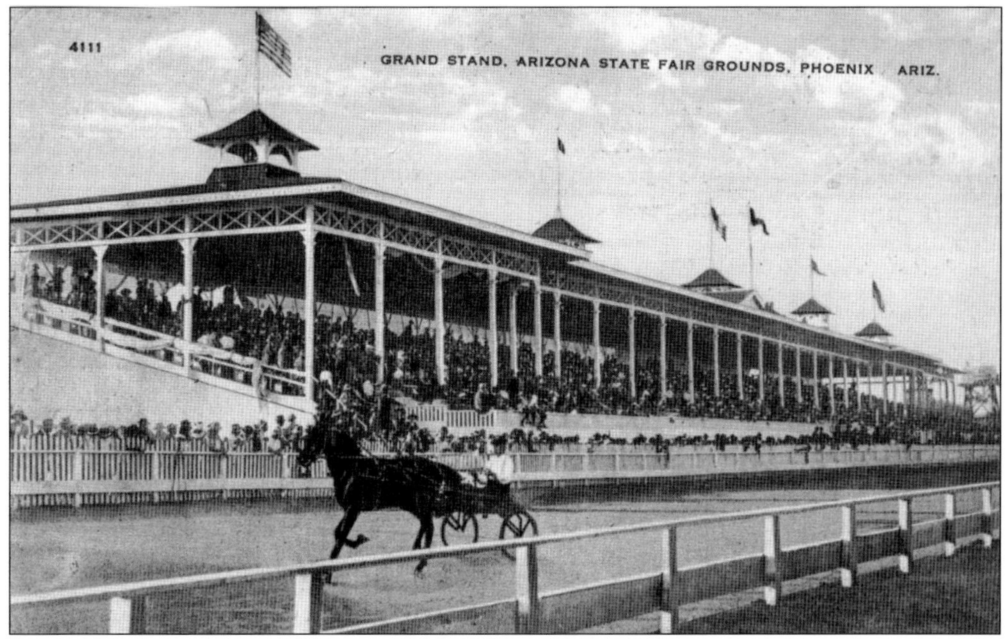

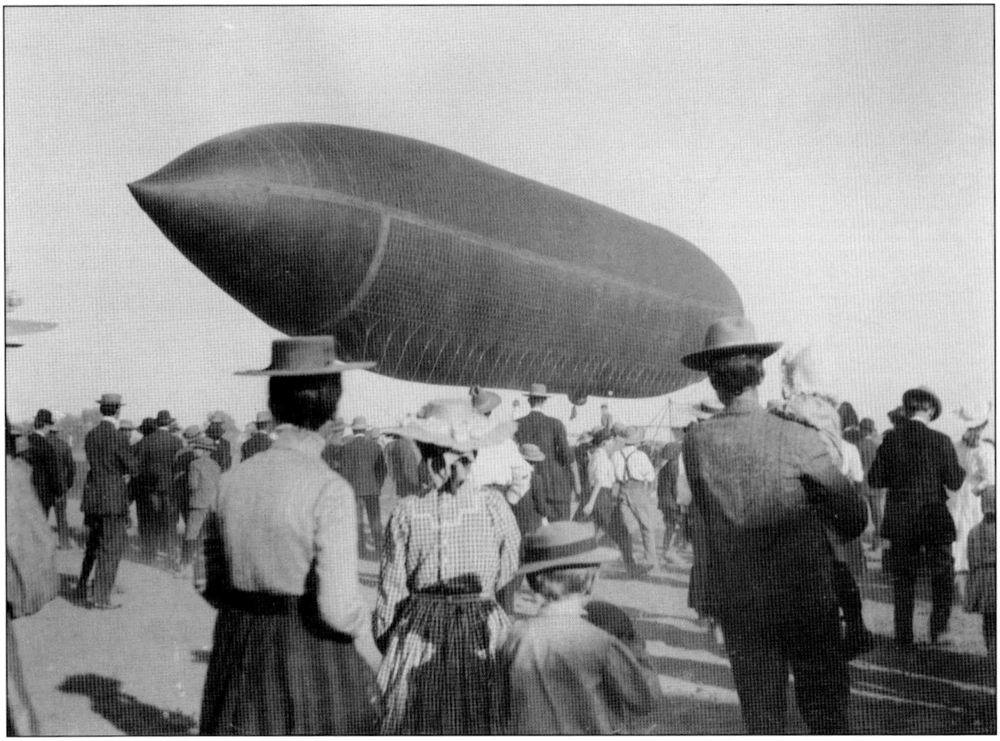

The first dirigible to make its debut at the fairgrounds was launched on November 9, 1908. A throng of adults and children gathered to watch the spectacle (above). Carrying pilot Roy Knabenshue and engineer George Duesler, the huge craft lifted off, and people looked on in amazement (below). Originally scheduled to fly over the Arizona capitol, the course was changed to go over downtown to make it visible to more people. Later that afternoon, Southern Pacific Railway agent L.H. Landis went up as a passenger and dropped 200 fliers out to advertise his transportation of choice. (Both, courtesy of Arizona Science Center.)

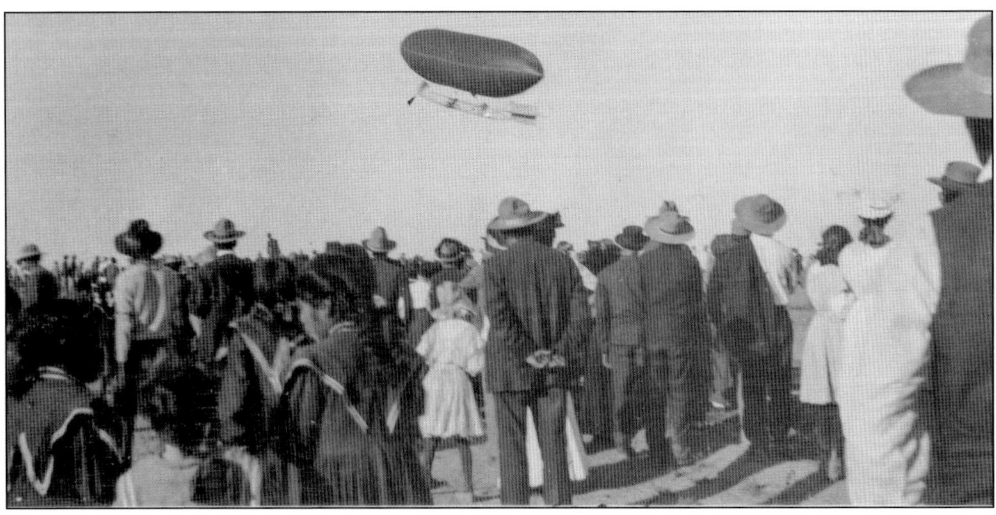

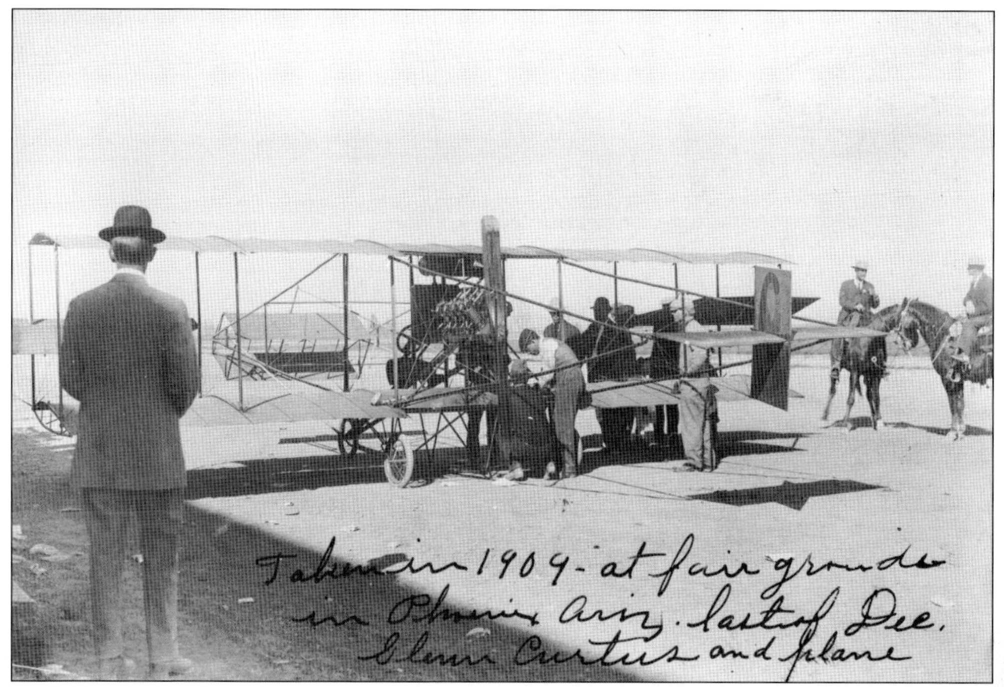

On December 31, 1909, famous aviator Glenn Curtiss, above, was aloft at the Arizona Territory Fairgrounds. As a member of the Aerial Experiment Association, Curtiss began flying in 1907. He piloted the *White Wing*, a heavier-than-air machine, in a flight of 1,017 feet in 1908. Management of the fairgrounds hosted two Phoenix Air Shows in 1910, one in February, below, and a second, less successful one in December. Another early aviator, Cal Rodgers, made the first pit stop at the fairgrounds in a coast-to-coast air race on November 2, 1911. His Wright EX biplane was named the *Vin Fiz* after the new grape soft drink by Armour. (Both, courtesy of Arizona State University Department of Archives and Special Collections.)

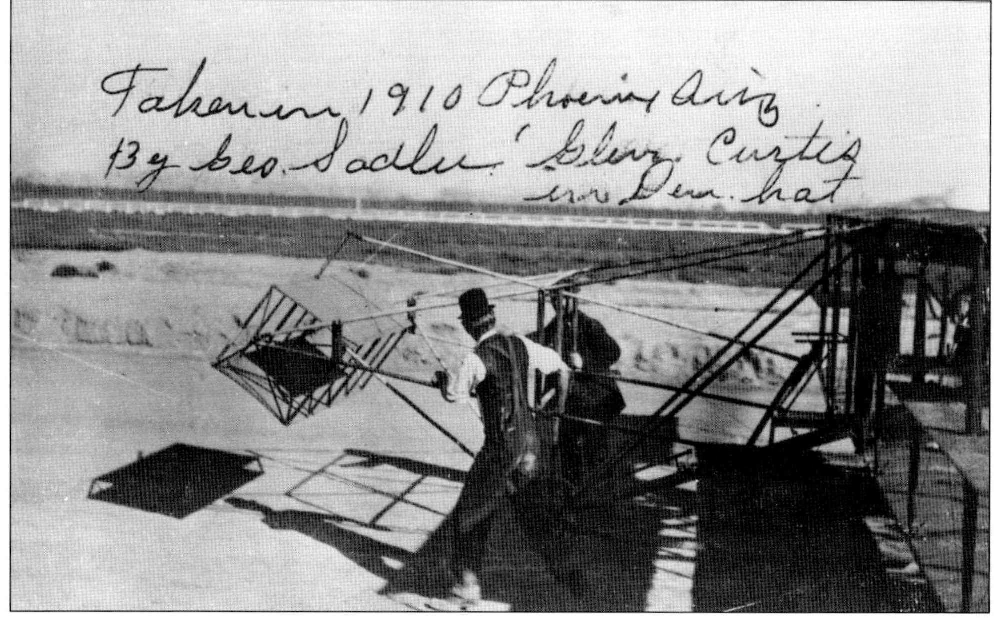

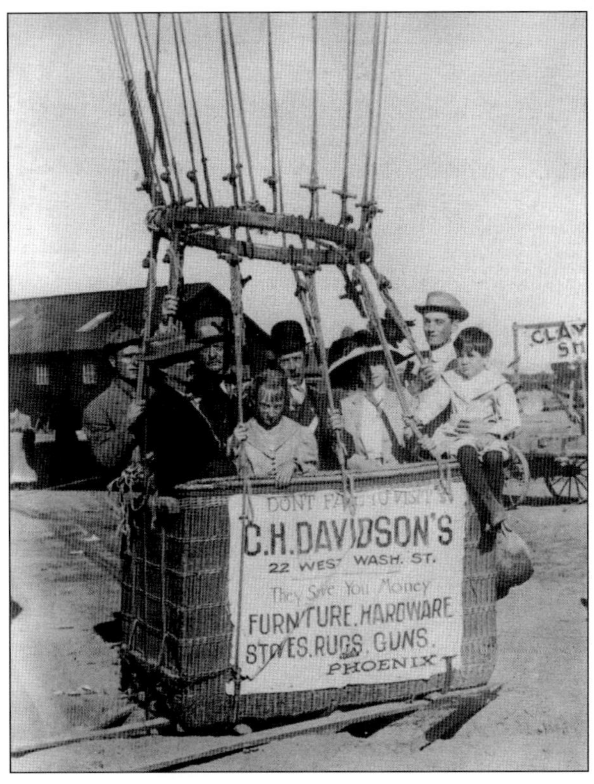

Residents were thrilled to see a balloon that could carry passengers at the early state fairs. The young girl on this balloon ride looks a bit skeptical. C.A. Davidson's mercantile establishment at 22 West Washington Street sold furniture, hardware, rugs, and guns, among other necessities of frontier life. The aerial image below of the dual tracks at the fairgrounds was taken from the passenger balloon in the photograph at left. It was a real point of pride that the fairgrounds boasted not one but two tracks. This balloon had a dual purpose, entertainment and advertising. (Both, courtesy of Arizona State Library, Archives and Public Records, History and Archives Division, Phoenix.)

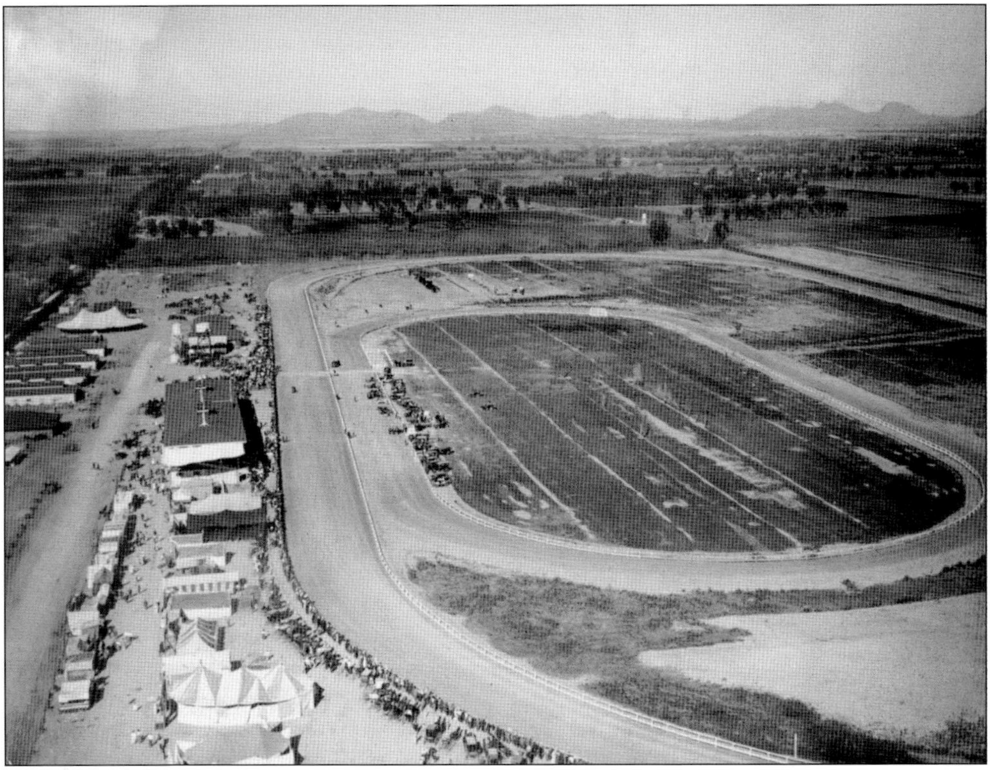

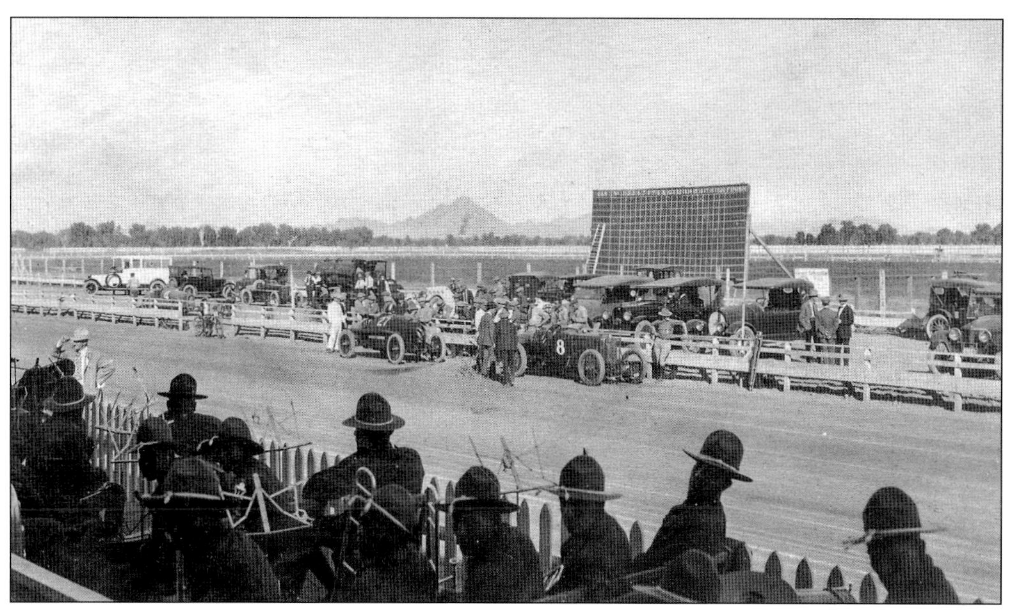

The excitement of speeding horses, airplanes, and cars was always a reason to attend the fair. The Cactus Derby, a road race starting in Los Angeles, going through Yuma, and ending in Phoenix, attracted racing fans as early as 1908. Races were over harrowing terrain or dangerous, unpaved roadways that could damage tires and the car body. In 1914, Barney Oldfield, the famous early driver, won the race. The Arizona State Fair held an inaugural road race from Douglas to Phoenix in 1916. Martin Gold's car had originally been declared the second-place finisher, but when the final times came in, his car was in third place. (Both, courtesy of Bob Bertram.)

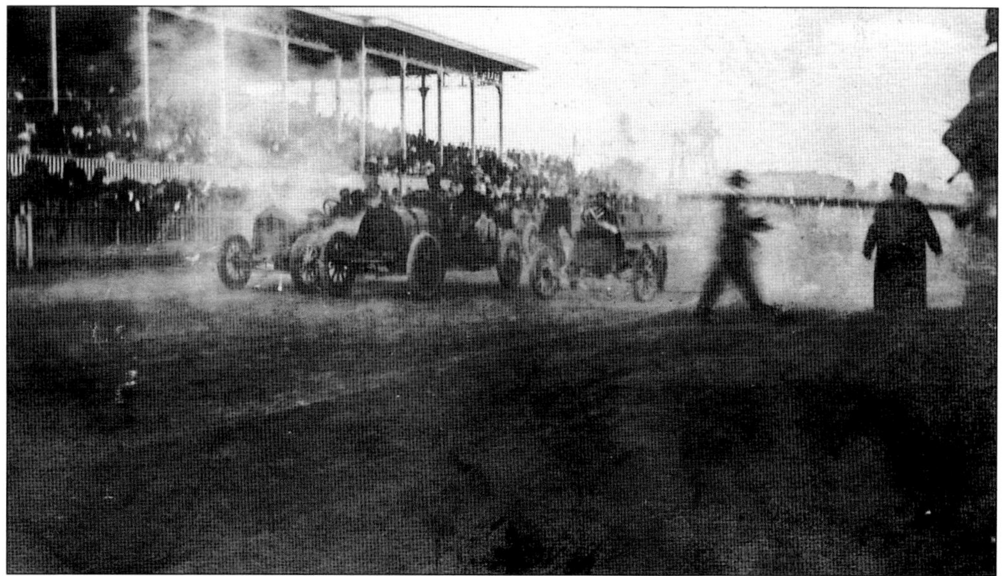

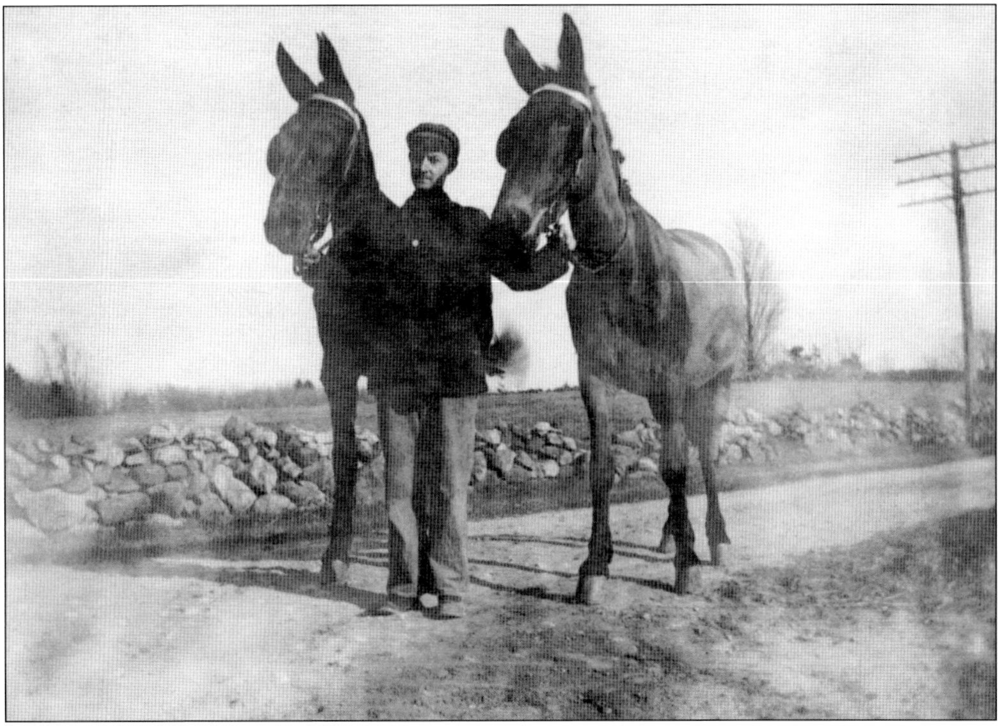

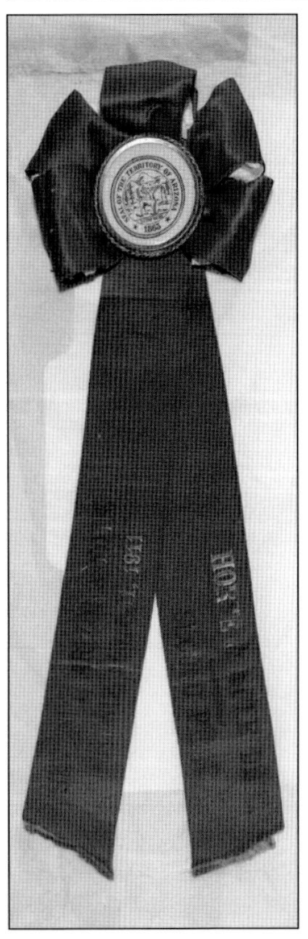

Mules were the original heavy-duty trucks of the territory. They were used to haul building materials, pull plows, and often raced. At the seventh territorial fair in 1911, the second prize in the horse and mule department was awarded to Christopher Dixon. He had hauled materials for several early hotels and the old jail. Sand and gravel for many of the sidewalks stamped by Frenchy Vieux in Phoenix had been hauled by Dixon. This prize ribbon shows the Territorial Seal of Arizona from 1863, featuring mountains, pine trees, and deer. The original red ribbon is intact and prized today, at left. (Above, courtesy of Tempe History Museum; left, courtesy of John Carl Maurin III.)

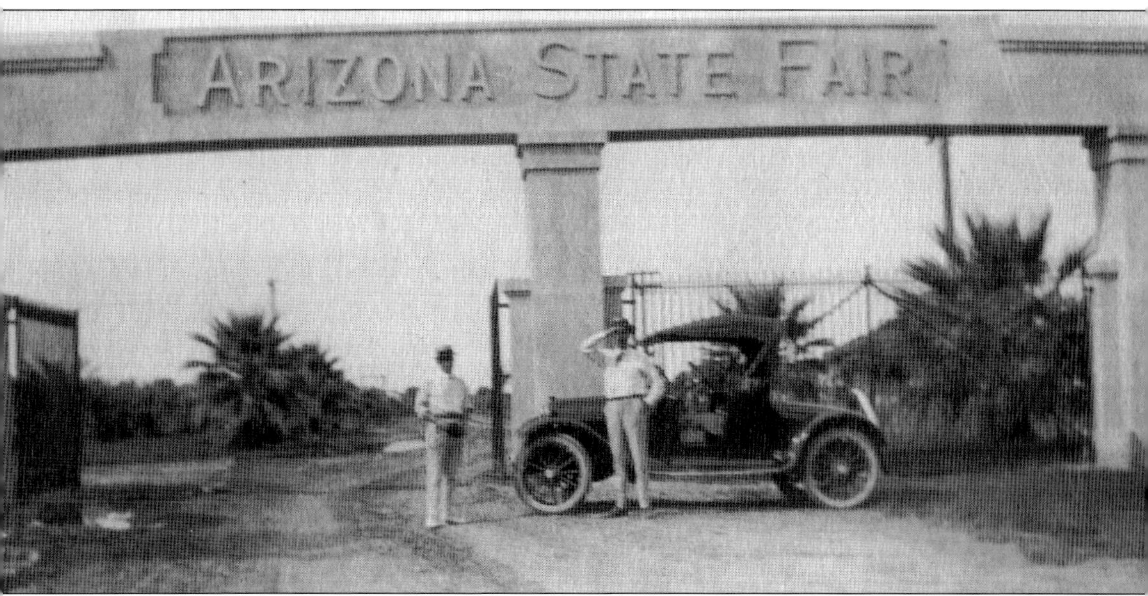

The residents of the Arizona Territory had been working toward statehood for several decades. In anticipation of Arizona's admission day, territorial governor Richard E. Sloan wrote to the governors of every state in the Union in early January asking each to declare the day a national holiday. On February 14, 1912, Arizona was finally admitted to the Union. Proclamations were read, bells were rung, and a general carnival atmosphere prevailed on that Valentine's Day. The entrance gate to the state fairgrounds, above, reflected the state's pride in finally being part of the great whole. Arizona boosters, long intent on statehood and with the cooperation of the Arizona Territorial Fair Commission, had hosted displays at various events, such as the Chicago Columbian Exposition of 1893 and the Louisiana Purchase Exposition of 1904 in St. Louis, to introduce the glories of Arizona to the world. (Courtesy of Carolyn Refsnes Kniazzeh.)

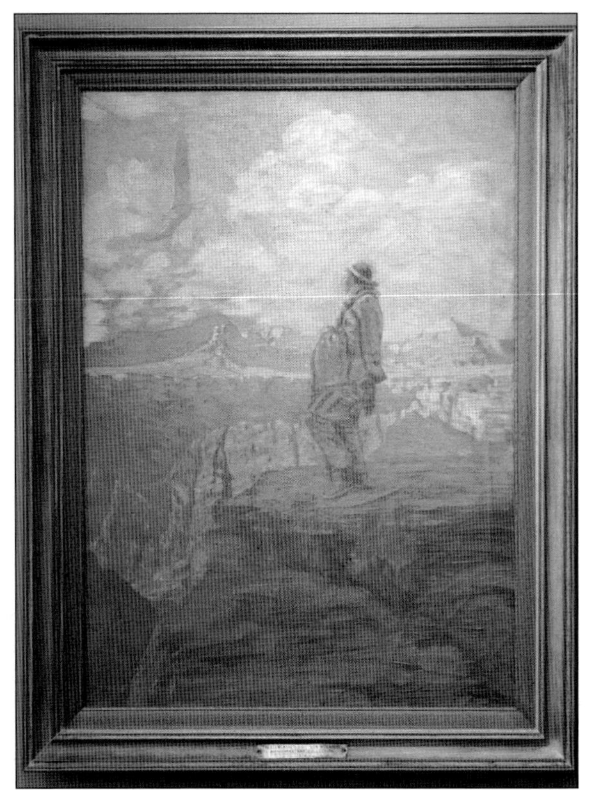

The Woman's Club of Phoenix formed an art committee to develop the community's interest in art. In 1915, the group chose the painting "Egyptian Evening" by Carl Oscar Borg at the state fair from professional artists' entries. It was paid for by the Phoenix City Council, thus beginning the city's art collection. Lon Megargee's painting "The Elemental," pictured left, was the Woman's Art Committee's purchase at the 1916 state fair. Megargee forged a strong bond with his adopted state and painted 15 large canvases for the Arizona State Capitol in 1913–1914, which are still displayed today. Visitors to the state capitol are pictured enjoying the cactus gardens during one of Arizona's mild winters. (Left, courtesy of the City of Phoenix Office of Arts and Culture; below, courtesy of McCulloch Brothers Photographs, Herb and Dorothy McLaughlin Collection, Arizona State University Libraries.)

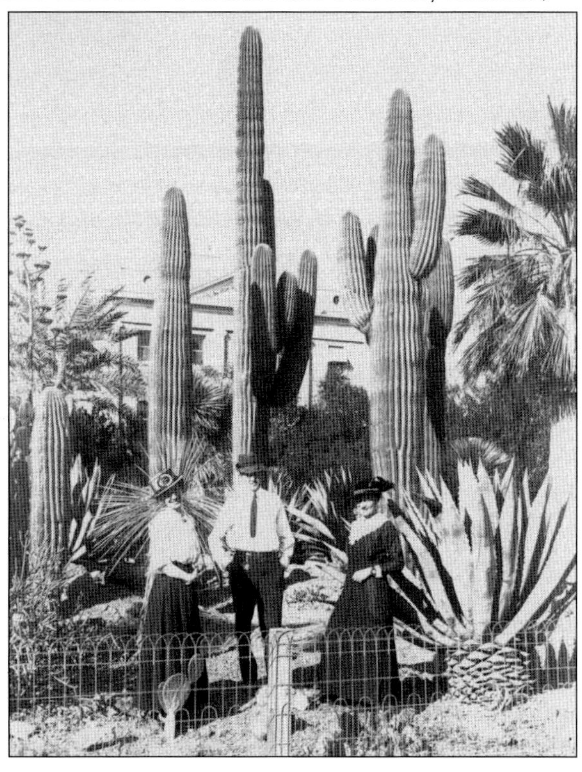

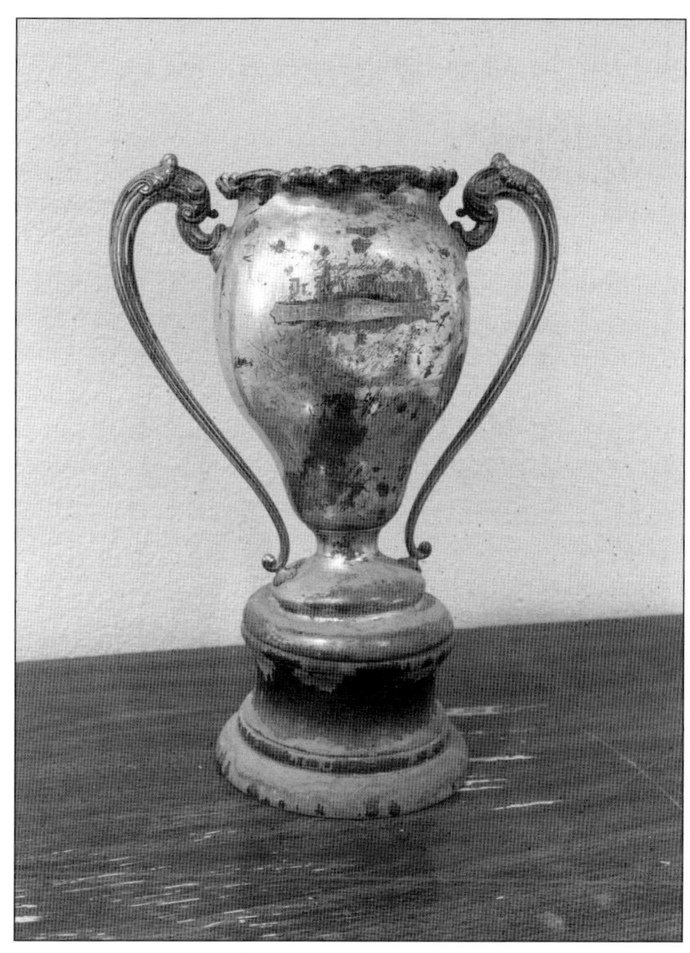

The Department of Public Health promoted the importance of sanitation at the fair for several years. The silver trophy, inscribed with "Presented by Dr. R.N. Looney / State Supt. Public Health / to the winner of / State Laboratory Contest / Pasteurized Cream," is on display in the fair offices. The Riverside Nursery sold remarkable roses, shrubs, and trees for homeowners throughout the valley. James Kellogg Wheat, pictured at the 1916 state fair, preferred the term "plantsman" for his work. The idea of Phoenix as a "Garden City" originated in the late 1800s because of crop diversification, which ranged from grain to fruit trees, and the year-round growing season. (Right, courtesy of Arizona State Fair; below, courtesy of James Kellogg Wheat.)

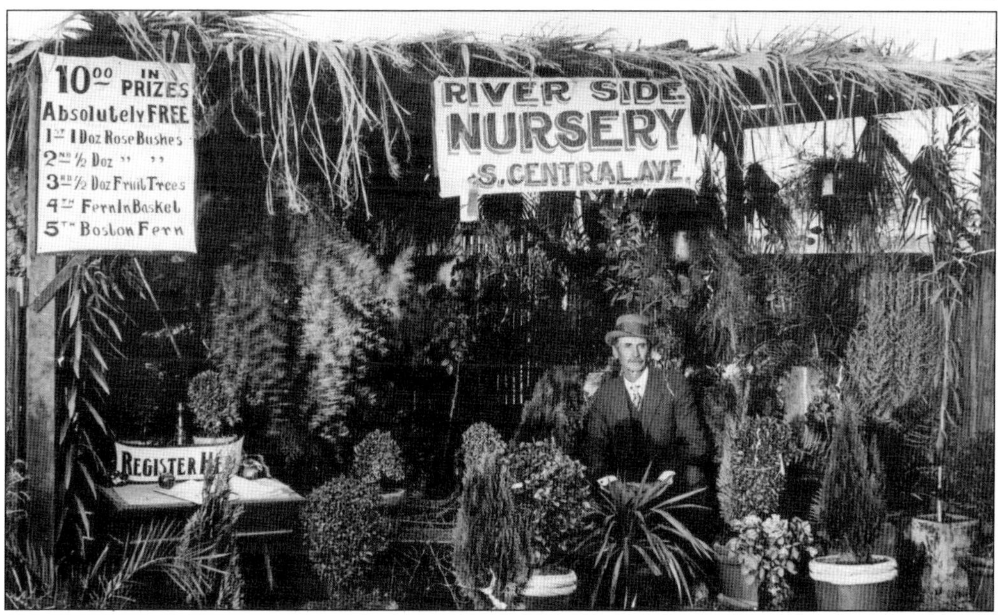

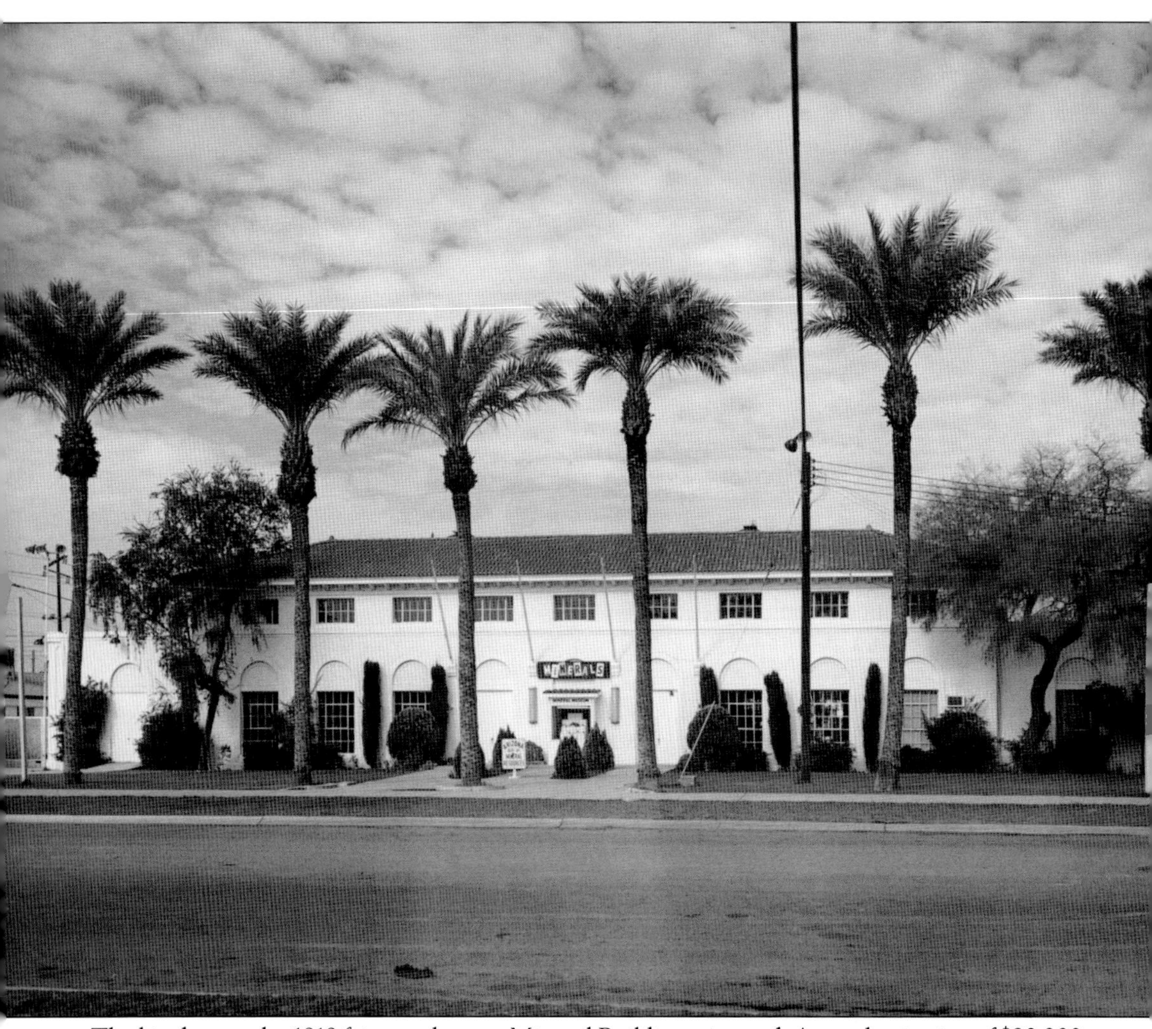

The big draw at the 1919 fair was the new Mineral Building, pictured. An authorization of $30,000 by the legislature gave life to the concept of the building in 1917. Half a dozen of Arizona's largest copper producers donated funds to complete the work. It was a symbol of the mining industry's pride and the largest building on the fairgrounds. The copper industry was a major force in Arizona economics for years. The huge structure, nearly 100 years old today, was designed by architect J.B. Lyman Jr. in the Second Renaissance Revival style of white-painted brick with a red tile roof. At nearly 90 feet long, it is imposing in its design and position on the fairgrounds, parallel to Nineteenth Avenue. Various names given to the building include Mining and Mineral Museum, Gem and Mineral Museum, and Party Gras Building. (Courtesy of Herbert and Dorothy McLaughlin Black and White Photography, Arizona State University Libraries: Arizona Collection.)

Innovative Switzer's Department Store owner Walter Switzer brought a different kind of first to Phoenix in 1919. He arranged with an aerial circus promoter to utilize a plane to deliver merchandise, not to the downtown store but to the state fairgrounds while the fair was in progress. The airplane soared over the packed grandstand, right, with the wings painted with "Switzer's Air Express." Switzer was occupying a Packard limousine parked off to the side of the racetrack. When the plane landed on the grassy surface inside the track, Switzer leaped out of the car, threw the package into the car, and then circled the racetrack several times to wild applause while the band played. Switzer's son is pictured below. (Right, courtesy of the Herb and Dorothy McLaughlin Collection, Arizona State University Libraries; below, courtesy of the family archives of Walter Switzer Jr.)

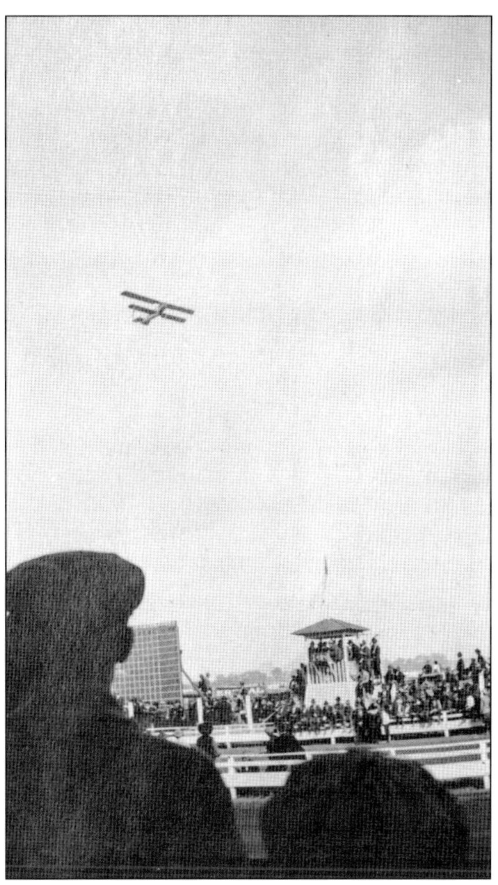

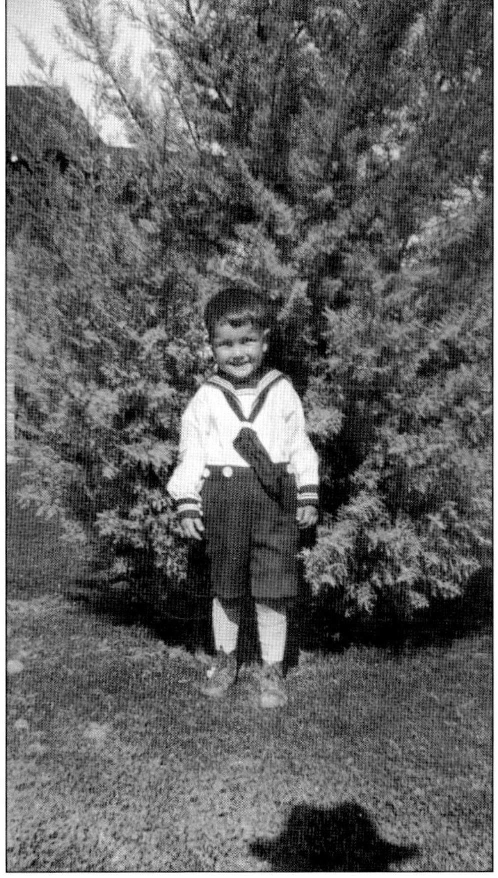

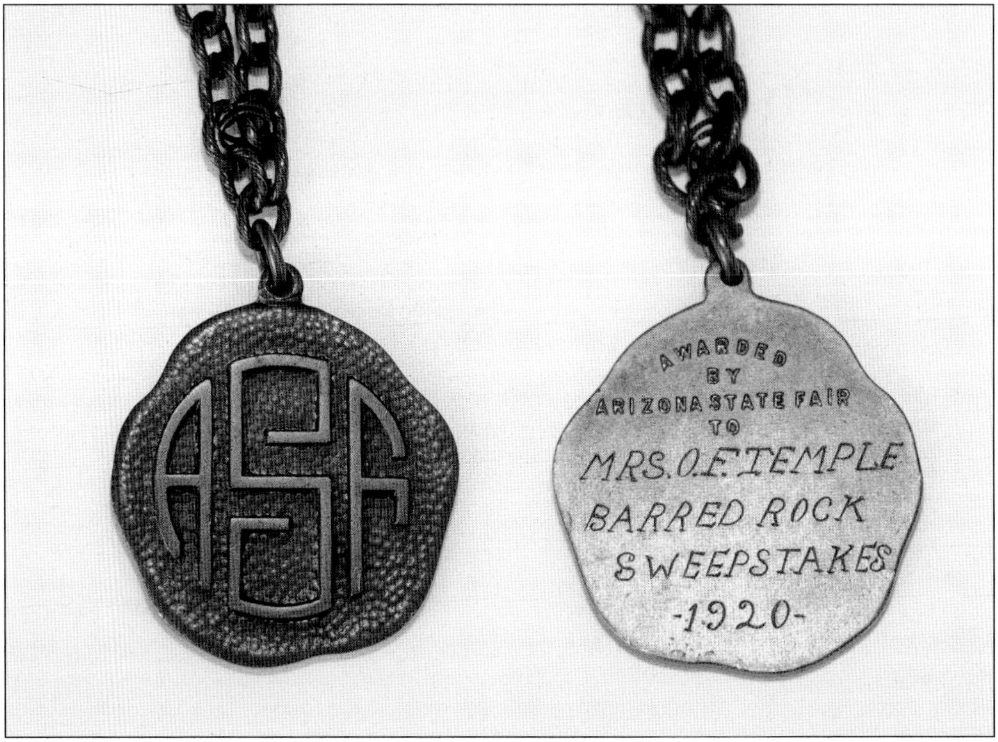

The solid copper medal above is inscribed with "ASF" on the front. On the reverse, it reads, "Awarded by Arizona State Fair to Mrs. O.F. Temple Barred Rock Sweepstakes 1920." Barred Rock chickens are year-round layers and excellent meat producers. The Temple Farm was at the northwest corner of Van Buren Street and Fifteenth Avenue. (Courtesy of Jodey Elsner.)

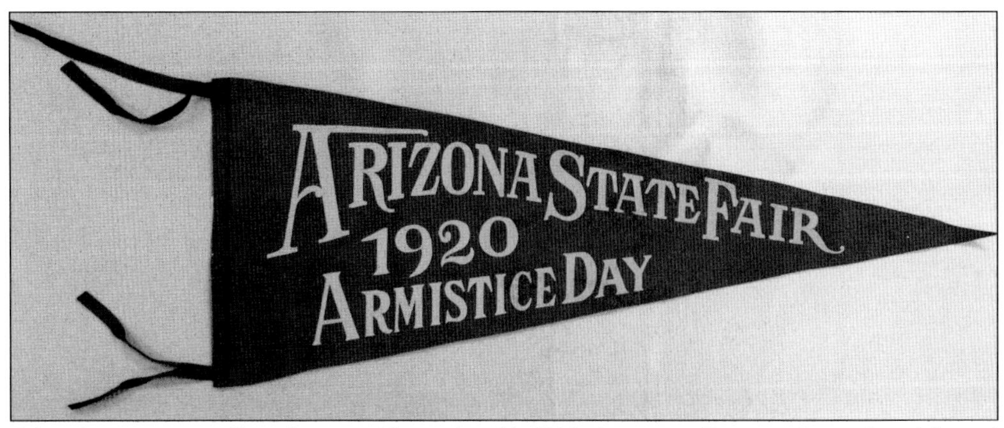

After the cessation of hostilities on November 11, 1918, Armistice Day was fervently celebrated annually at the state fair in the years following the end of the Great War. "The War to End All Wars" resulted in increased pride in the abilities of the United States. Patriotism and pride were the hallmarks of Armistice Day. (Courtesy of Tempe History Museum.)

Advertising catering to the new motoring public was glamorous in the early part of the last century. The exotic, elegantly dressed woman carrying an armful of flowers in the Texaco advertisement at right was an example of the excitement attached to motor cars. A Model T Ford in 1926 was an affordable $260. William "Billy" Wayne Hurt, below, and his dog Rex participated in a footrace involving entrants racing with their leashed dogs at the Arizona State Fair in 1927. They were the first-place winners of the Shell Handicap "Doggone" Race. The friendly competition was fun for all. The prize was a "special build" Model T Ford. The dog looks as happy as the boy. (Right, courtesy of the Arizona Science Museum; below, courtesy of Karen Mancuso.)

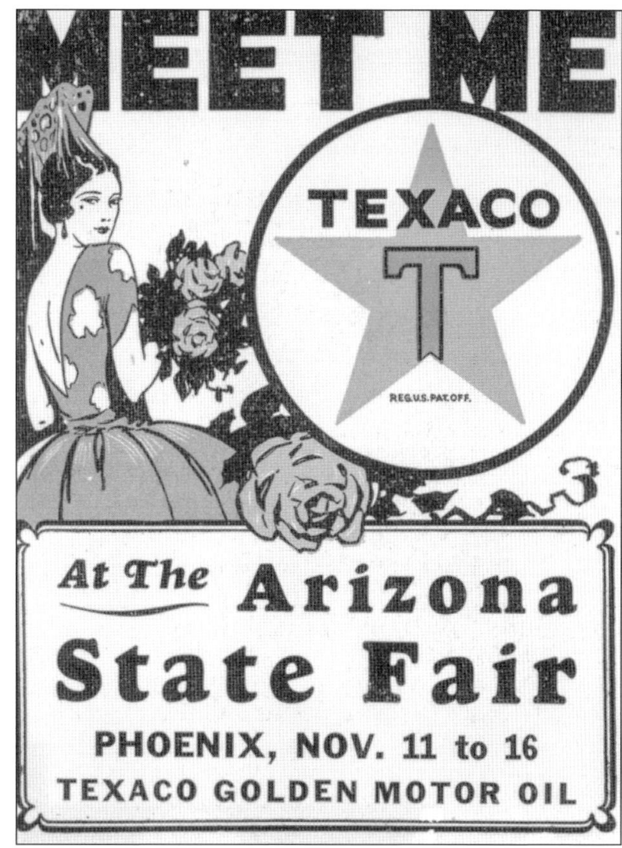

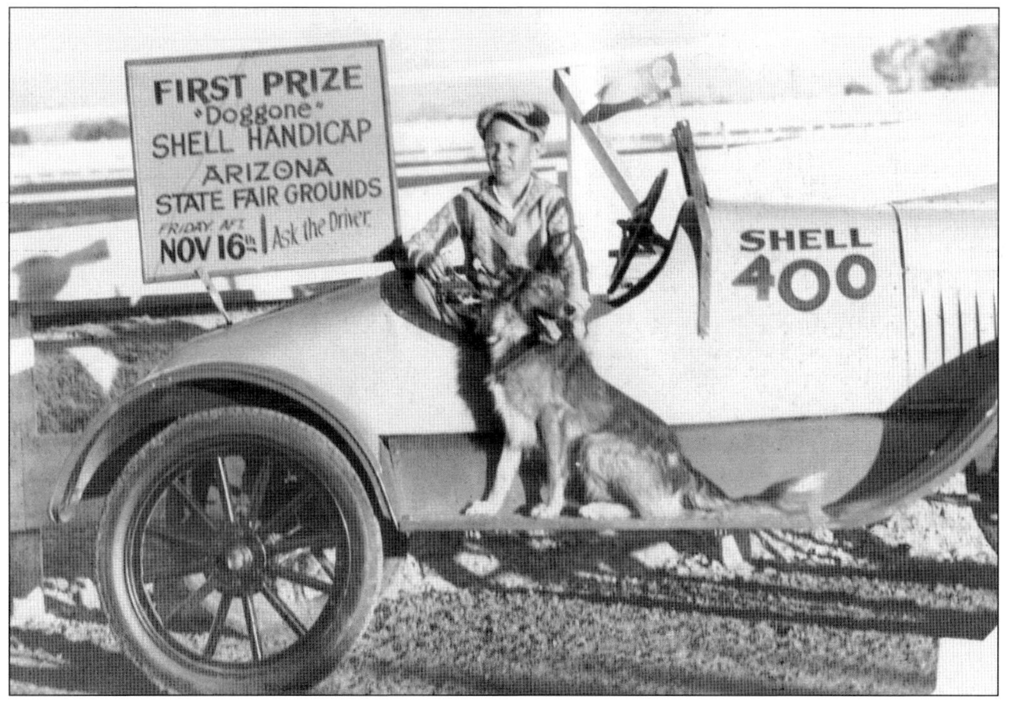

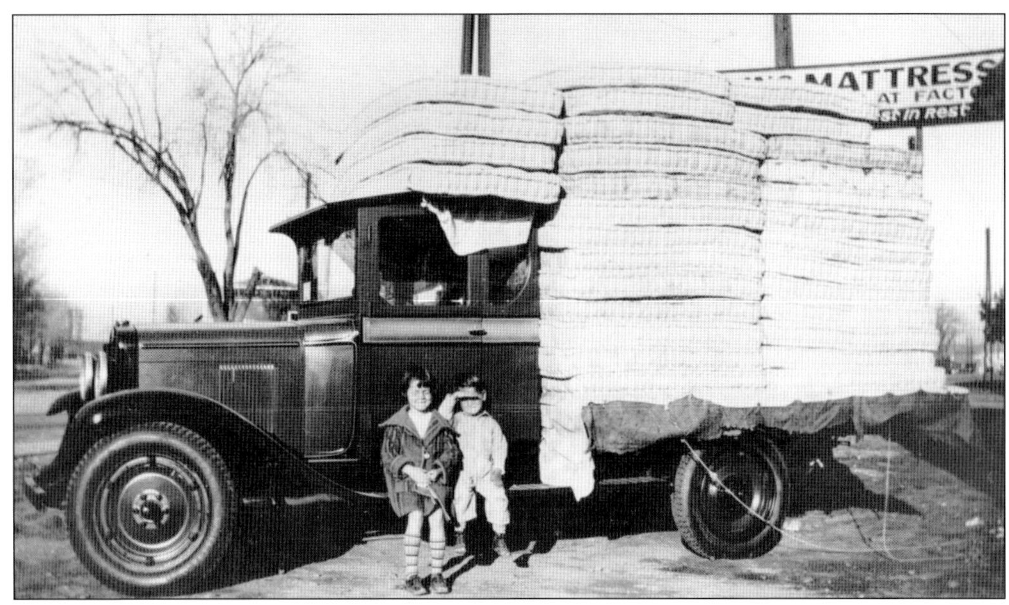

In the 1920s, Noble Ewing suffered from respiratory illness and had moved from Arkansas to Texas. In search of a healthier climate, he wrote to many cities. All except one responded with the advice to stay put unless he had money to return home if plans failed. The Phoenix Chamber of Commerce responded optimistically along the lines of "great opportunities, great climate and friendly people." The Ewings packed their children into their 1929 Model A Ford and headed west. The Ideal Court on Grand Avenue, just below McDowell Road, became the family's first home as they established a mattress renovating factory across the street at 1754 Grand Avenue, above. They became part of the Grand Avenue community, consisting of small businesses, gas stations, bars, and a church. Prospering, the mattress company moved to larger quarters at 1804 Grand Avenue in 1932, below. (Both, courtesy of Charles Ewing.)

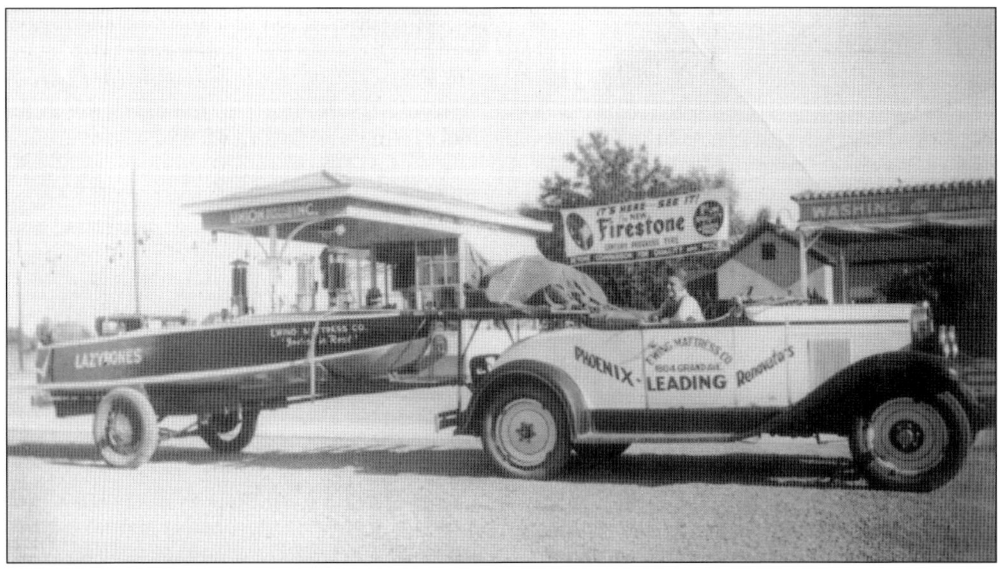

Two

New Deal at the Fairgrounds

The Great Depression began with the stock market crash in 1929, and by the early 1930s it seriously affected Arizona's economy. With Franklin Roosevelt's 1932 election, New Deal programs were initiated in 1933 to address the devastation produced by lack of work affecting one quarter of the population. President Roosevelt named Frances Perkins as secretary of labor, the first woman ever named to a cabinet post. Federal money began to flow to the states to put people back to work, but Arizona's economy was so bad in 1933 that the state could not fund a fair that year, nor several years thereafter. However, the fairgrounds were still being used. The largest New Deal agency, the Works Progress Administration, was financing projects on the site by the mid-1930s that put Arizonans back to work.

The 1905 fairgrounds grandstand burned in 1934. Rebuilt with insurance money and federal funds, it was named B.B. Moeur Stadium in honor of Gov. Benjamin Baker Moeur, who championed the project. Dedicated in September 1936 by Harry Hopkins, one of FDR's closest advisors, Moeur Stadium became a grand example of federal and state cooperation. Two cattle barns, with distinctive lamella truss roofs, were constructed in 1936–1937. The WPA Administration Building was built in 1938, facing West McDowell Road. Another new building north of the WPA headquarters, similar in style, was the Agricultural or Home Arts Building. These projects on the fairgrounds joined the immense Mineral and Mining Building finished in 1919.

More than eight decades later, construction projects in Phoenix that emerged from the New Deal programs are today's prized landmarks. They include not only the buildings on the state fairgrounds, but also the addition to the Arizona State Capitol with Jay Datus murals, the Arsenal in Papago Park, South Mountain Park structures, Phoenix Homesteads neighborhood, Encanto Park, buildings on the Phoenix College campus, and the post office on Central Avenue at Fillmore Street.

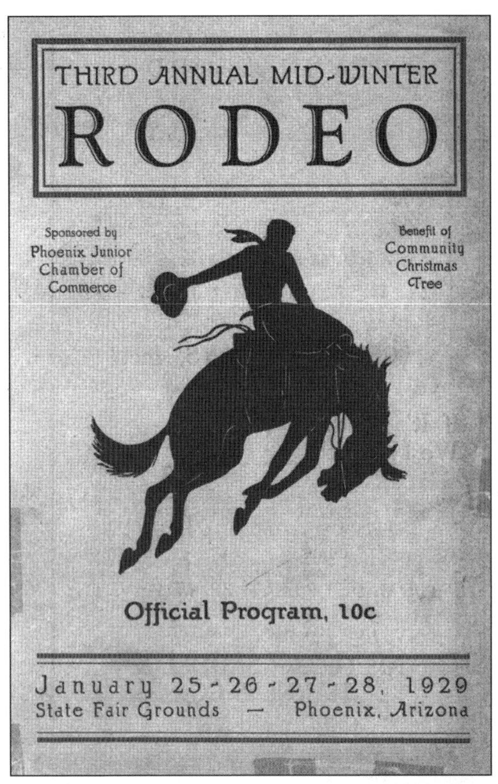

The spirit of Arizona was typified by members of the Phoenix Junior Chamber of Commerce, called Jaycees. Their midwinter rodeo enhanced the connection with the Old West. In failing health, hotelier John C. Adams asked the Jaycees to take on a philanthropic tradition he had begun years earlier. Adams not only provided a Christmas tree in the lobby of the Hotel Adams, pictured below, but also provided food and clothing for the underprivileged shoeshine boys who came into his hotel to get warm. The Jaycees took over Adams's project to provide relief for the impoverished children. The annual Phoenix Jaycees Rodeo of Rodeos in 1929 at the state fairgrounds (left) raised money for "unfortunate tots unable to have a Christmas of their own." In the early 1930s, the need for assistance had outstripped the Jaycees' efforts. By 1933, Arizona had a Board of Public Welfare. (Left, courtesy of the Phoenix Jaycees; below, courtesy of Picture of the Past Antiques.)

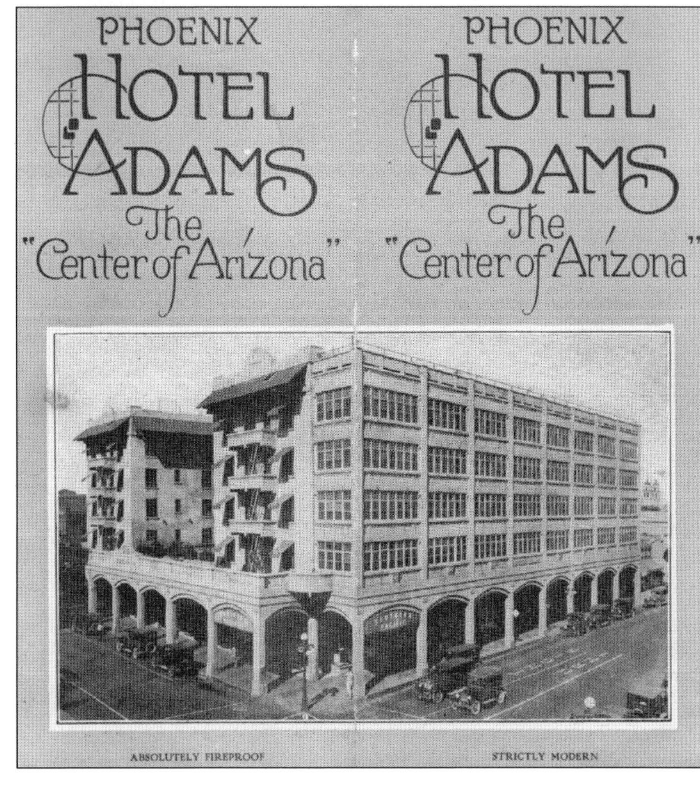

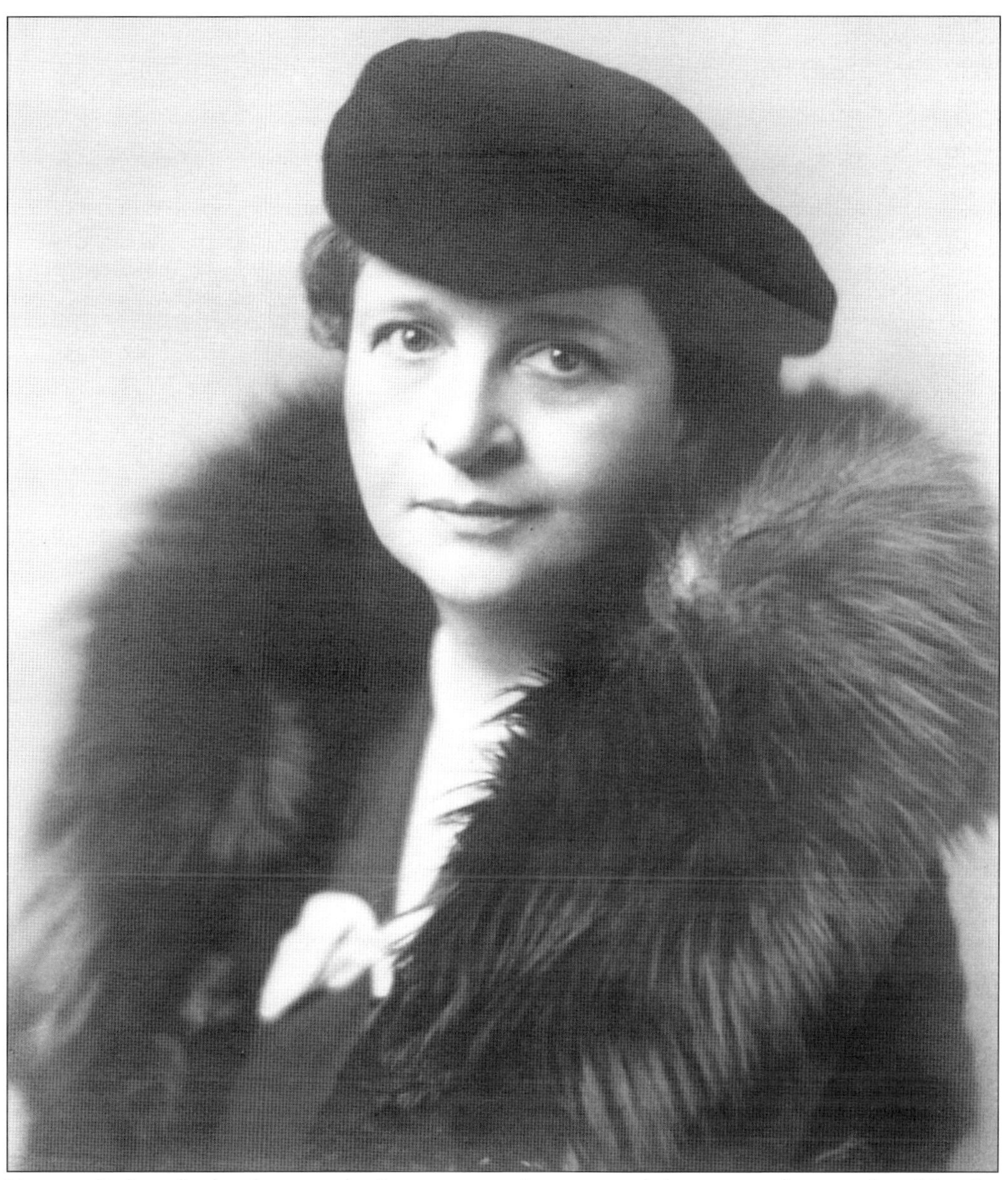

Frances Perkins had a distinguished career as a champion of the poor and unemployed by the time she was named by President Roosevelt in 1933, to be his secretary of labor. The first woman to serve in a presidential cabinet, Perkins had been executive secretary of the New York City Consumers League and was an expert in worker health and safety issues. New York governor Al Smith had appointed her to the New York State Industrial Commission. When Smith lost his 1928 bid to become president of the United States, he was succeeded as governor by Franklin Roosevelt. New York's new governor recognized Perkins's ability and asked her to become the state's industrial commissioner. Perkins had publicly challenged President Herbert Hoover's contention that employment was on the rise in 1930, making headlines in the process. With Roosevelt's election in 1932, she eventually made history with her advocacy for programs to bring the nation's unemployed back to work. Perkins famously said, "I came to Washington to work for God, FDR, and the millions of forgotten, plain common workingmen." (Courtesy of Frances Perkins Center.)

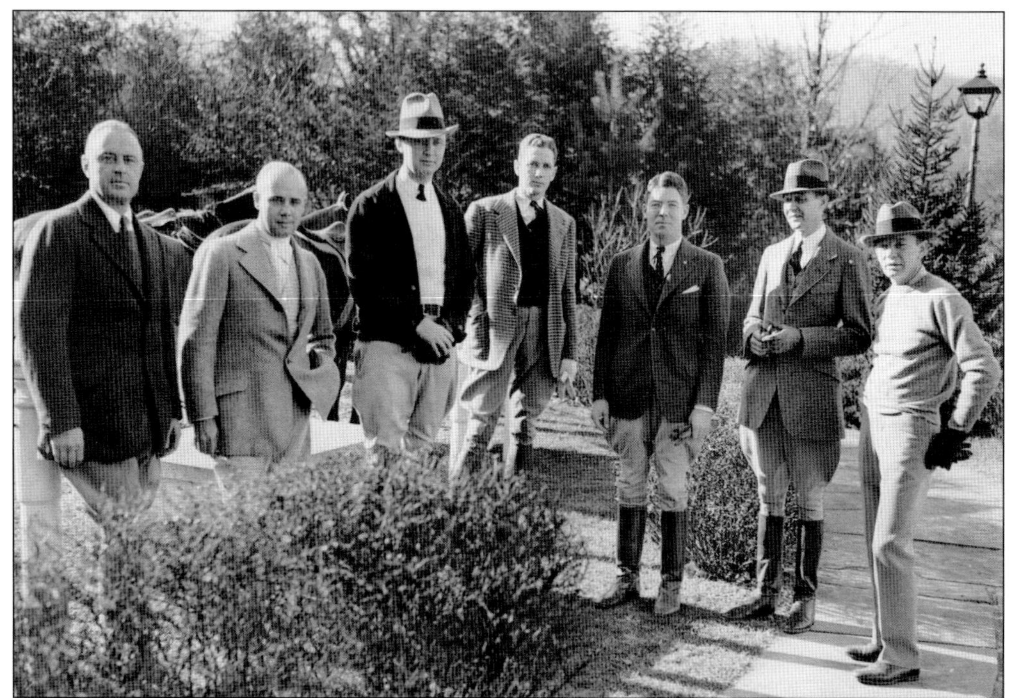

Joseph E. Refsnes opened J.E. Refsnes & Company, an investment firm in 1931, prior to the passing of the Glass-Stegall Act, known as the Banking Act of 1933. Part of the New Deal, the Banking Act prohibited bank sales of securities and prevented banks from using depositors' funds for risky stock market investments. The Investment Bankers Association had its 1932 annual convention in White Sulphur Springs, West Virginia. The riding group is assembled with Joseph Refsnes at right, above. The c. 1933 photograph below shows the Refsnes, Ely, Beck & Company's employees. Joseph E. Refsnes is the third from left. Years later, the firm handled the bonds for the coliseum. (Both, courtesy of Carolyn Refsnes Kniazzeh.)

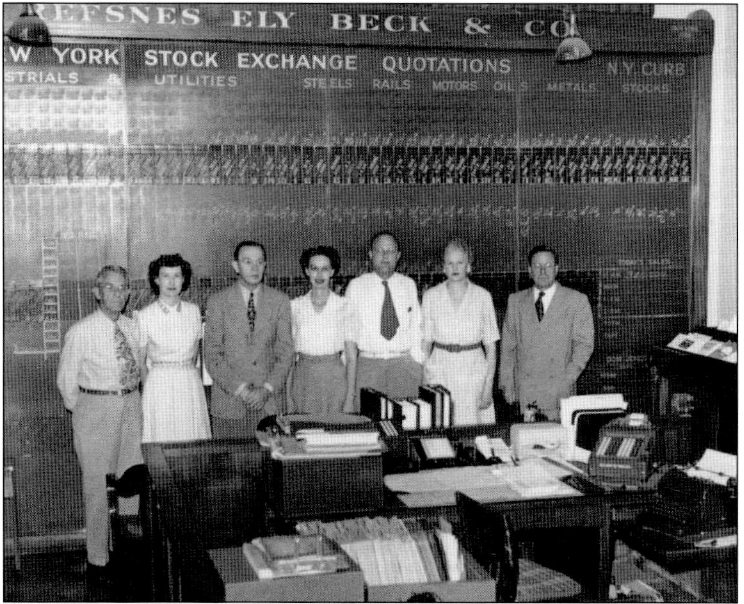

Benjamin Baker Moeur, a Tennessee native, worked as a young man in Texas as a cowboy. In 1896, after graduating from medical school in Arkansas, he married Honor G. Anderson. The couple, pictured right, moved to Tempe, Arizona, where he practiced medicine. He was a country doctor, who often traveled miles to make house calls, and was a college physician at Arizona State Teachers College. Dr. Moeur participated in a variety of businesses that prepared him for his public role. Always involved, he attended the 1910 Arizona Constitutional Convention as a representative from Maricopa County. Elected governor in 1932, he served Arizona during the Great Depression from 1933 to 1937. (Both, courtesy of Susan Moeur.)

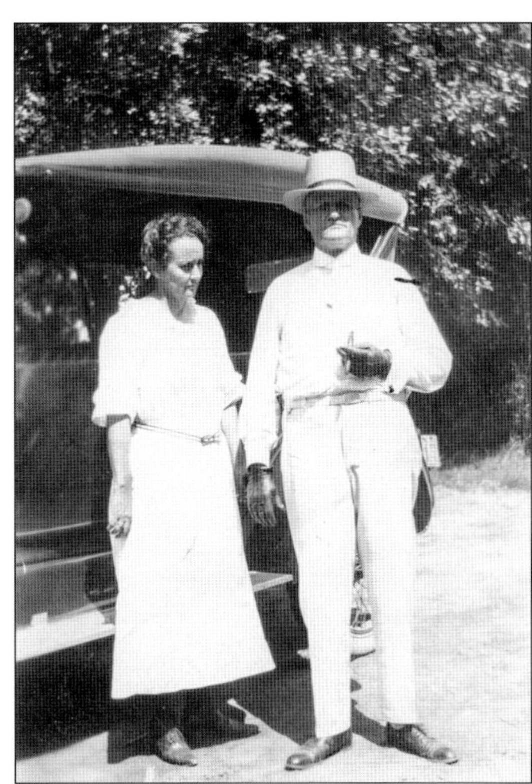

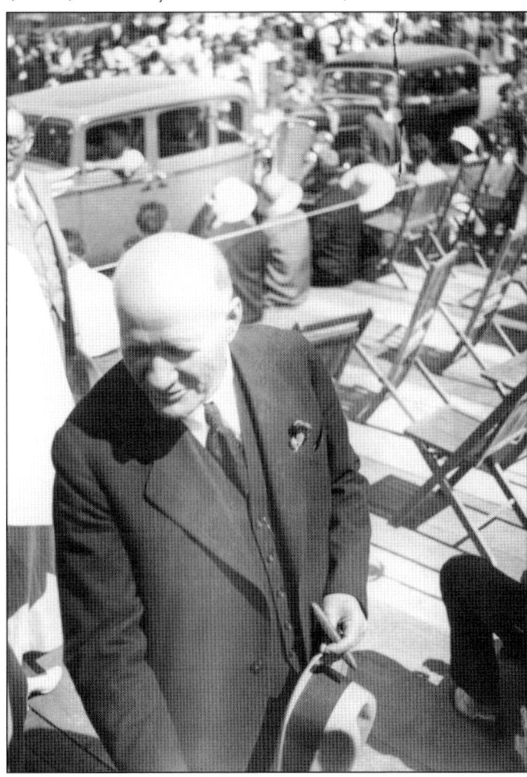

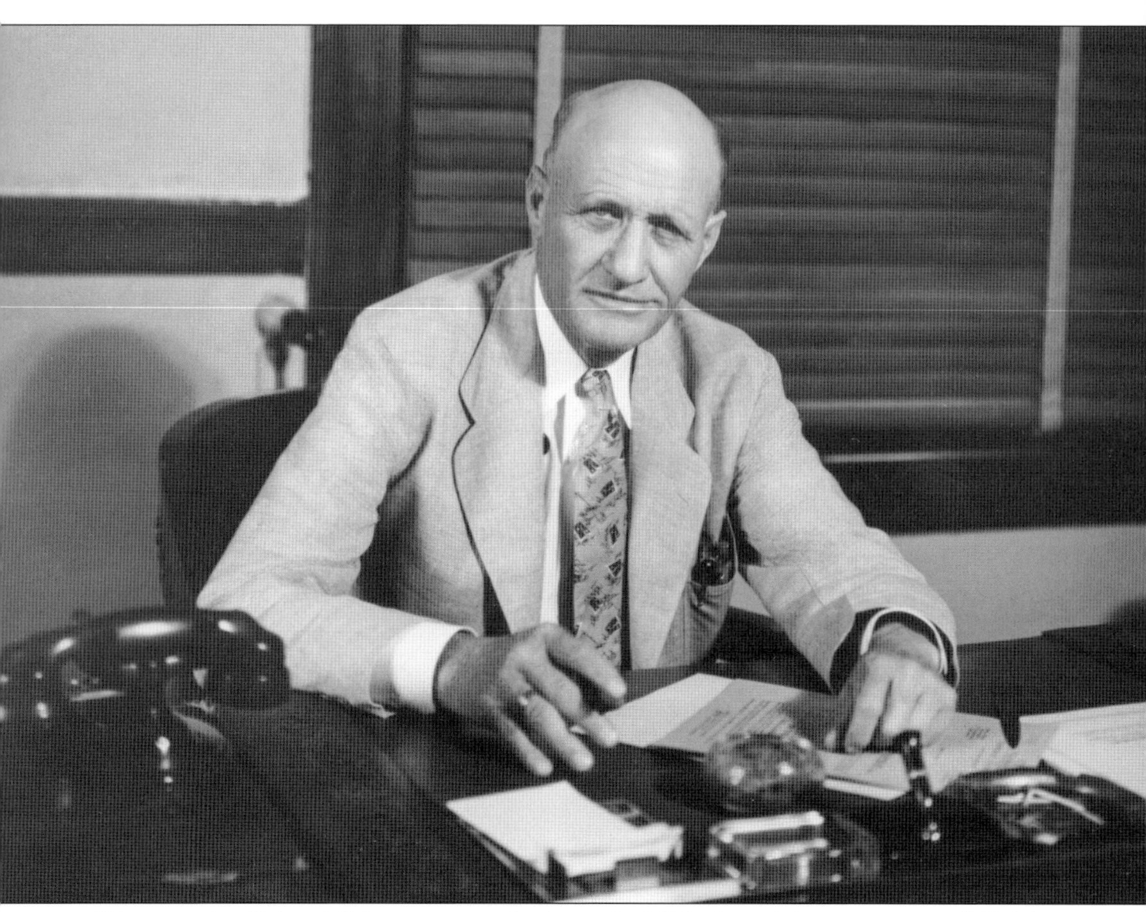

"Guns on the Colorado" became a catch phrase in 1934 when Arizona governor B.B. Moeur mobilized the National Guard to preserve Arizona's water rights. In 1922, the Colorado River Compact originated when six of seven states signed it. Arizona refused to sign because the state's entitlement was inadequate. Governor Moeur believed that Parker Dam, to be constructed by California and the Metropolitan Water District, had never been properly authorized by the Bureau of Reclamation. Soldiers were dispatched to Parker, Arizona, to observe and protect Arizona's water rights. Troops patrolled the Arizona side for months, and Governor Moeur declared martial law to block the construction of a bridge on the Arizona side. Secretary of the Interior Harold Ickes intervened, and the governor recalled the Arizona troops. Governor Moeur was vindicated when the US Supreme Court ruled that the dam project had never been authorized. (Courtesy of Susan Moeur.)

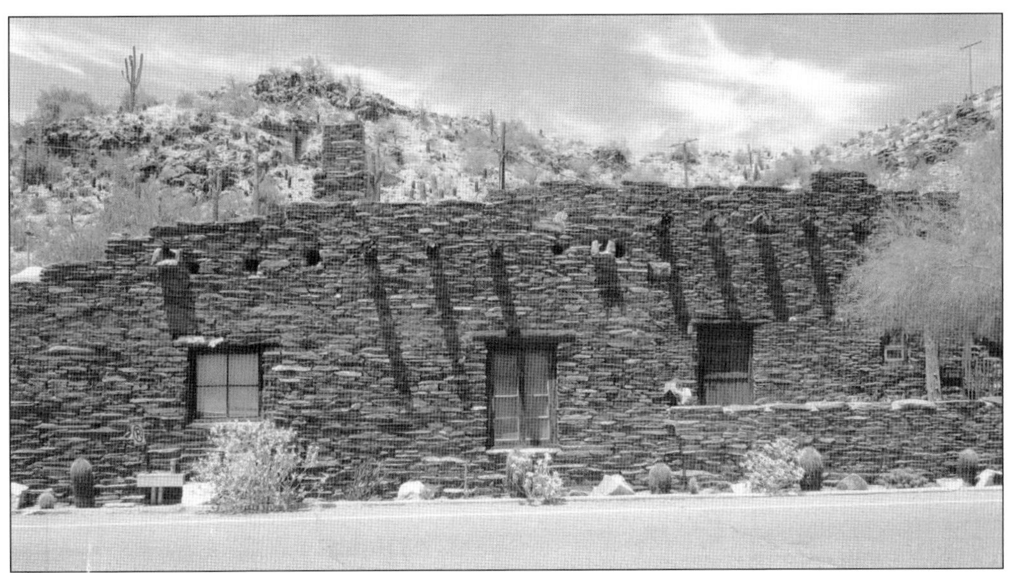

The picturesque stacked-stone buildings, pictured above; ramadas; picnic tables; and other structures in South Mountain Park are emblematic of the New Deal Emergency Conservation Relief Act. In 1933, the Civilian Conservation Corps (CCC) was created to put unemployed young men to work building highways, planting trees, and constructing useful structures. Paid reforestation and construction projects for the conservation of vulnerable areas were ideas that caught the public's imagination. Designed by the National Park Service to reinforce the rustic setting of South Mountain Park, the structures, like the one pictured below, increased the use and enjoyment of this giant park. The small stipend paid for the men's service provided the intangible commodity of hope. (Above, courtesy of Encanto Citizens Association; below, courtesy of Phoenix Parks and Recreation Department and George Hartz.)

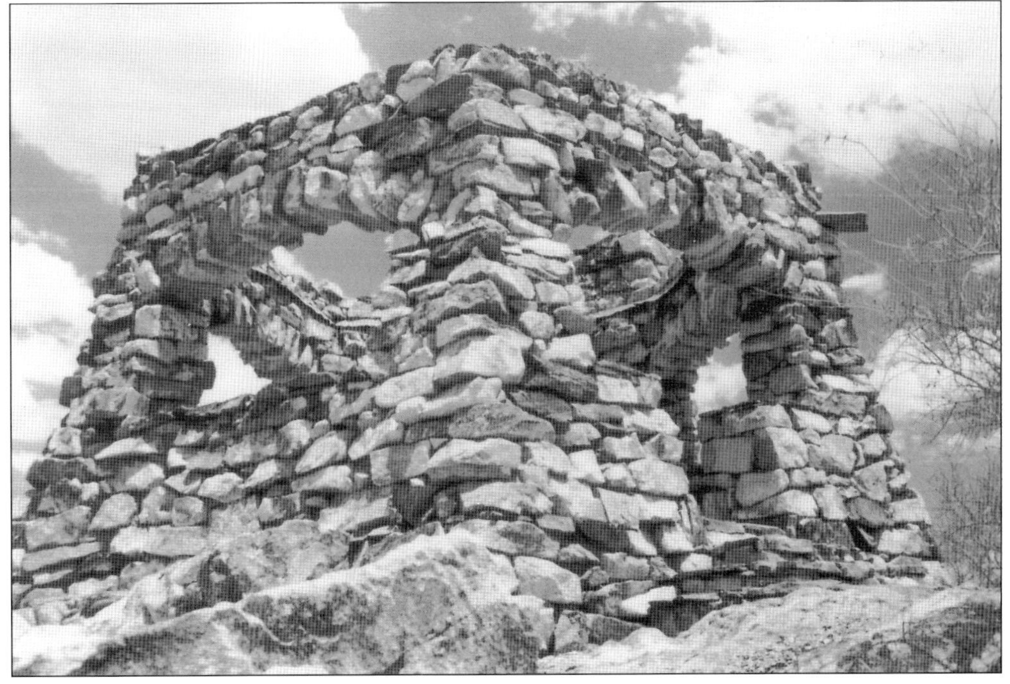

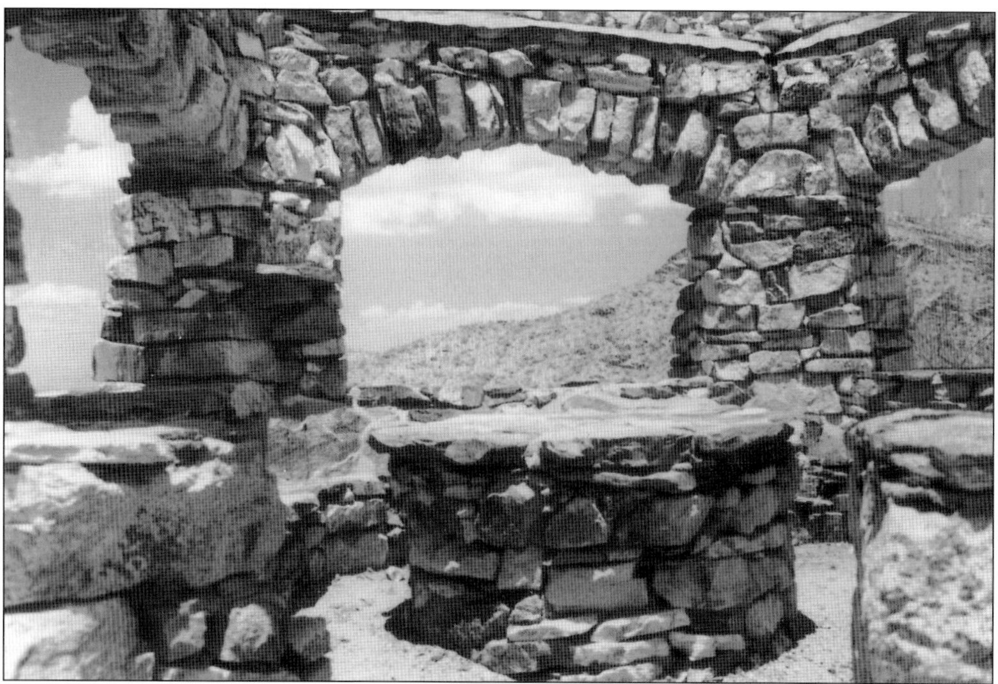

Enhancement of the appearance of the desert setting at South Mountain was of prime importance to the National Park Service architects who designed the structure pictured above. There was a CCC campsite at South Mountain and one in the vast desert landscape of Papago Park from 1933 to 1938. The military use of Papago Park began in 1909, when the northwest corner of the large park was withdrawn from the public domain. The plaque below, honoring the history of the park, was placed by the Arizona State Society and the Grand Canyon Chapter of the Daughters of the American Revolution. (Above, courtesy of Phoenix Parks and Recreation Department and George Hartz; below, courtesy of Edward Jensen.)

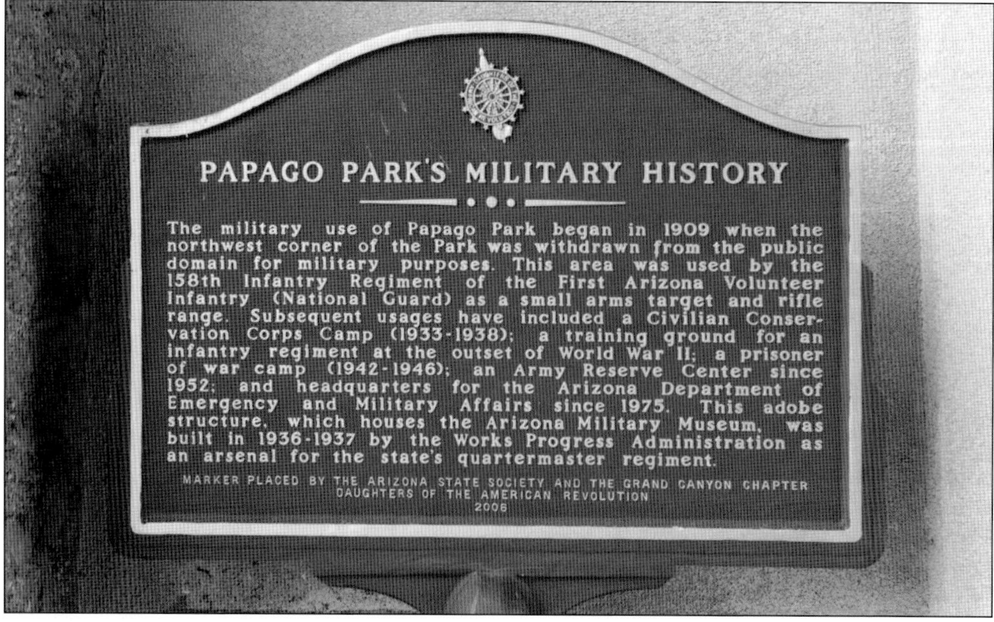

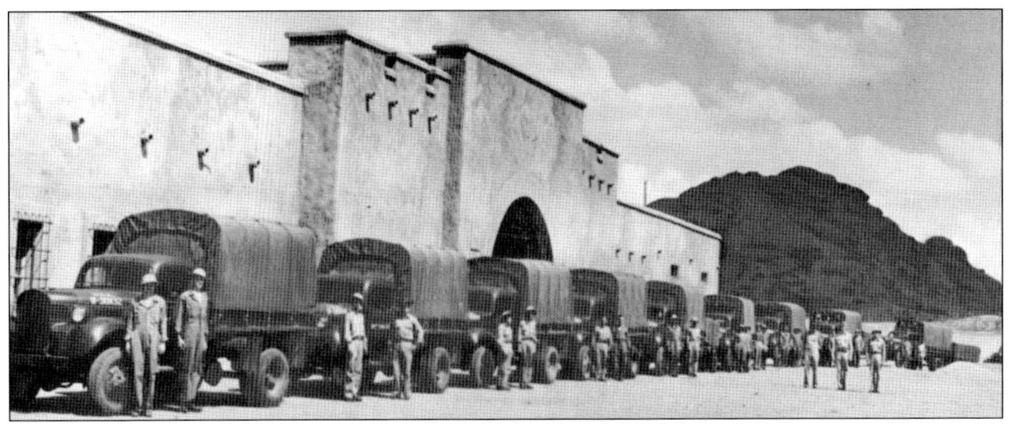

Papago Park today is the location of the Arizona National Guard Headquarters at 5636 East McDowell Road. The 1936–1937 Arsenal built by the Works Progress Administration (WPA) during the New Deal is the largest adobe building in continuous use in Arizona. Company D of the 120th Quarter Master Regiment is shown in 1940, above, prior to World War II with members of the National Guard training for battle. The Arsenal was also used as a maintenance shop during the war (below). The old Arsenal now houses the Arizona Military Museum showcasing original and reproduction uniforms, weapons, and a Vietnam-era helicopter. (Both, courtesy of Arizona Military Museum.)

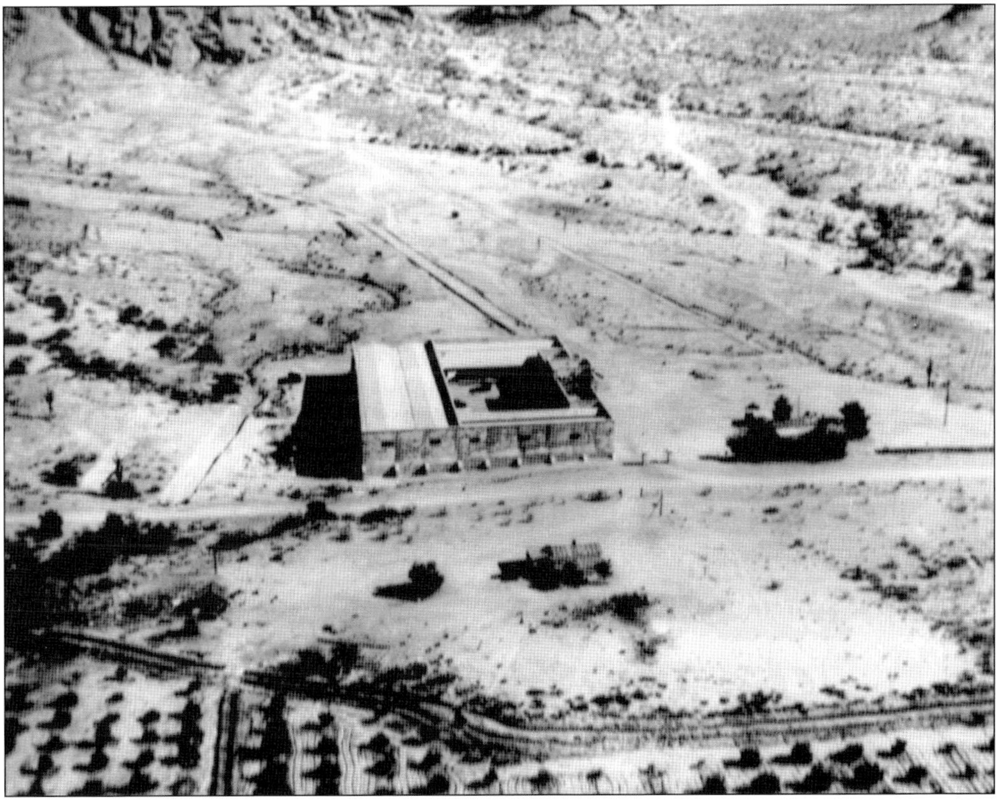

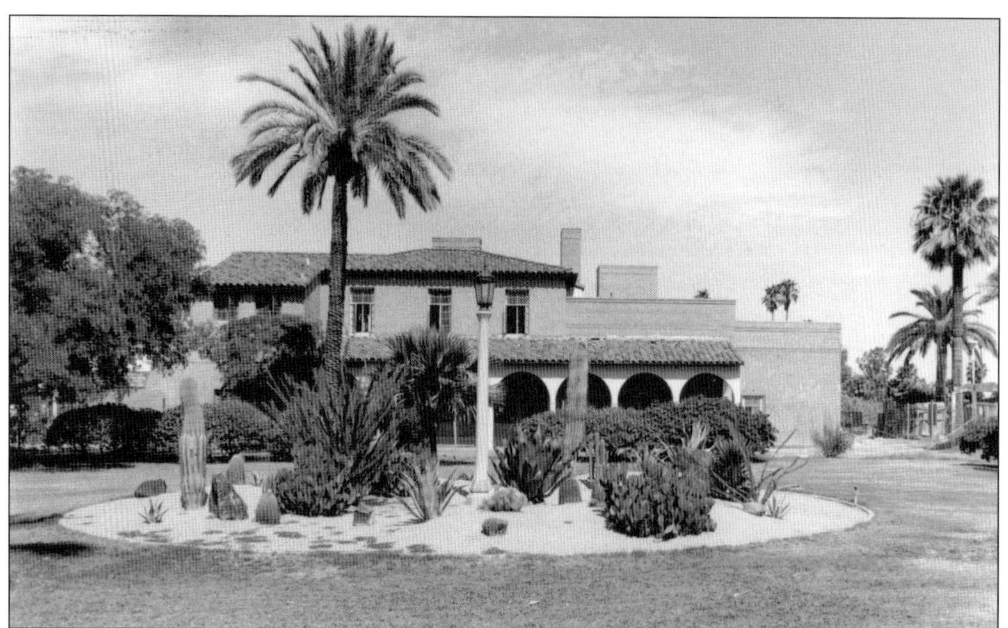

The City of Phoenix created a beautiful green space from former farmland with New Deal funding. The Public Works Administration put Phoenicians to work building Encanto Park. Created in the mid-1930s, the long-term benefits of the park cannot be overestimated. The clubhouse, seen from the winding drive on the west entrance to the park, was designed by the architectural firm of Lescher and Mahoney in the Spanish Revival style. (Courtesy of the Encanto Citizens Association.)

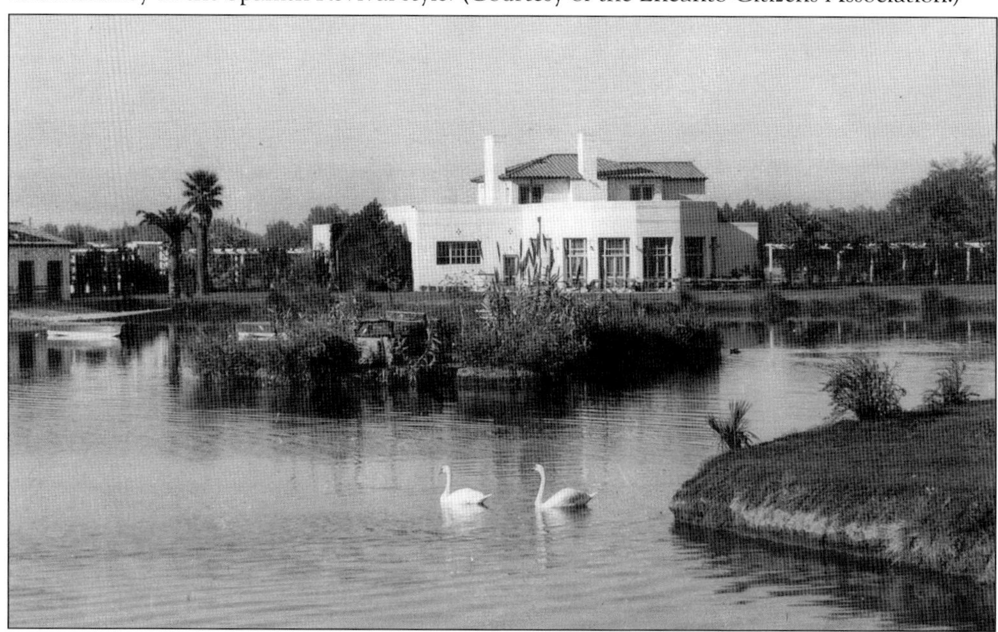

The naturalistic setting for Encanto Park was the idea of William G. Hartranft, known as the father of the Phoenix Parks System. The lagoon, boathouse, and clubhouse reflect the tranquil oasis Encanto Park has become amid a very large city. The park is listed in the National Register of Historic Places and has been named one of the best parks in America. (Courtesy of the Phoenix Parks and Recreation Department.)

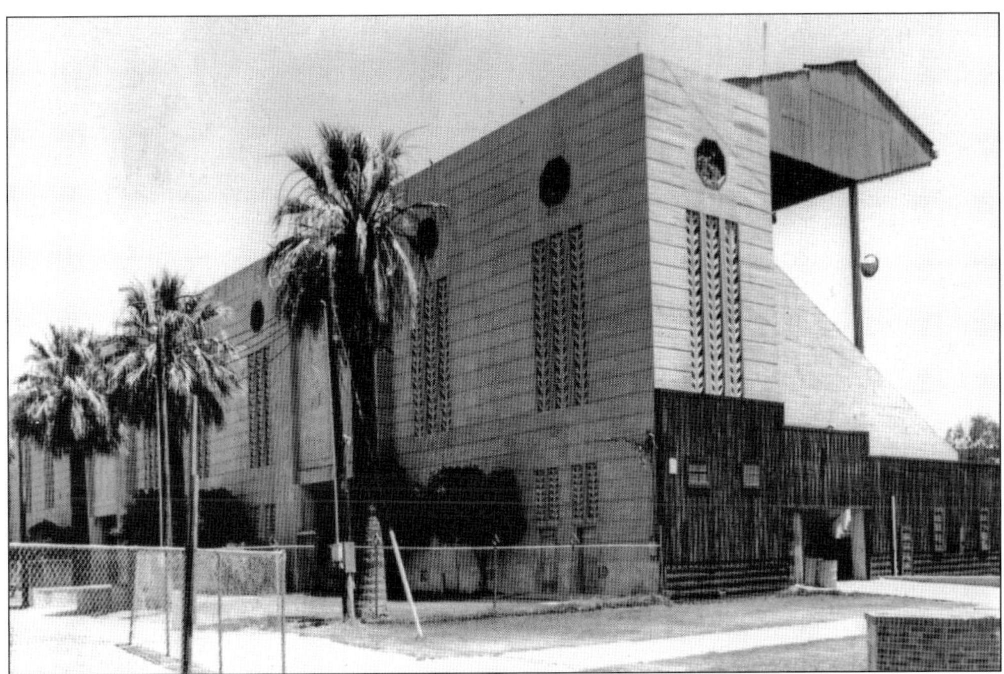

The original grandstand on the fairgrounds burned in 1934. It was a loss to the site; however, Governor Moeur considered it to be an opportunity to put people to work on a new grandstand. It would be built with the insurance money and a Works Progress Administration grant. Designed by architect H.H. Green, the grandstand provided work for the steel and concrete industries and opportunities for artists to embellish the structure in a variety of jobs. More than utilitarian, the replacement provided a grand showcase for public art. Local artists David Carrick Swing and Florence Blakeslee, under the Federal Arts Project, collaborated on 23 bas relief medallions commemorating Arizona scenes, at right. National administrator of the Works Progress Administration Harry Hopkins dedicated the B.B. Moeur Stadium in September 1936. (Above, courtesy of the Encanto Citizens Association; right, courtesy of Jack Bell, Arizona State Fair.)

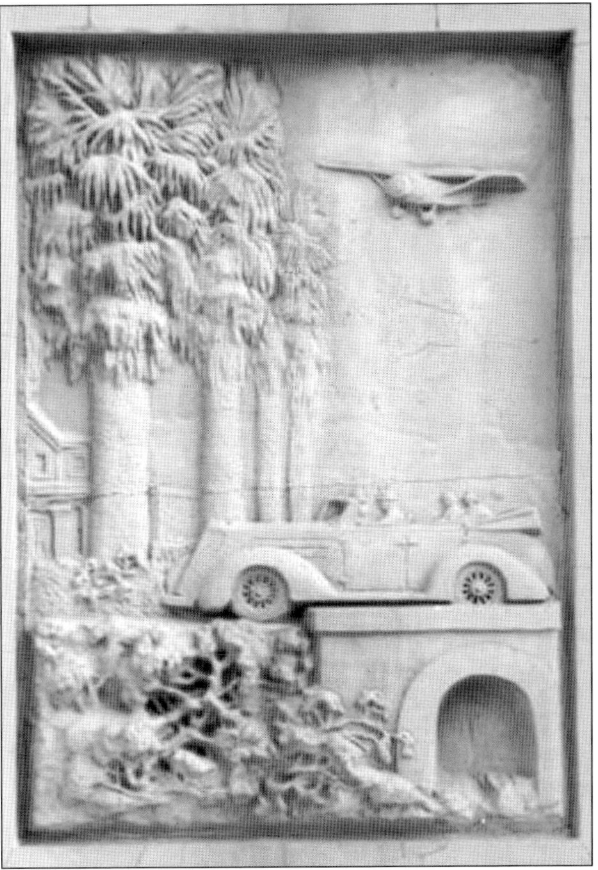

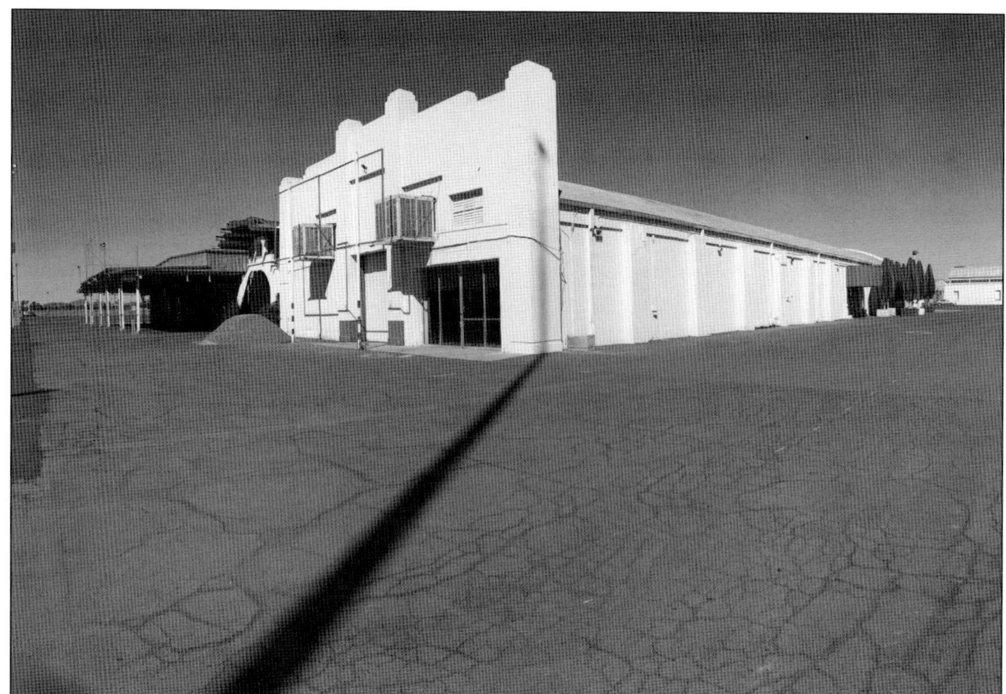

The Home Arts Building, above, was constructed under New Deal programs, as were the cattle barns. Both have distinctive lamella roofs and reinforced-concrete frames with adobe walls. The roof construction consisted of a diamond pattern made with relatively short timbers that made the roof exceptionally lightweight yet strong. Cattle had always been important to Arizonans and even more so during the Depression. It was vital to plan for the well-being of cattle. When money became available for such projects, two large cattle barns were constructed on the western side of the fairgrounds in 1937. No ordinary barns, these had concrete floors and vaulted lamella roofs (pictured below). These barns have been in continuous use since their construction. (Both, courtesy of Phil Allsopp.)

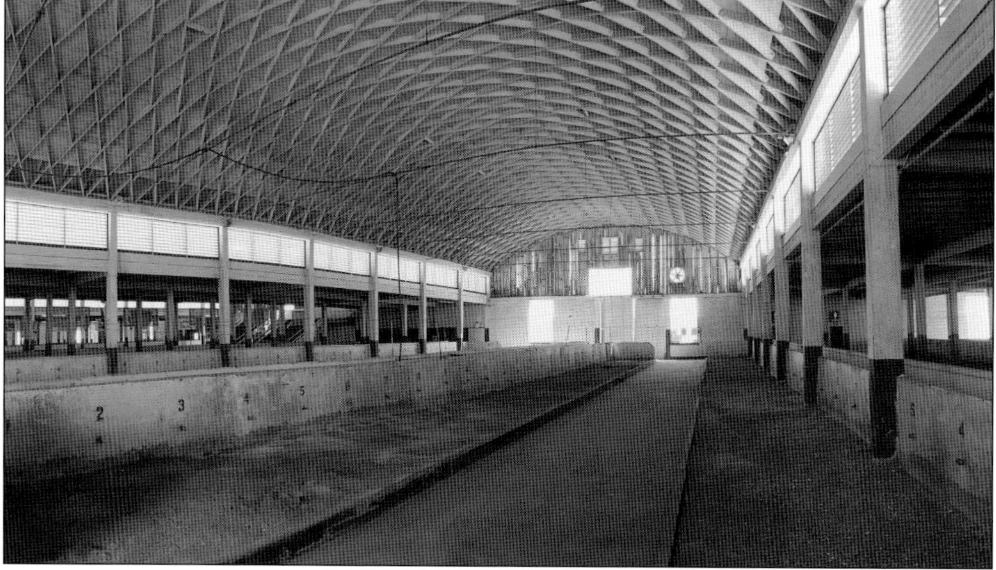

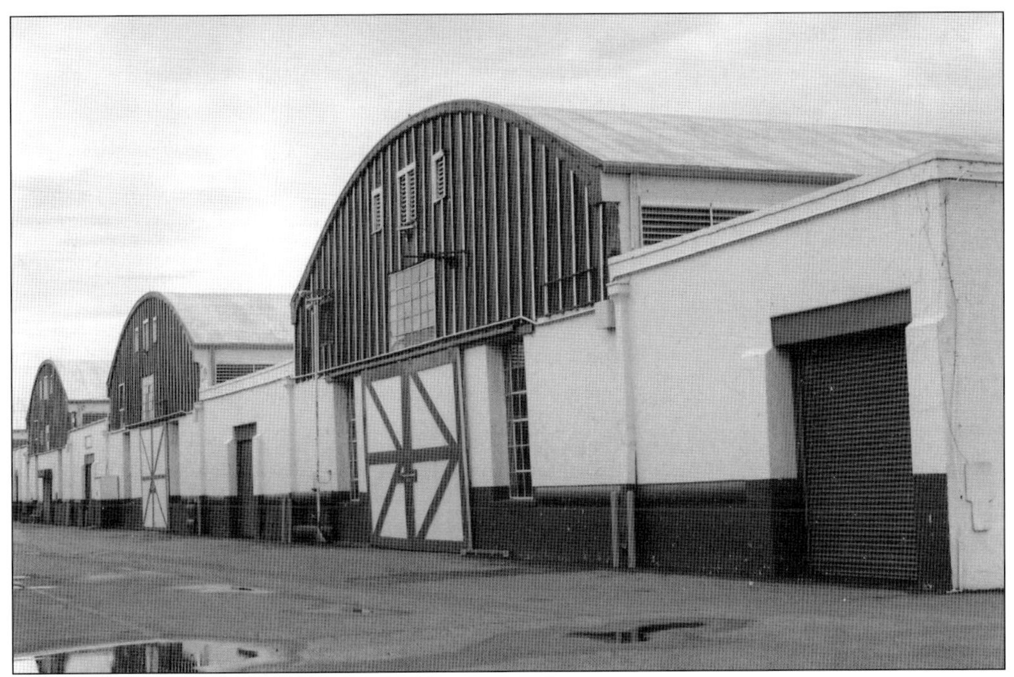

The two original barns that sheltered troops and sometimes workers during World War II had proven successful. Located to the east of the first barns, two nearly identical cattle barns were added in 1947, pictured above. The unusual diamond-pattern lamella roof was again utilized. The intricate construction is shown in detail, below. Fairs were so successful after the war that the bronze plaque on the last two barns reads, "This building erected without expense to the people with funds earned by the Arizona State Fair." (Both, courtesy of Patrick and Terry McCue.)

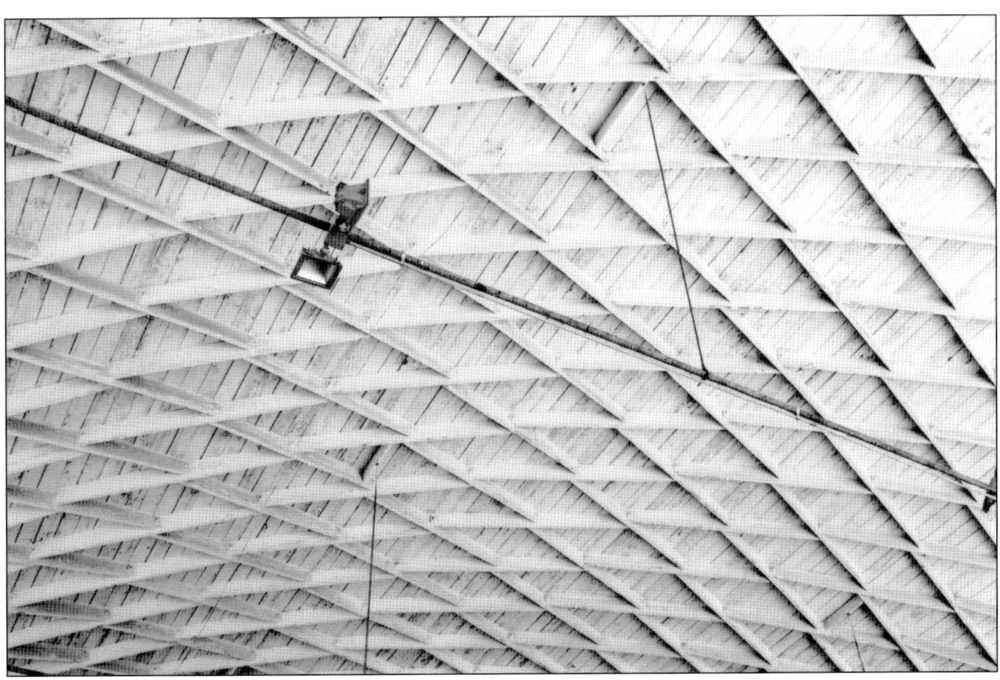

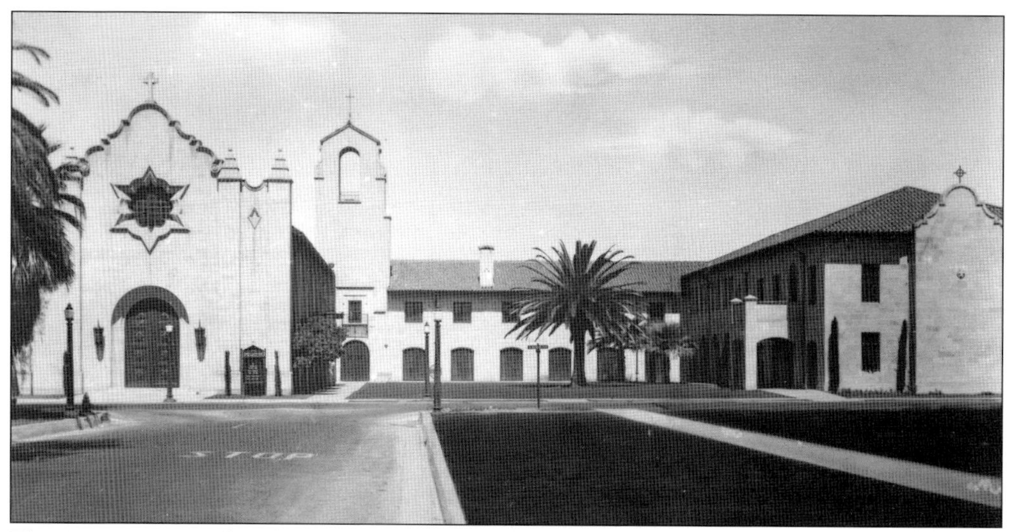

The Mission Revival–style Trinity Episcopal Cathedral, above, has been concerned with the welfare of Phoenicians for over a century. Located on Roosevelt Street at Central Avenue, early on, the church established a camp for people suffering from lung ailments. During the Depression, in conjunction with the Works Progress Administration, the cathedral cosponsored recreational activities for children on the grounds. The youngsters shown below were given the opportunity to improve their physical health amidst a beautiful, serene setting. According to historical records, many Phoenix churches offered hot lunches to undernourished children. Working mothers wrote heartfelt appreciation letters about the WPA lunch project. (Above, courtesy of McCulloch Brothers Photographs, Herb and Dorothy McLaughlin Collection, Arizona State University Libraries; below, courtesy of Arizona State Library, Archives and Public Records, History and Archives Division.)

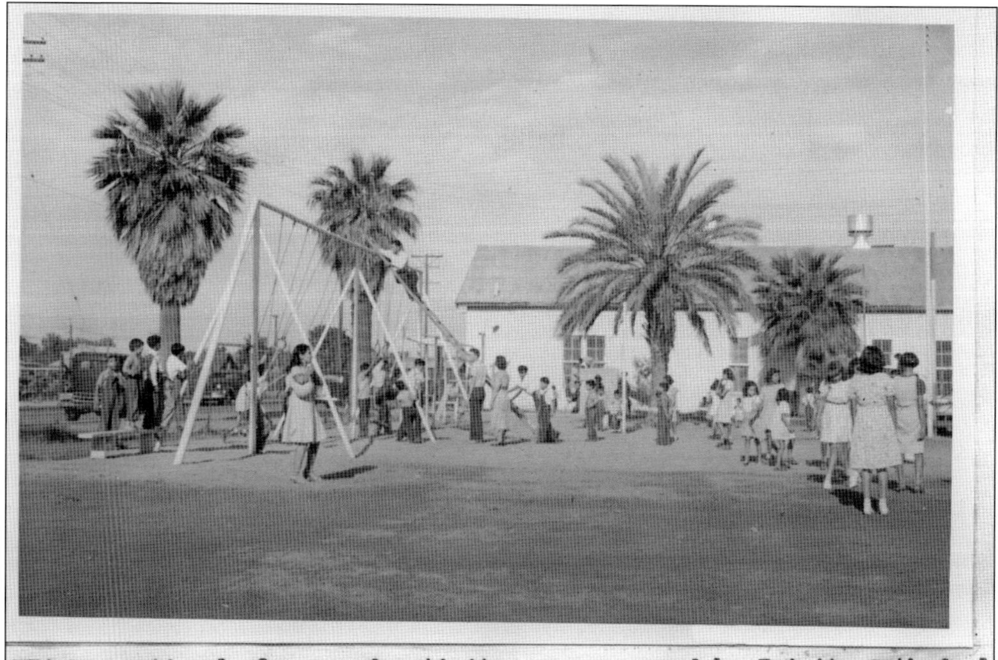

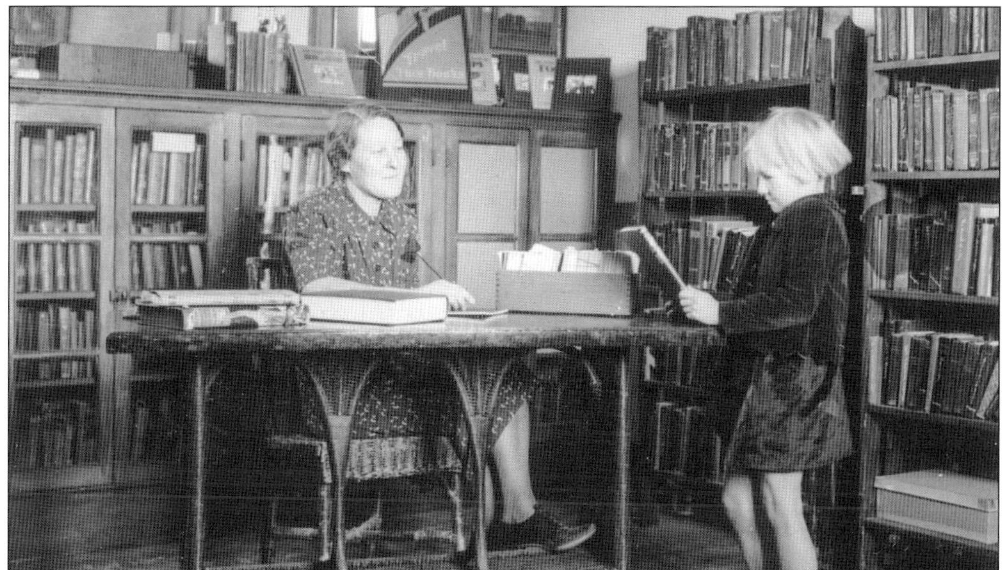

Efforts administered out of the WPA headquarters on the fairgrounds were educational projects. The woman running the library, pictured, went to work, as many women did during the Depression, to support her family. The beautiful child enthralled by the book would have her horizons broadened with reading material either from a rural library or the advent of a bookmobile nearby. (Courtesy of the Arizona State Library, Archives and Public Records, History and Archives Division, Phoenix.)

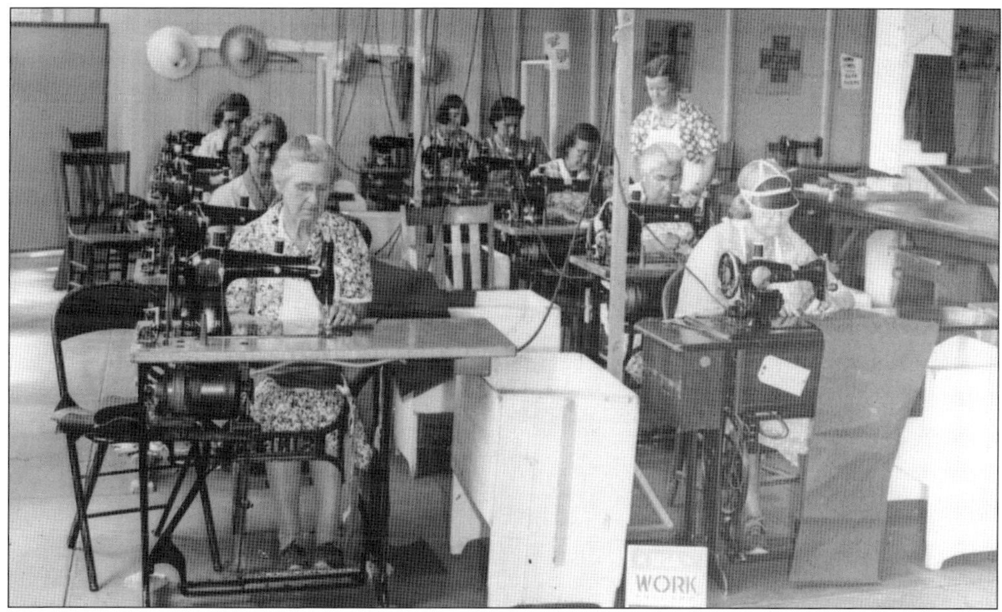

The women working at the sewing machines typified other WPA projects. There were spinning, weaving, and sewing projects constructing drapes out of Arizona long-staple Pima cotton for the new Women's Activity Building at the Arizona State Teachers College in Tempe. The president of the college, Grady Gammage, wrote a letter to the state director of women's projects in Phoenix extolling the new drapes. (Courtesy of the Arizona State Library, Archives and Public Records, History and Archives Division, Phoenix.)

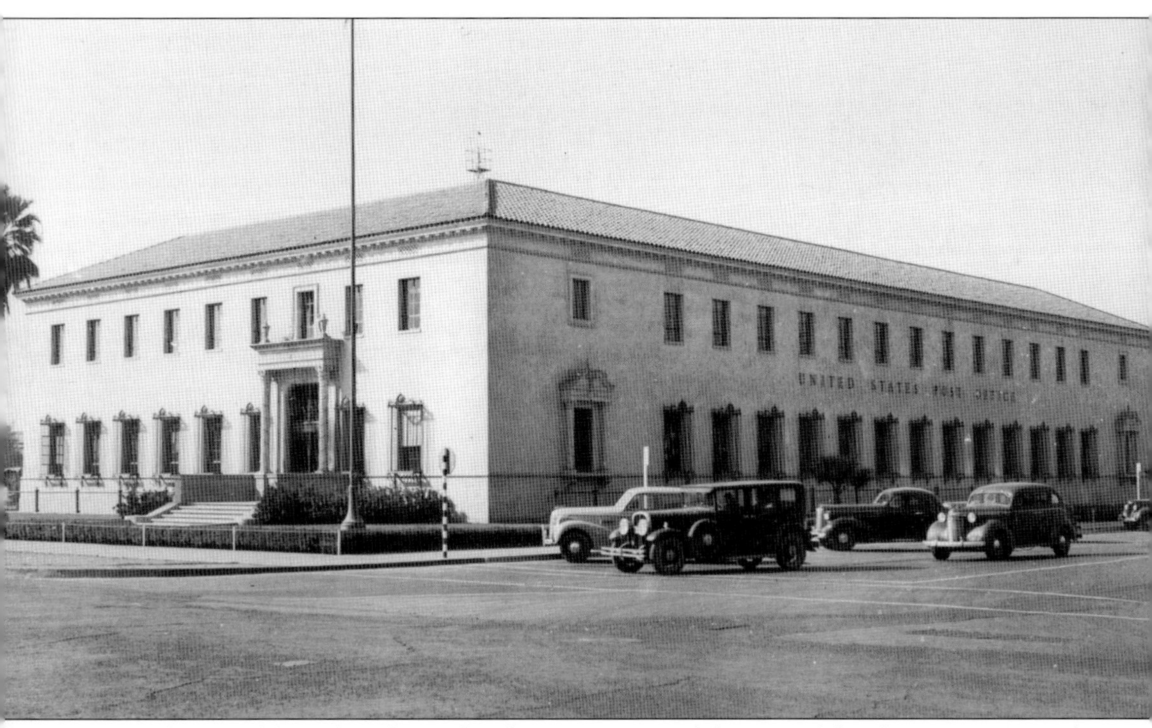

The architectural firm of Lescher and Mahoney constructed this Spanish/Mediterranean Revival federal post office at southwest corner of Central Avenue and Fillmore Street. The 1936 building has been a landmark in central Phoenix for 80 years. Royal Lescher began his architectural firm in 1910 in Arizona. By 1914, the group, then known as Lescher and Kibbey, had completed an addition to the original wooden grandstand at the fairgrounds. The firm became Lescher and Mahoney in 1923. The murals in the lobby were completed under the New Deal Federal Art Project. They are vivid depictions of early Spanish exploration and Native American culture. There was a national competition to design the murals, which was won by Oscar Berninghaus and Laverne Nelson Black. The post office function remains, but the building is now part of the Arizona State University Downtown campus. (Courtesy of Derek Horn.)

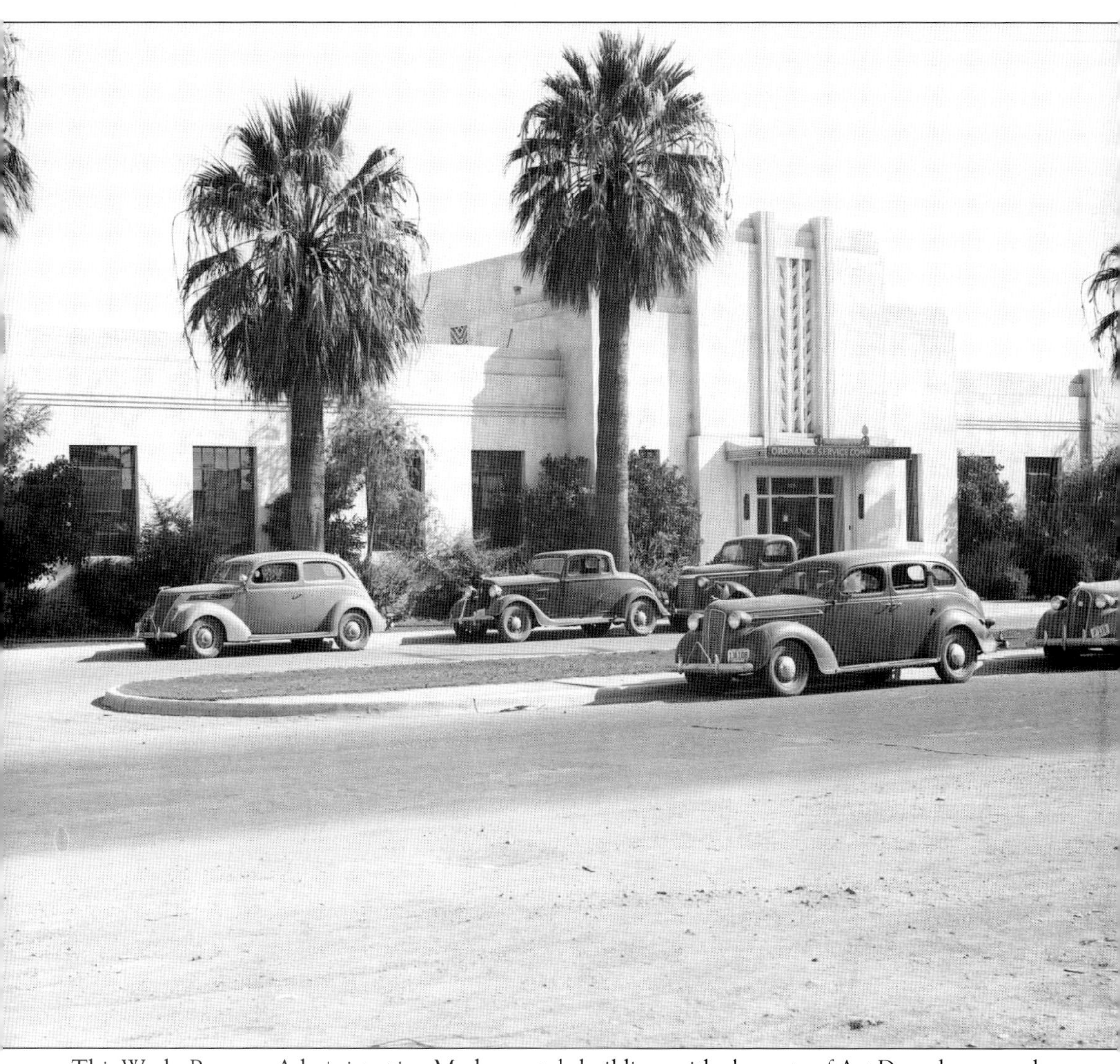

This Works Progress Administration Moderne-style building, with elements of Art Deco, has served many functions. It was constructed in 1938 as Arizona's headquarters for the WPA's Depression-era programs. Economic revival resulted when laborers, road builders, artists, seamstresses, and others went to work for modest stipends from the federal government. During World War II, it became offices for Garrett AiResearch, a military aircraft parts manufacturer, and headquarters for the Ordnance Service Command. After the war, it was renamed the Floricultural Building and served exhibitors. Later, it provided office space for the Phoenix Roadrunners hockey team. The cast-concrete and adobe structure lay dormant for years. When demolition was considered, a widespread group of preservation advocates rallied to save the building. In 2016, allocations from the City of Phoenix, the Phoenix Industrial Development Authority, businesses, and neighbors made more than $200,000 available to stabilize the building (see page 124). The state allocated $120,000. Considered the "Face of the Fairgrounds," the building will hopefully be revitalized and again become an asset to the community. (Courtesy of Arizona State University Libraries, Department of Archives and Special Collections.)

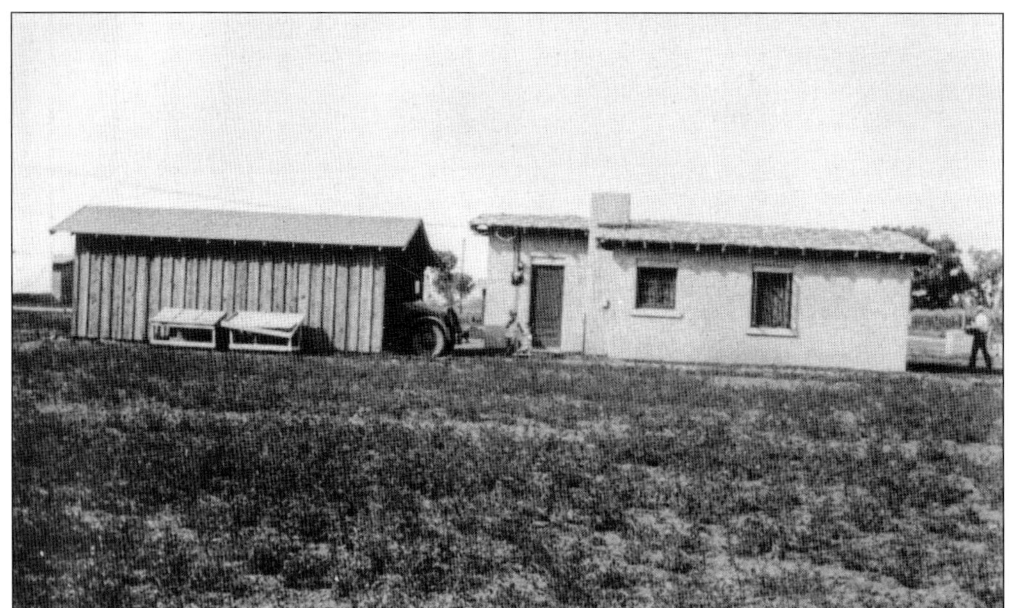

The New Deal Subsistence Homestead Program created small farms in concentrated geographic areas. Designed to help families feed themselves, the plots allowed room to grow food and to raise chickens and a cow. The adobe homes with cowsheds, designed by Phoenix architect Robert T. Evans, were on 40 acres north of Indian School, above. Christened Rural Homes of Arizona, it provided a close-to-town opportunity that allowed work in the city and work on the family farm. A second section, Arizona Part-Time Farms, was located slightly north, with a community building and a dairy. It was designed by architect Vernon deMars, supervisor of the Resettlement Administration, Western Division. (Both, courtesy of the Phoenix Homesteads Association Collection, Arizona Collection, Arizona State University Libraries.)

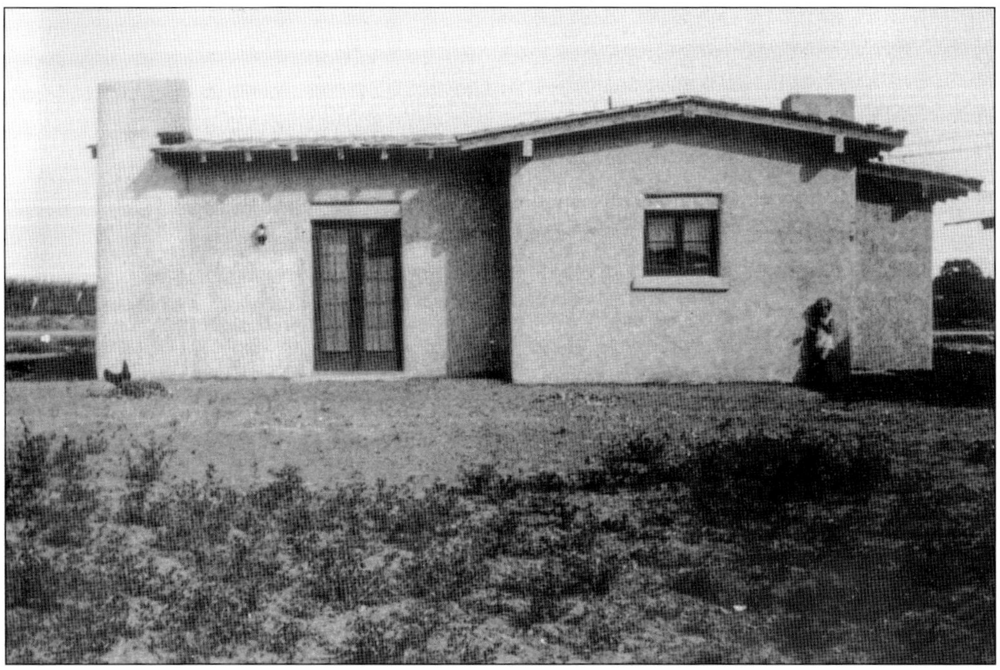

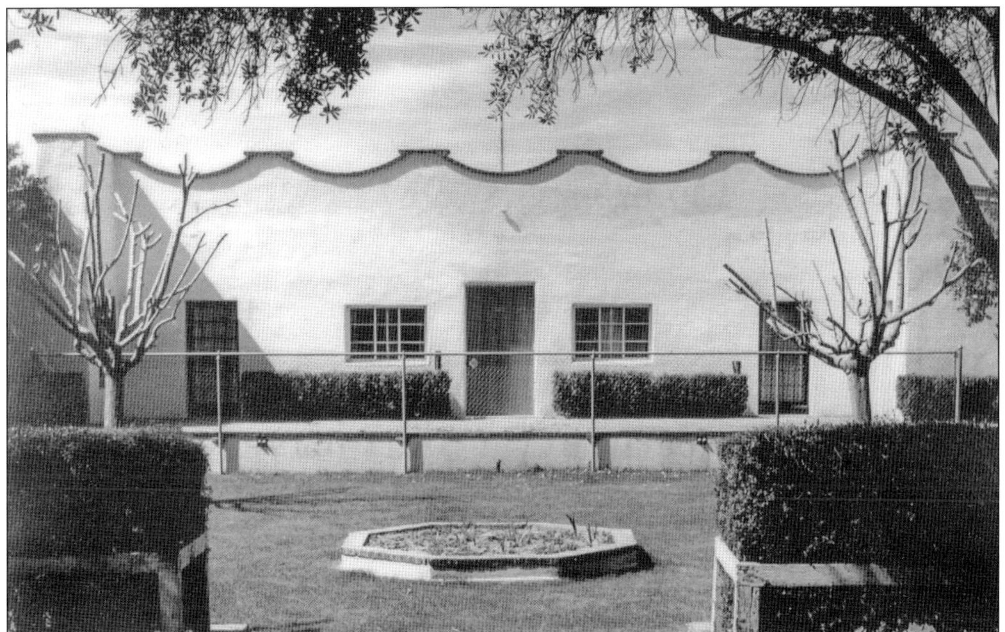

There was division of opinion in the United States on the benefits of subsistence farms in the 1930s, but the program proved valuable to generations of Americans. Today, homes in the Phoenix Homesteads Historic District continue to provide an attractive and a desirable place to live. It is irrefutable proof of the usefulness of the original program. Most of the homes remain in the bucolic setting of the Phoenix Homesteads Historic District, listed in the National Register of Historic Places, and are shaded by 80-year-old trees. The community building, pictured above and below, was purchased by the Creighton School District and remains in service today. (Above, courtesy of the Creighton School District; below, courtesy of the Encanto Citizens Association.)

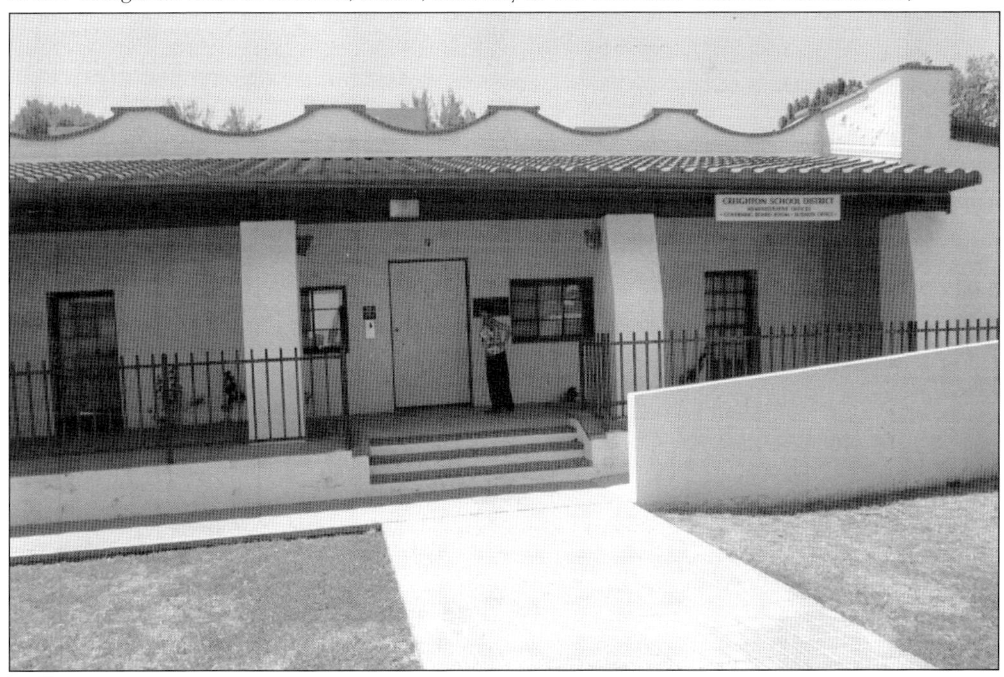

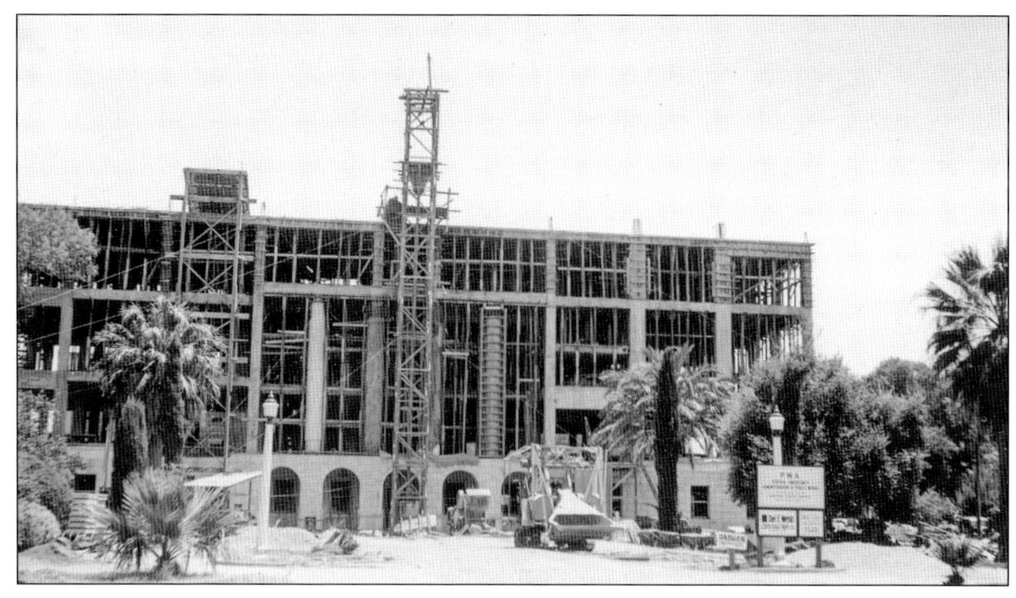

The historic Arizona Capitol was in need of an addition during the 1930s to house the library, archives, and public records that had accumulated during many decades. A rising Arizona contractor, Del Webb, was chosen. The work on the addition was started in 1937, above, and was completed in 1938. The addition and the art within were funded by the New Deal Public Works Administration. Jay Datus, a 23-year-old Michigan artist who had studied at prestigious art schools, created the eight murals in the capitol addition after intense study. The murals titled the Pageant of Arizona Progress depict Native Americans, early explorers, and pioneers and nod to the future. (Both, courtesy of the Arizona State Library, Archives and Public Records, History and Archives Division.)

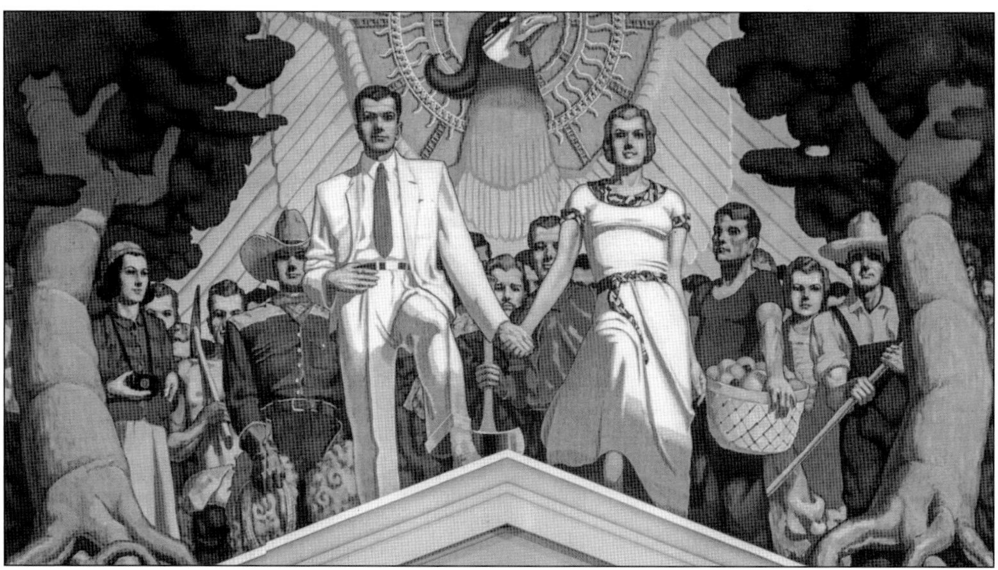

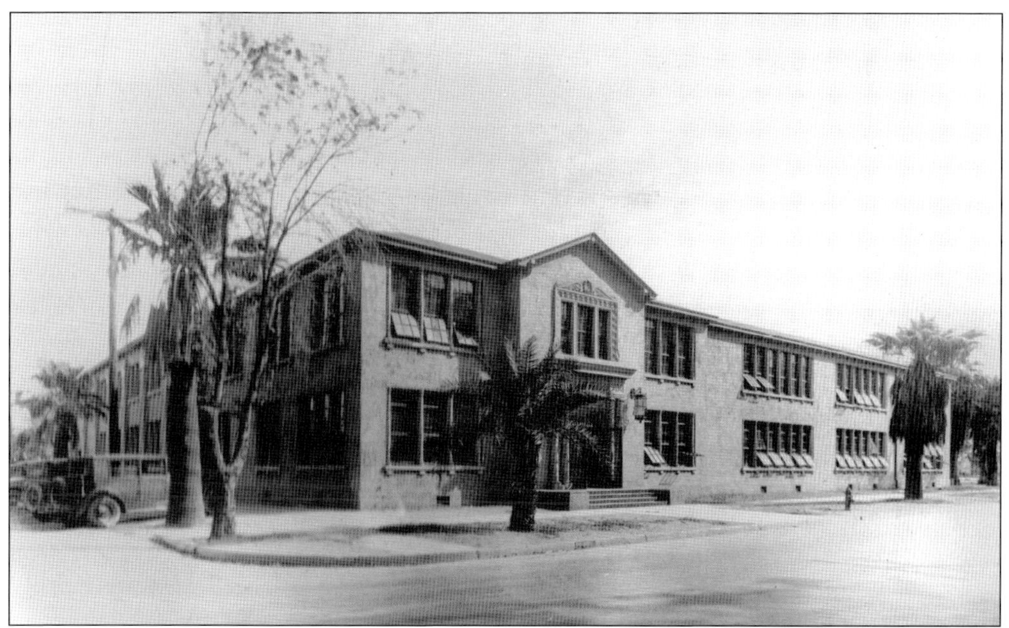

Phoenix Junior College originated in 1920, in a wooden building on the now historic Phoenix Union High School campus. In 1929, the beautiful structure, pictured above on Seventh and Van Buren Streets, was erected for the expanding student body. The burgeoning student population had rapidly outgrown that building, and expansion plans were made. By 1938, substantial funding had been obtained from the Public Works Administration and the Works Progress Administration. A parcel at 1202 West Thomas Road was selected for several new school buildings. Several of the best-known and creative architects working in Phoenix were chosen for different buildings. The Lescher and Mahoney firm designed the E Building, below, now the Noble Engineering–Science Building. (Both, courtesy of Phoenix College.)

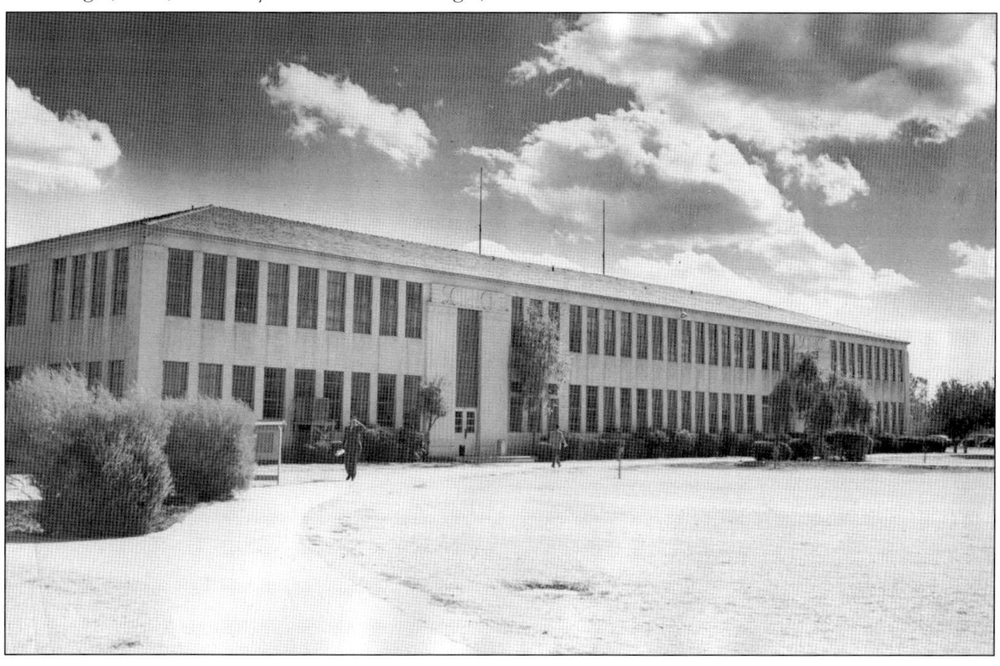

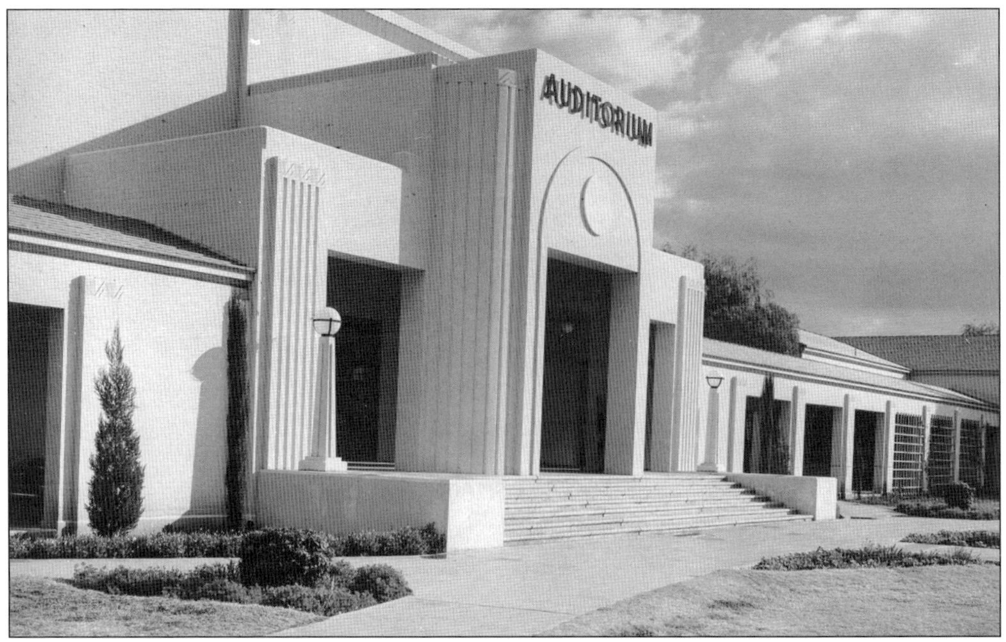

The beautiful Art Deco Phoenix Junior College Auditorium, above, was the centerpiece of the new campus. The stylistic fluted pilasters, ornamental lighting columns, rounded features over the door, and strong horizontal lines of the stairs speak to the hopeful and optimistic mood of the times. The 1939 New York World's Fair motto "the world of tomorrow" highlighted the rush toward the new by architects and designers. The Liberal Arts Building, below, opposite the E Building, was designed by architect Frederick Wallis Whittlesey in 1938 and funded with $250,000 from the Works Progress Administration. The rounded entryway and glass blocks above the door give it a modernistic style in addition to admitting light to the second story. (Both, courtesy of Phoenix College.)

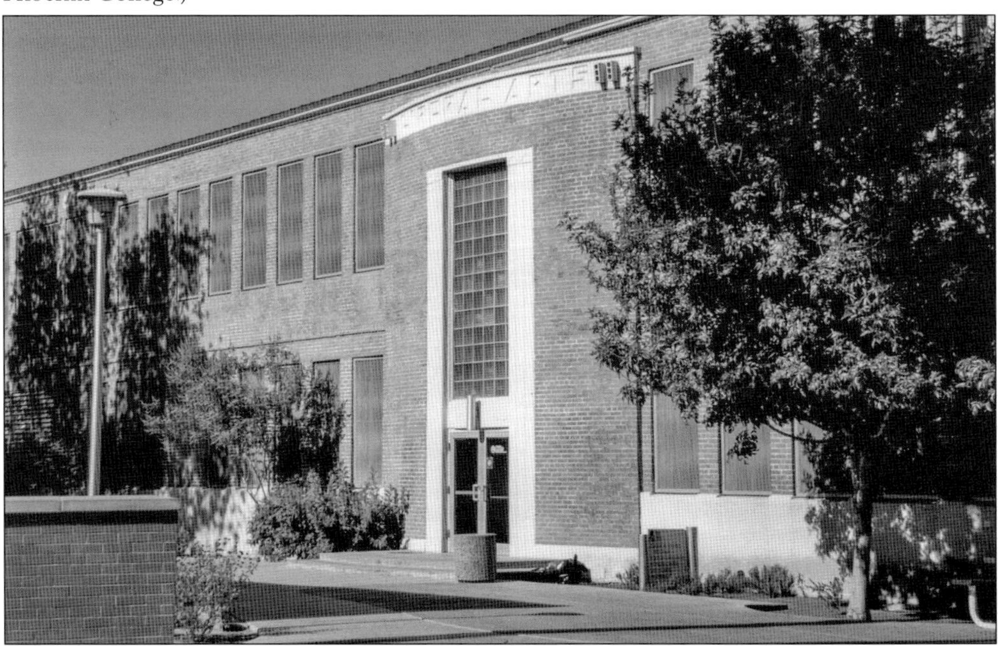

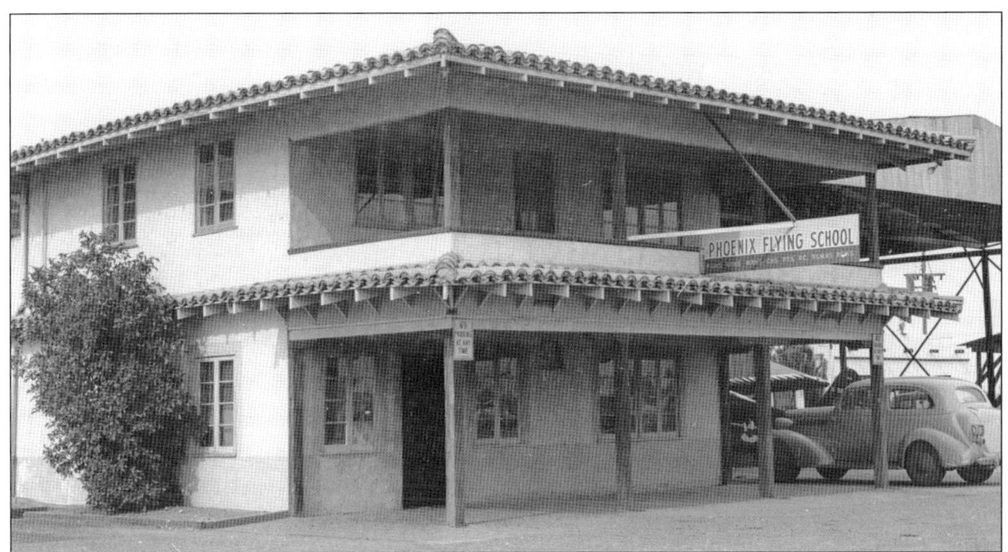

The D Building on the Phoenix Junior College campus, above, was designed by the noted architect H.H. Green in 1938. He designed many wonderful residential properties in Phoenix. Originally designed as the college's library, it housed the college's radio station on the second floor. It was funded by $250,000 in Works Progress Administration money. In later years, it was used for computer and media services. Beginning in 1939, Phoenix Junior College was one of three public schools in the nation to offer an aviation pilot training program. Flying instruction was given on the campus, and field instruction took place at Phoenix Flying School at Sky Harbor Airport, below. (Both, courtesy of Phoenix College.)

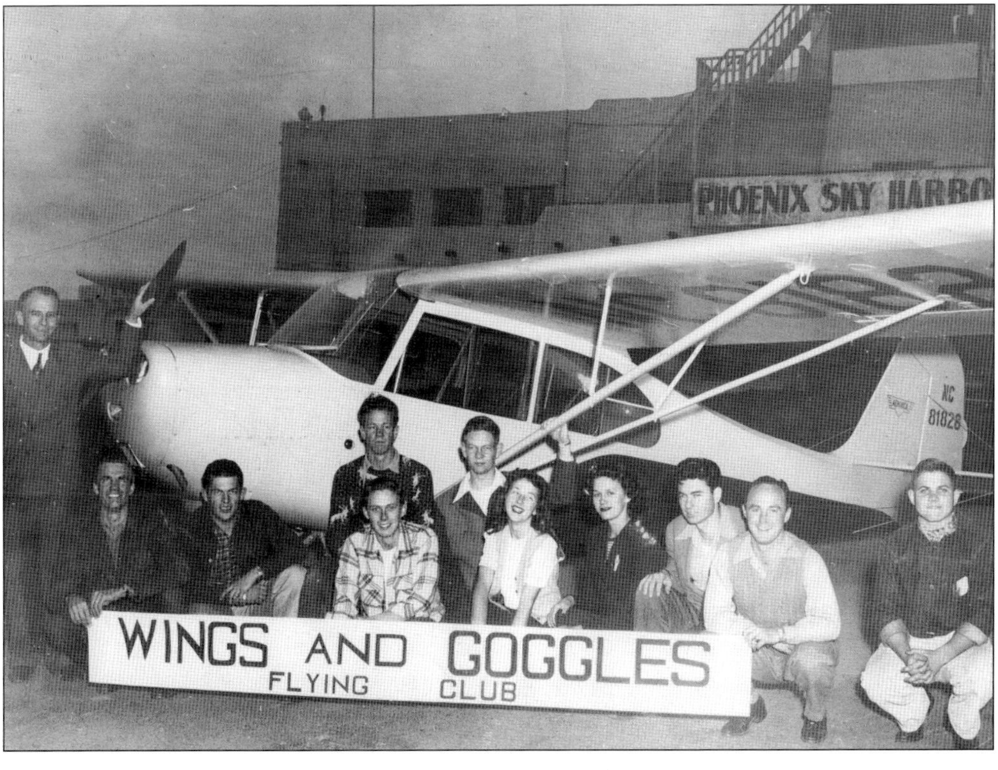

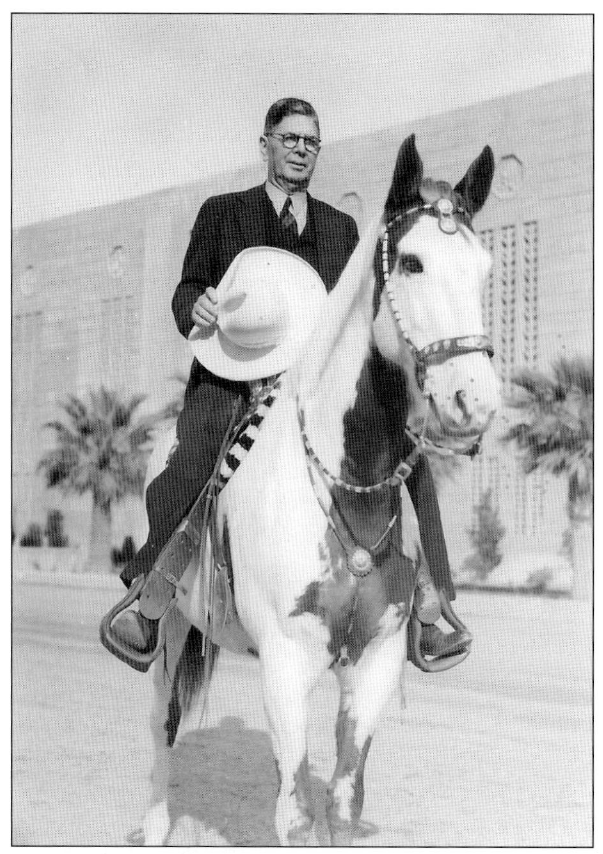

Famous Arizonans had always been pictured on horseback, and even though they traveled by air for business, for many men in the state, their horse was their favorite method of travel. Gov. Robert Taylor "Bob" Jones, left, is pictured in 1939 in front of Moeur Stadium at the fairgrounds. Jones readied Arizona for war by strengthening the National Guard. He had also served in the state senate, where he passed legislation for old-age pensioners' relief and coauthored a minimum wage act for women. Joseph E. Refsnes, below, a prominent stockbroker is shown on his horse Nick Carter in 1939. (Both, courtesy of Carolyn Refsnes Kniazzeh.)

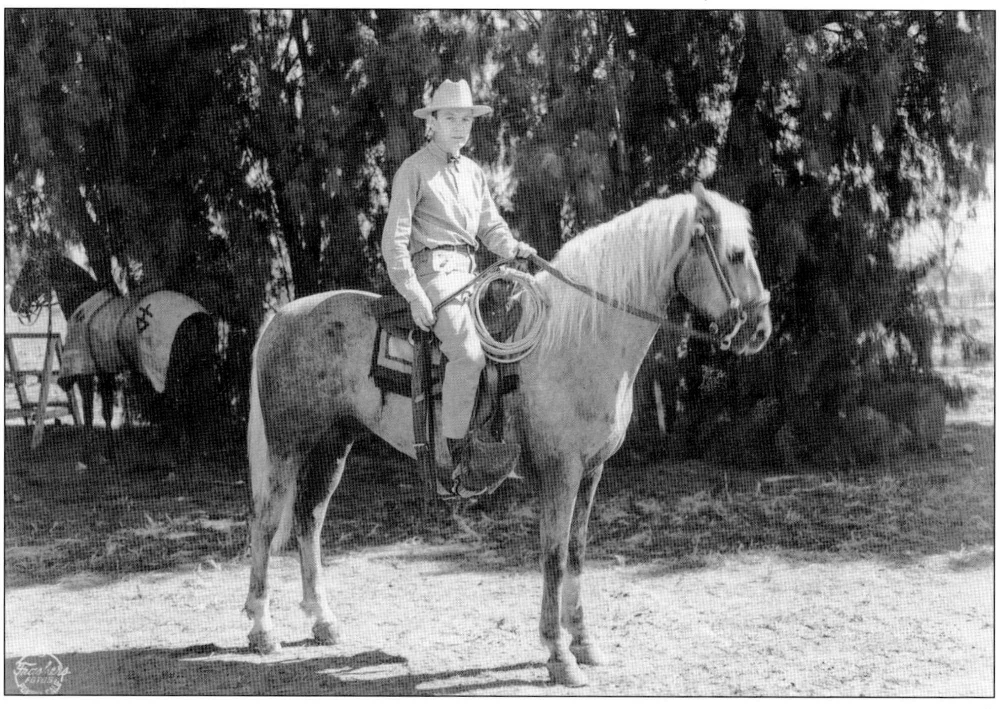

Three

Fairs Resume But War Intervenes

State fairs resumed in 1940. By 1941, Paul F. Jones was named secretary to the fair commission, and things seemed normal after years of cancellations. However, the United States entered World War II in December 1941. The fairgrounds were commandeered soon afterward by the Department of War for the duration of the war. Years went by without a fair, but the grounds were not idle. The Phoenix Junior Chamber of Commerce continued its Rodeo of Rodeos throughout the war years to raise funds and keep spirits high in the community. Their efforts and proceeds supported the Red Cross canteen at the Union Railroad Station, scrap drives, and other projects.

Army equipment was repaired and stored on the grounds. Officers and soldiers bivouacked there. The ordnance department supplied combat units with weapons and ammunition. Troop trains passing through Phoenix allowed soldiers to sleep in the cattle barns overnight.

According to an eyewitness during one particularly memorable episode in 1942, authorities discovered a shortwave radio hidden in the basement of a market belonging to a Japanese family facing Grand Avenue at the Six Points intersection. McDowell Road, Nineteenth Avenue, and Grand were cordoned off, and all access to the fairgrounds was closed by the highway patrol, sheriff's posse, and Military Police while the situation was neutralized.

With year-round perfect weather for flying, Phoenix became an ideal spot for training pilots. Defense plants opted to locate away from the West Coast since it was believed that enemy bombers could not fly this far inland. Garrett AiResearch from California occupied the original Works Progress Administration (WPA) headquarters at the fairgrounds around 1943. In the book *Out of Thin Air*, a history of the Garrett AiResearch Company, a line about the Phoenix operation mentions "working temporarily at a nearby race track." The book neglected to mention that the racetrack was located on the famous Arizona State Fairgrounds.

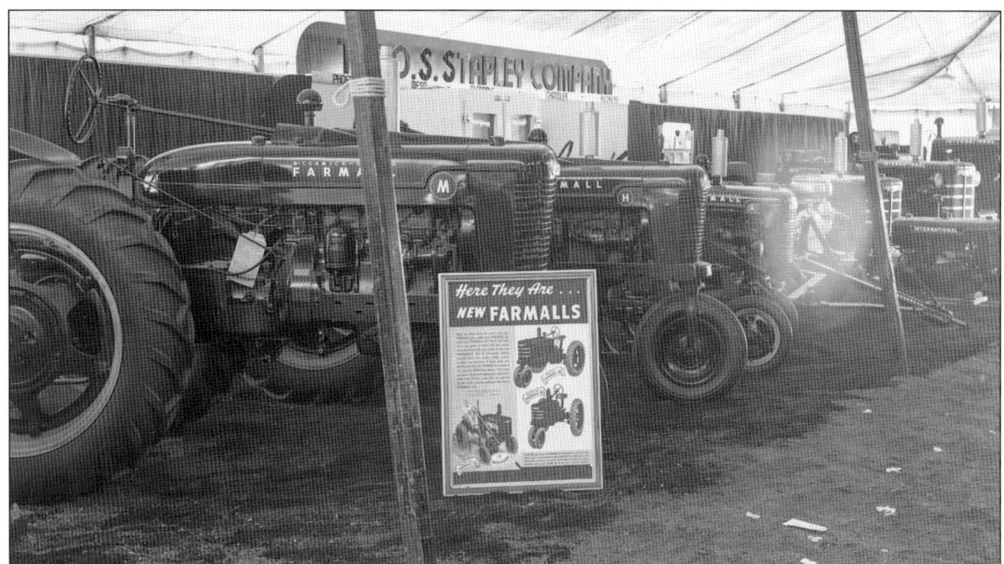

The hardest years of the Depression were fading by 1940, and there was hope for the future when life would return to normal. The O.S. Stapley Company, located at 723–747 Grand Avenue, stocked everything for the farm. These new Farmall tractors, above, were the centerpiece of their display at the fair that year. (Courtesy of the McCulloch Brothers Photographs, Herb and Dorothy McLaughlin Collection, Arizona State University Libraries.)

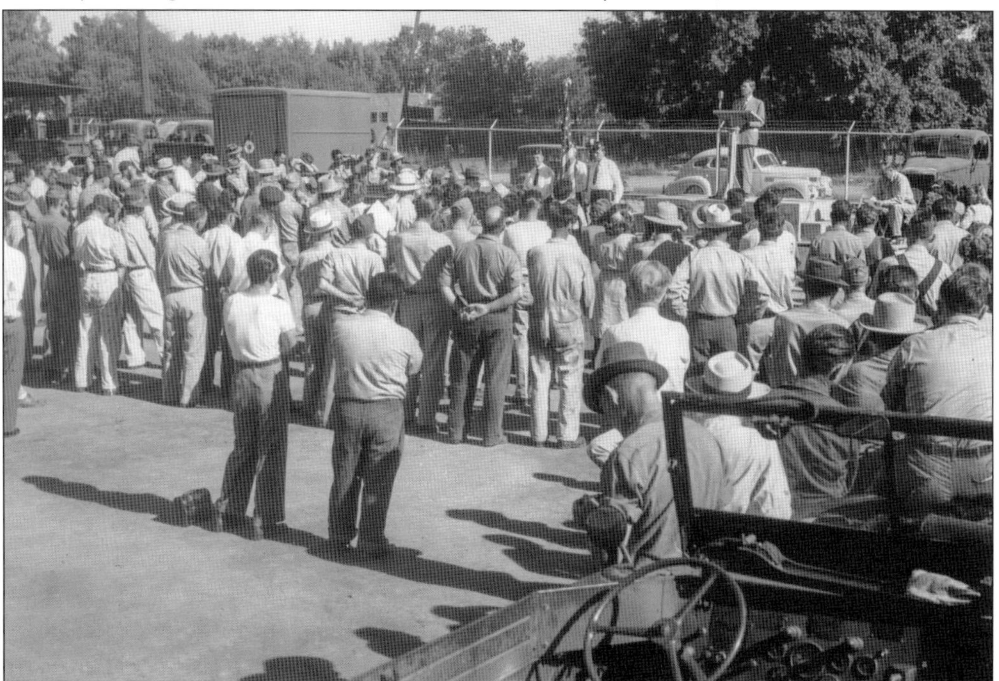

Americans were jolted by World War II in 1941, and thereafter, fairs were canceled for years. Gov. Sidney P. Osborn, pictured on the fairgrounds, is selling the crowd on the importance of purchasing war bonds to support the troops. The US government issued a savings bond for $18.25 that could be redeemed in 10 years for $25. War bonds financed the tremendous war expenditures. (Courtesy of the Arizona State Library, Archives and Public Records, History and Archives Division.)

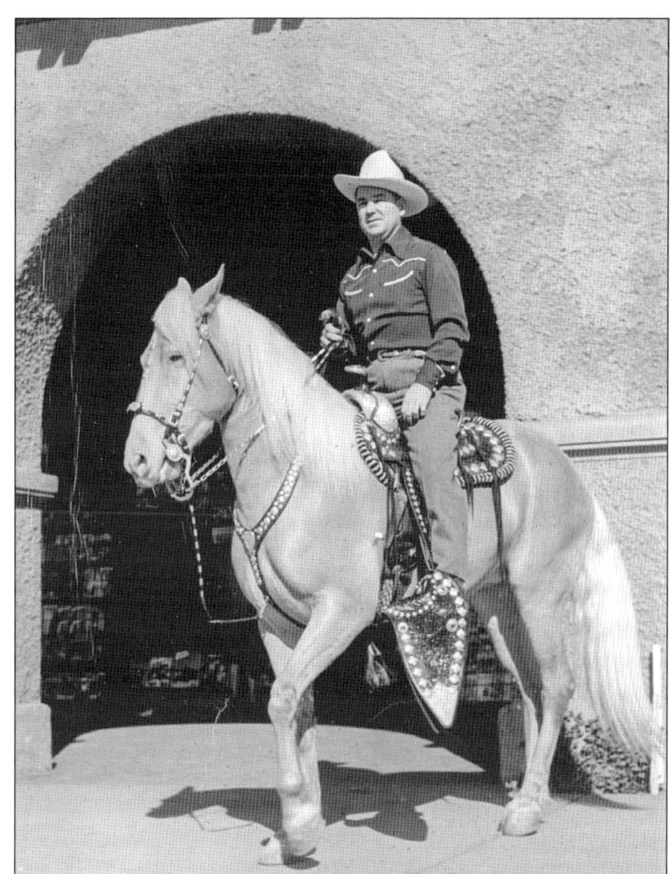

Andy Womack, well-known as a member of the Phoenix Junior Chamber of Commerce, homebuilder, and rodeo clown, kept the rodeo functioning through the war to earn money for the Jaycees' charity projects. Andy owned a famous Palomino horse named War Bond, pictured right. People would attend the Jaycees scrap drives just to see the horse. War Bond was recognizable in the Jaycees parade because of his distinctive pale-honey color. Andy's trained livestock, such as Brahma bulls, greeted dignitaries arriving for the rodeos during the war, pictured below. Known as Jaycee No. 1, Womack was eventually named to the Pro Rodeo Hall of Fame. (Both, courtesy of Karen Womack Vold.)

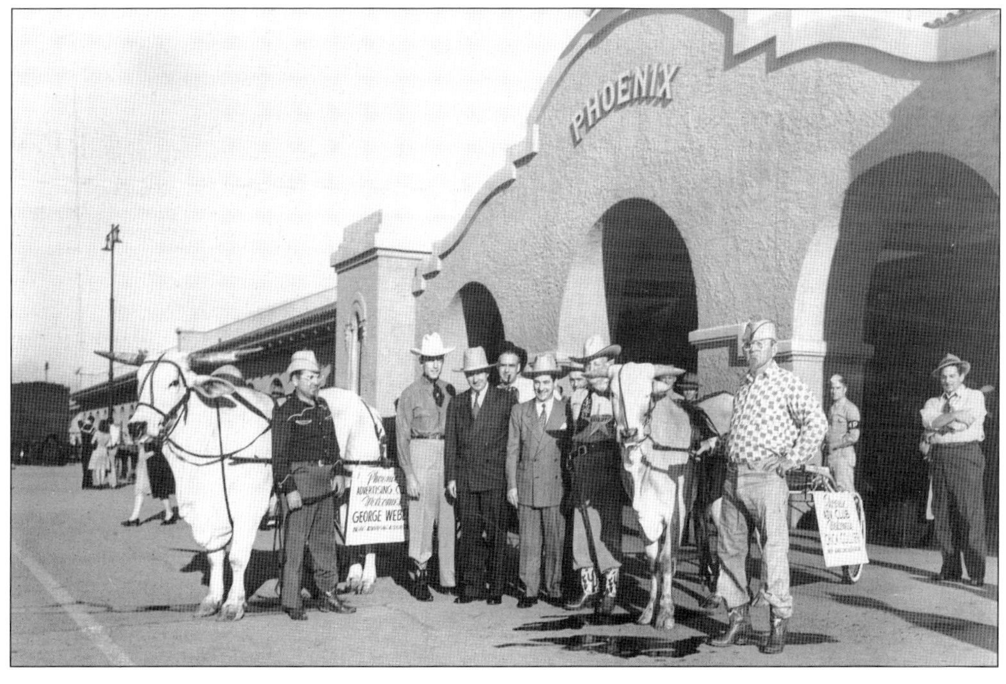

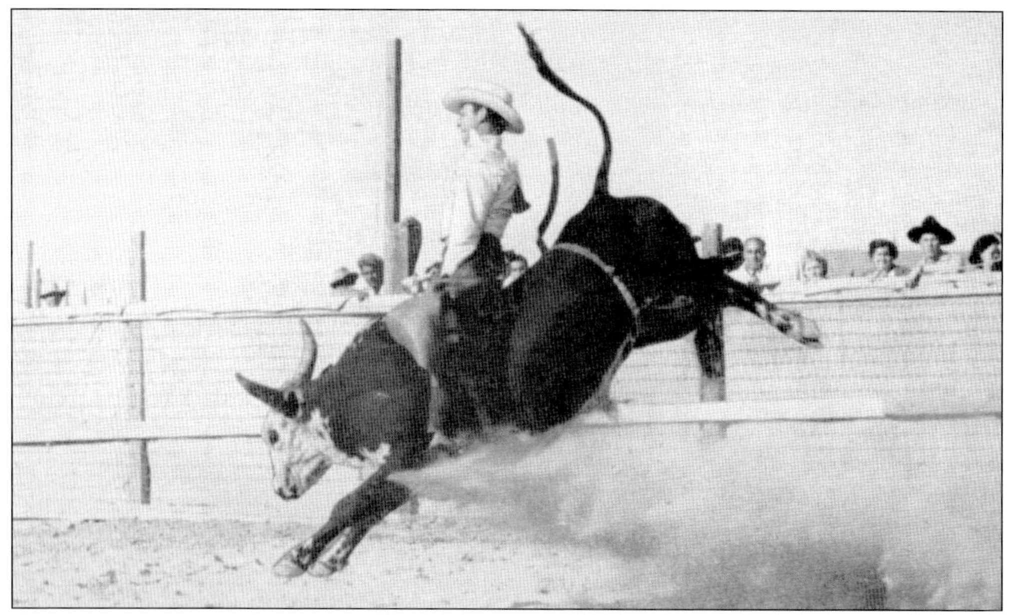

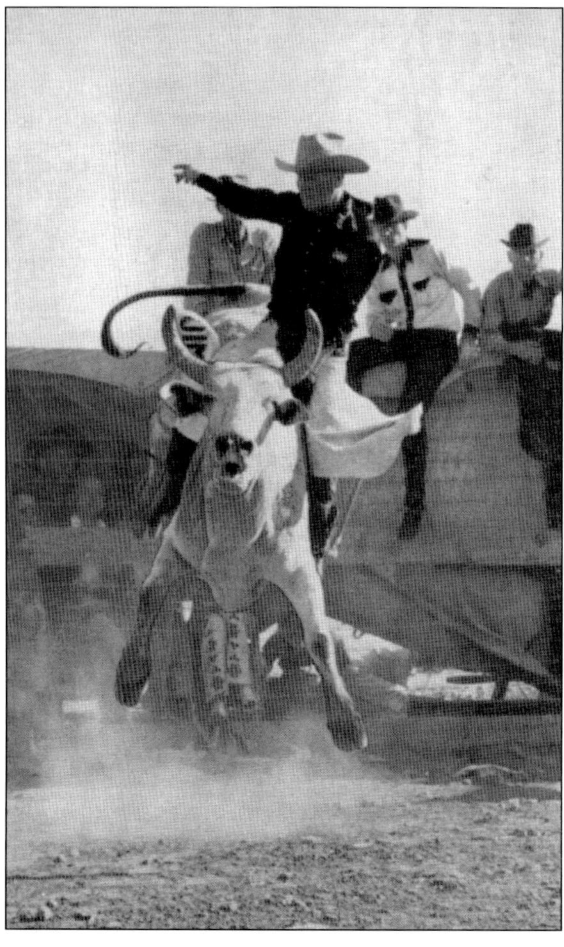

For every Brahma bull that has been tamed and trained, there are innumerable ones that are used in rodeos for bull riding contests. Rodeo photography is an art because the action moves fast. DeVere Helfrich was a well-known rodeo photographer from 1939 until 1967. He and his wife, Helen, traveled to rodeos throughout the country documenting the sport. Above is a DeVere photograph of Dick Griffith, a four-time World Champion bull rider, riding a Brahma at the 1942, Phoenix World's Championship Rodeo. The rider must stay on the bull eight seconds. At left is a DeVere photograph of Paul Gould riding a white Brahma at the 1943 Phoenix Rodeo. (Both, courtesy of Derek Horn.)

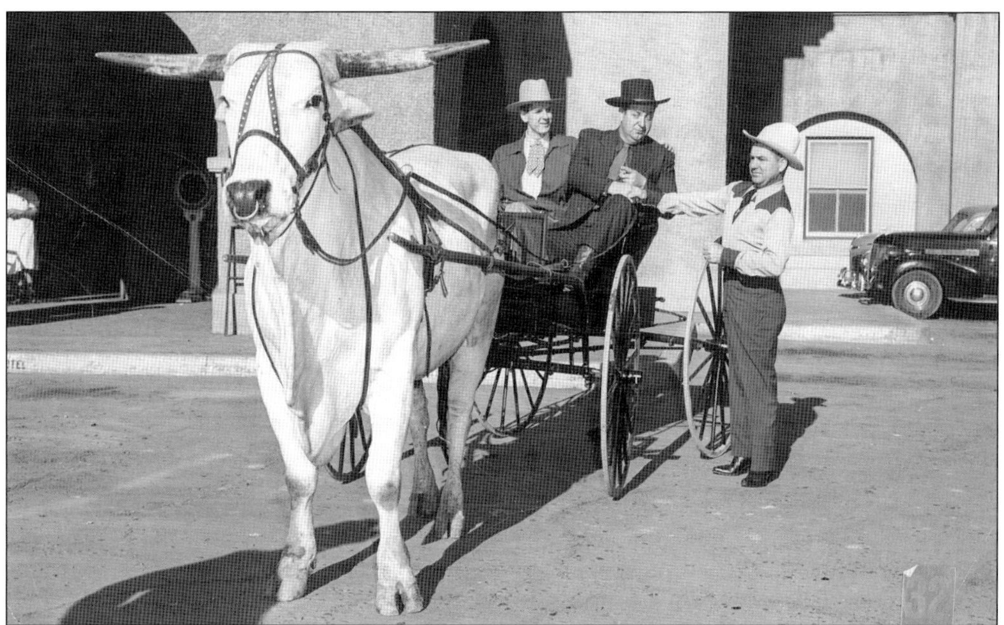

Andy Womack is standing with his trained Brahma bull Silver Dollar, pulling a cart with actor Smiley Burnette (in the dark hat) and a friend. Andy was skilled with animals. He was known as a barrel man, a rodeo clown who distracted the bulls away from a thrown rider in the bull riding events. He worked the rodeo as a performer and served as chairman. Mimicking the pose of the famous sculpture "End of the Trail" created by James Earle Fraser, he is shown below with Silver Dollar. The original sculpture shows an exhausted Native American holding a lance atop his very weary horse. (Both, courtesy of Karen Womack Vold.)

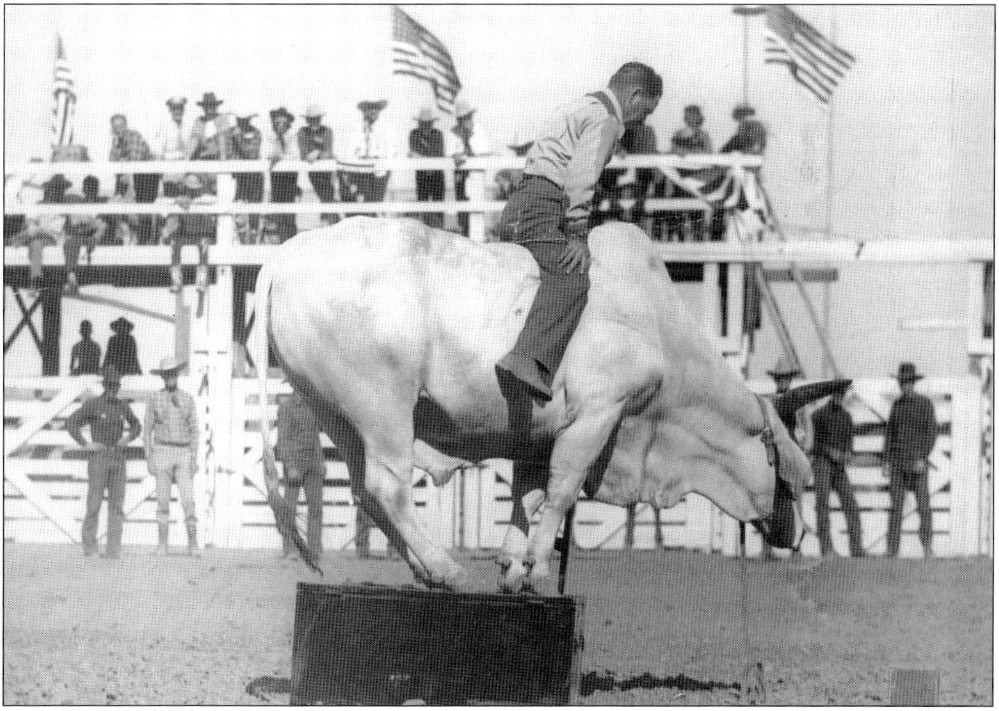

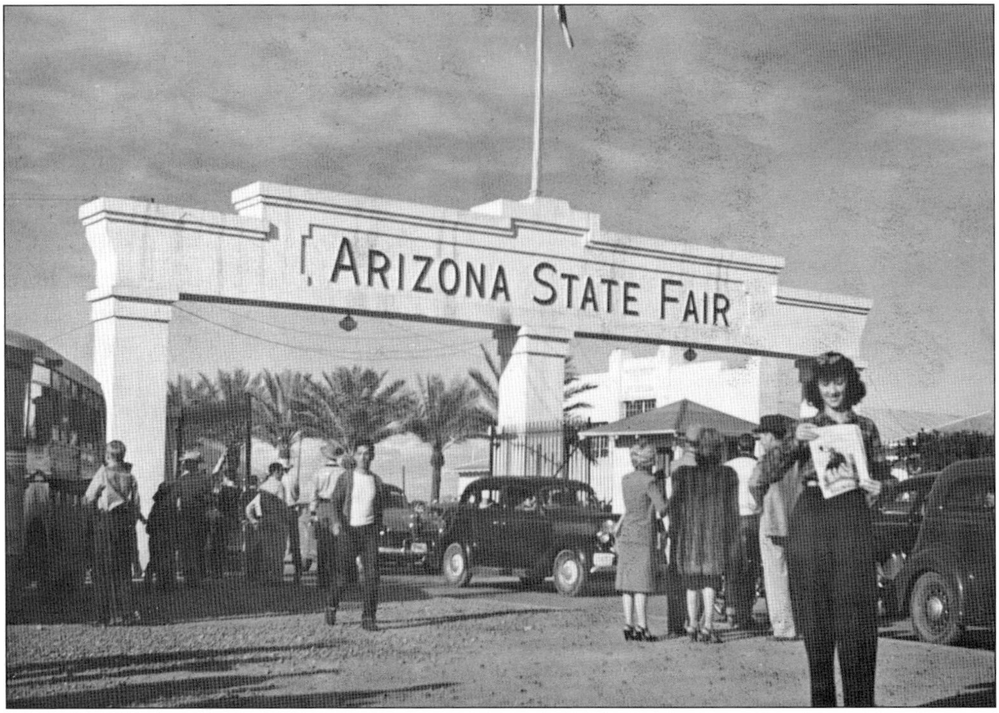

Beatrice and Bob Markow attended the Phoenix World's Championship Rodeo in March 1943. In the photograph above, Beatrice is holding a program at the original front entrance. Bob was stationed in Phoenix with the Army and became one of the most notable photographers in the city. The Jaycees' rodeo took place every March for 70 consecutive years, beginning in 1927. The Grand Entry Parade, pictured below, was a thrilling sight when all the bands, flags, and galloping horses signaled the beginning of the show. Note the abundance of soldiers in the stands. The program for that year was headlined "'A Command Performance' for You, Soldier!" (Both, courtesy of the Markow family archives.)

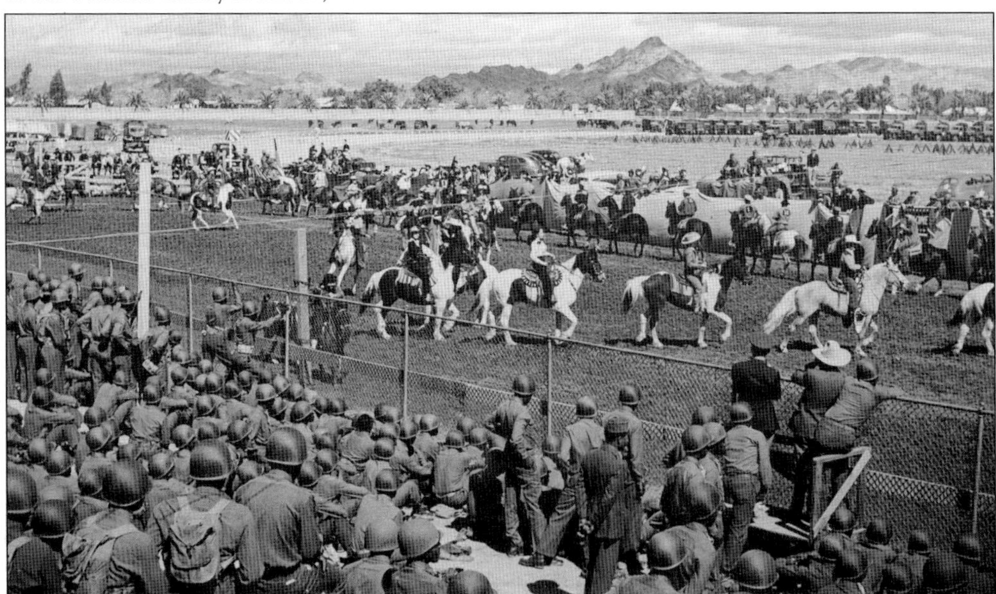

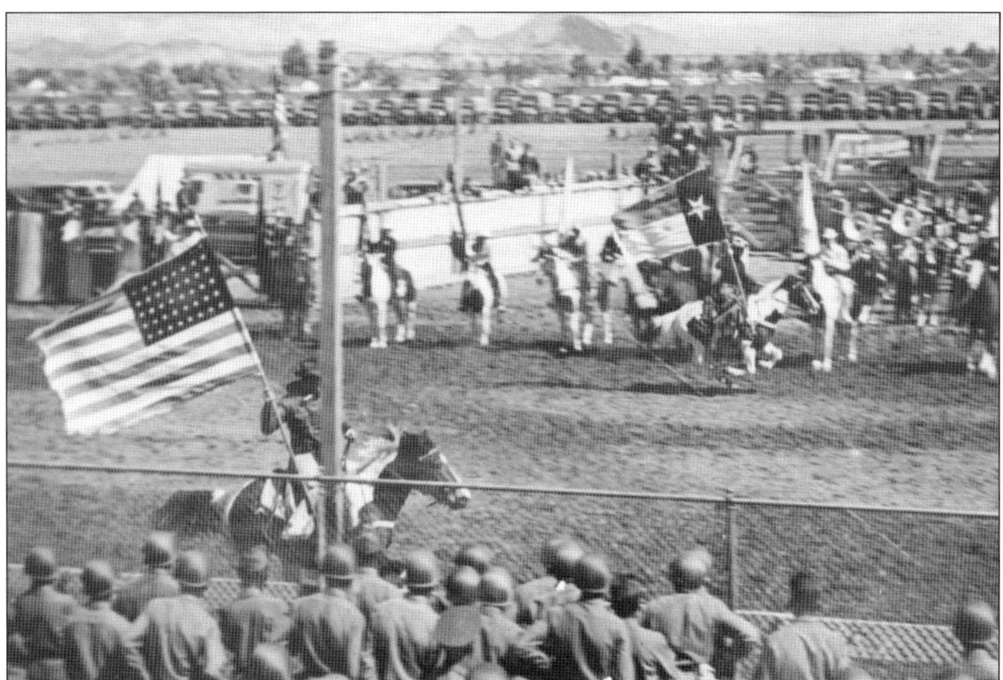

This 1943 photograph shows a rider circling the racetrack with the US flag prior to the opening performance of the rodeo. Gov. Sidney P. Osborn and Phoenix mayor Newell Stewart welcomed attendees in the Jaycees Souvenir Program. The program's theme was "Salute to the C.O.," and it featured the commanding officers from Lake Field, Williams Field, Thunderbird Fields Nos. 1 and 2, Falcon Field, and pilots from overseas. Phoenix was the largest military aviation training center in the entire nation. Note the clear view of Camelback Mountain. The wooden corrals, pictured below, were hand built by Jaycee volunteers prior to every annual rodeo. (Both, courtesy of the Markow family archives.)

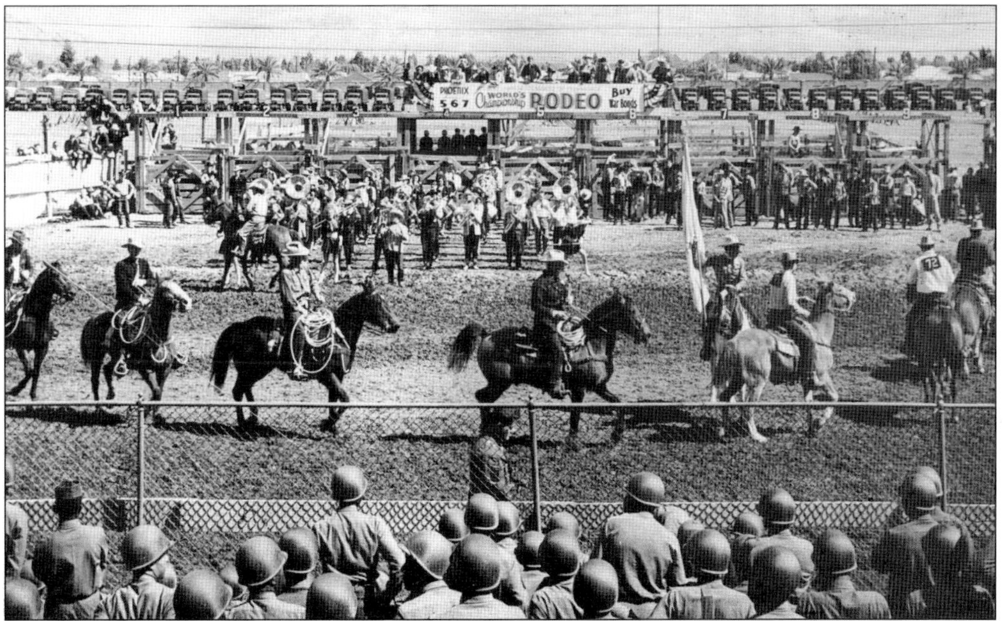

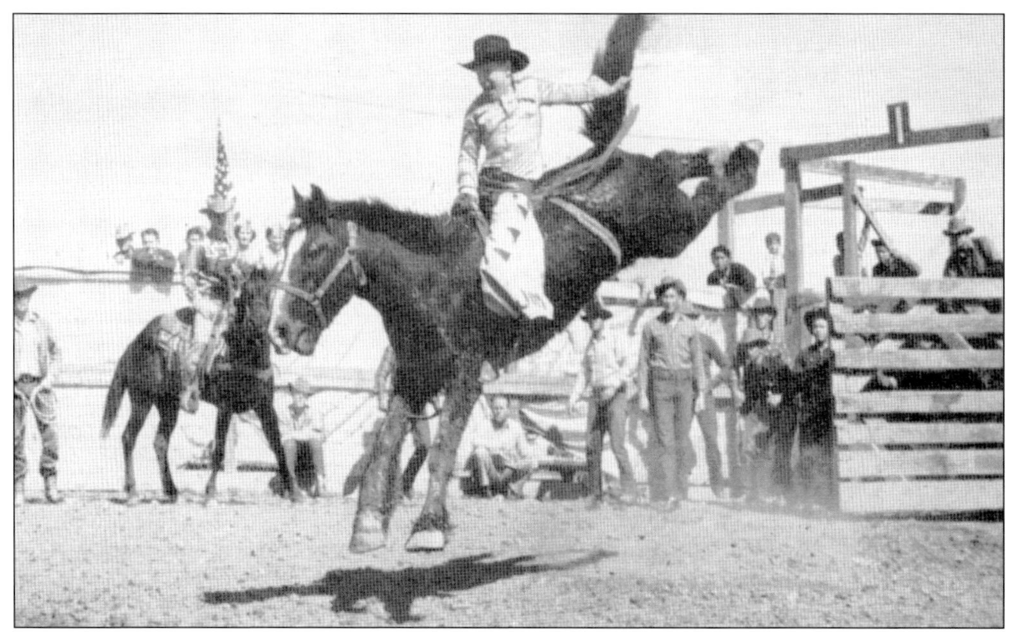

This photograph taken by DeVere Helfrich shows Jimmie Sloan on Rocket participating in the exciting and challenging sport of bronc riding. While using his/her spurs to make the unbroken horse buck, the rider can only use one hand to hold on. Several famous artists, such as Lon Megargee and Paul Coze, illustrated the Phoenix rodeo programs during the late 1930s and 1940s. (Courtesy of Derek Horn.)

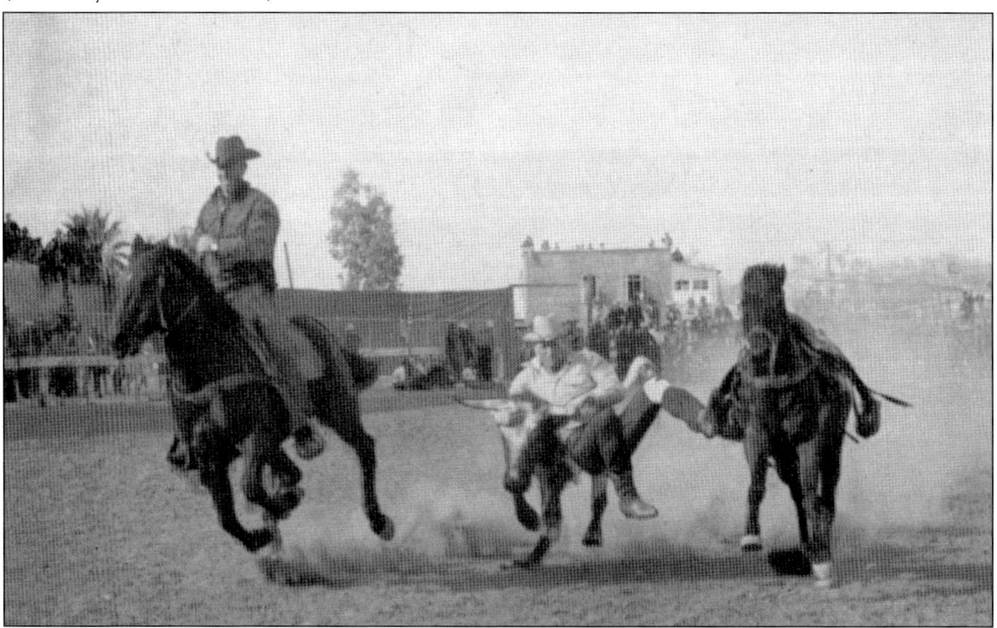

This 1942 DeVere Helfrich photograph shows Steve Hancock bulldogging, also known as steer wrestling, at the Phoenix rodeo. Bulldogging is a quick way of catching and throwing cattle without a rope. The "hazer" on the horse at left keeps the animal running straight. The Jaycees rodeo kept the fairgrounds in the spotlight from 1942 through 1945, during World War II when fairs were canceled. (Courtesy of Derek Horn.)

Gene Autry, far right, is shown clowning with Andy Womack, who entertained at many rodeo events. Gene was famous on radio, television, and the movies. He served in World War II and, later, in Special Services. Gene also owned a radio station and Western clothing store at the Hotel Adams. (Courtesy of Karen Womack Vold.)

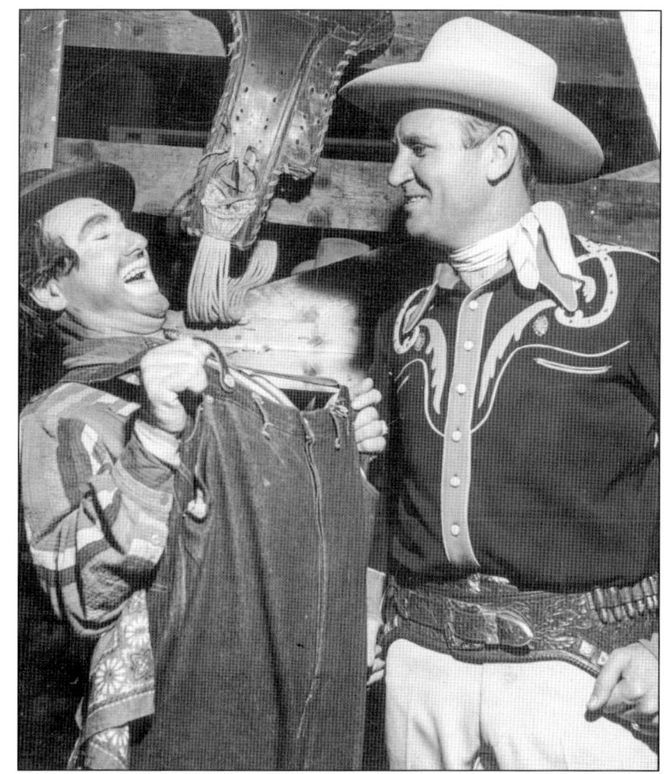

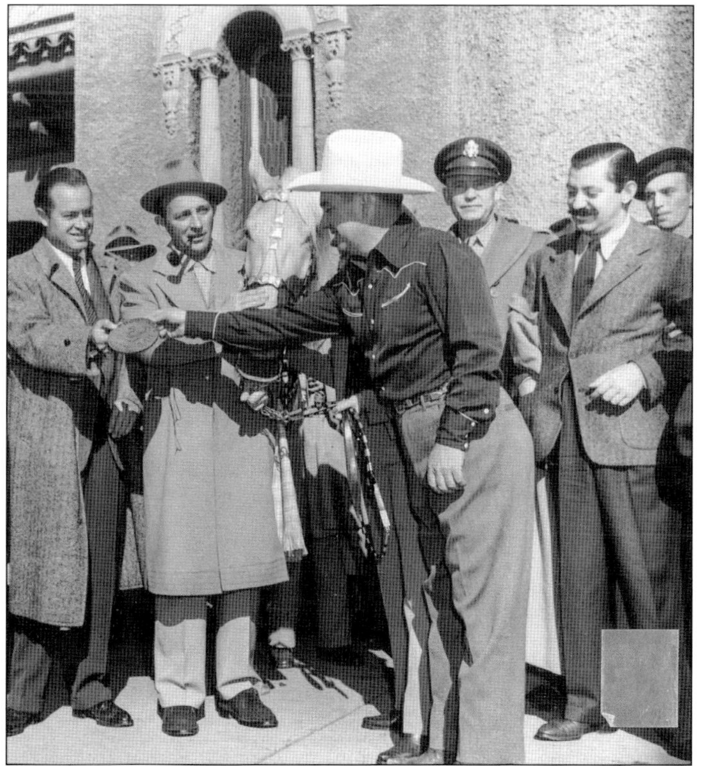

Andy Womack's roles in the Jaycees included meeting visiting entertainers at Union Station and helping build the chutes and corrals on the fairgrounds. Bob Hope and Bing Crosby, from left to right, are being welcomed by Andy and his horse War Bond, while mustachioed Jerry Colonna and servicemen wait to be greeted. (Courtesy of Karen Womack Vold.)

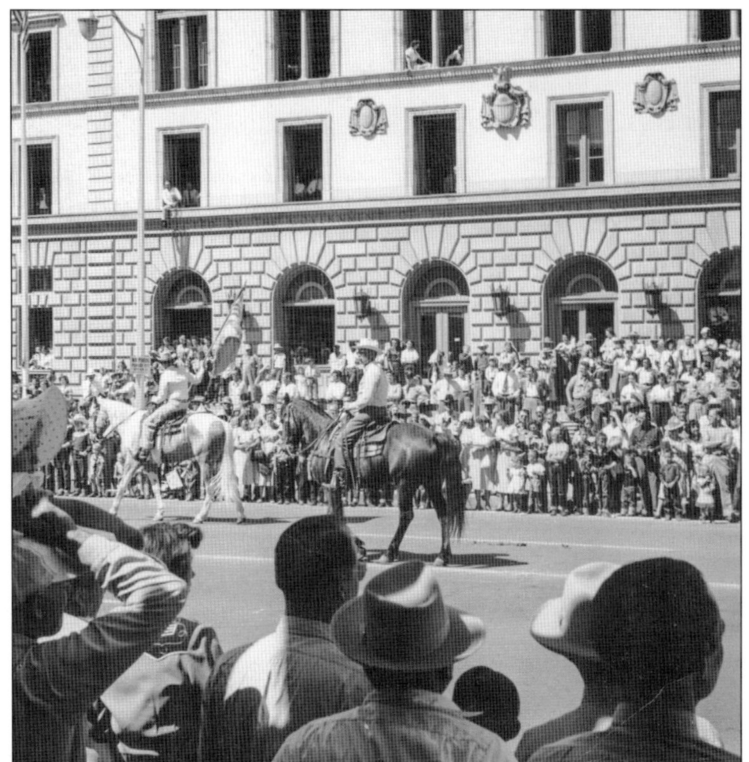

Here, the Jaycees rodeo parade was moving past the old federal building at 230 North First Avenue. The magnificent structure was constructed in 1913 and housed courts and FBI offices. This distinguished building, today often referred to as "architectural eye candy," was demolished in the late 1950s. (Courtesy of the Phoenix Jaycees.)

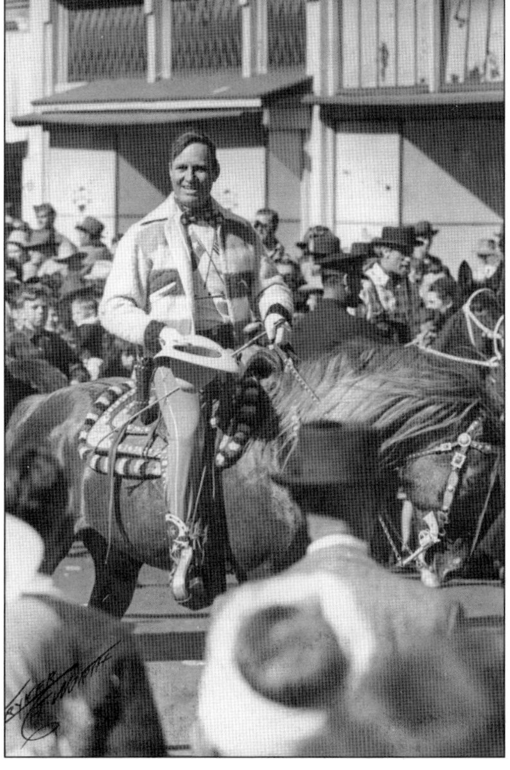

Gene Autry, a frequent visitor to Arizona, is shown in the Jaycees rodeo parade. His fictional radio ranch was located in Paradise Valley, a Phoenix suburb. "Rudolph, the Red-Nosed Reindeer," recorded by Autry in 1949, is a perennial holiday favorite. Gene Autry has five stars on the Hollywood Walk of Fame. (Courtesy of Karen Womack Vold.)

Maynard Dixon, pictured at right in 1909, was a dashing Californian whose true passion in life was the desert landscape of Arizona, New Mexico, and Utah. His artistic career began as an illustrator for newspapers and magazines. He won a medal at the Panama-Pacific International Exposition of 1915. During the Depression, he painted realistic canvases of humanity affected by the Great Depression, while his wife, Dorothea Lange, photographed those affected by the devastation. During the last 10 years of his life, he split his time between Mount Carmel, Utah, and Tucson, Arizona. Dixon died in Tucson in 1946. His last great artistic masterpiece was "The Grand Canyon of the Colorado," pictured on the following pages. (Both, courtesy of the Medicine Man Gallery, Tucson, Arizona.)

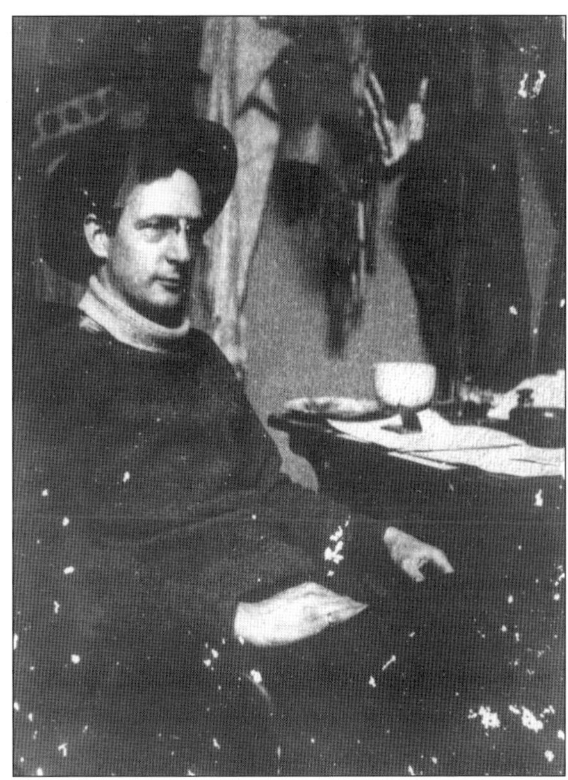

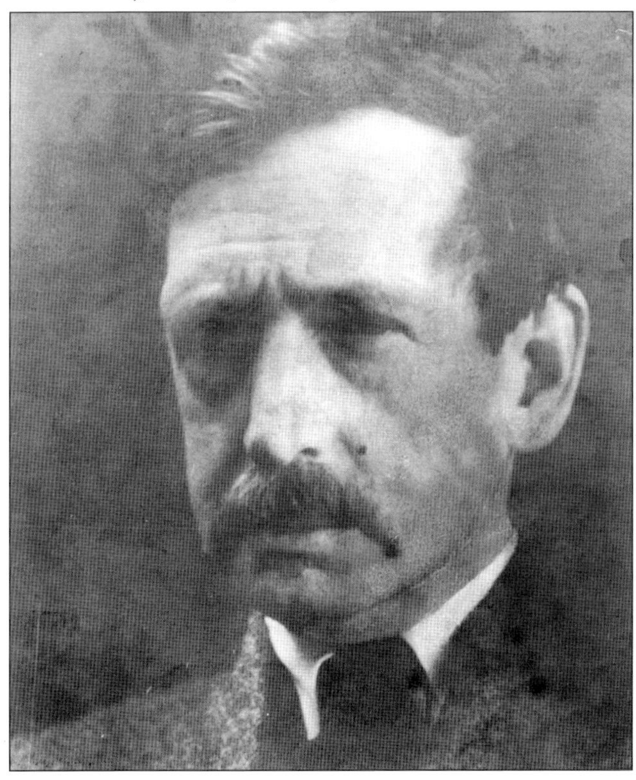

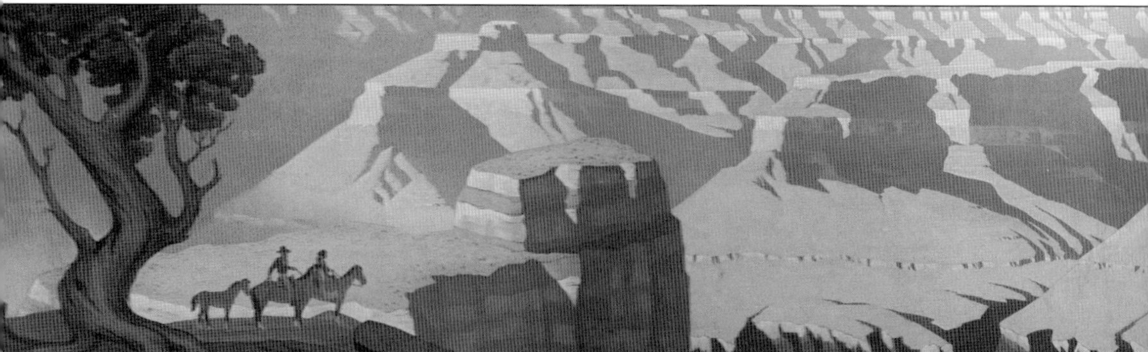

Artist Maynard Dixon conceived his mural "The Grand Canyon of the Colorado" on a monumental scale befitting the subject. Dixon, in failing health, directed the execution of this art at his Tucson studio in 1946. The immense size of the canvas, measuring 34 feet long and 5 feet high, originated as a commission for the Santa Fe Railroad's ticket office in Los Angeles, California. Later, it hung in the Veterans Memorial Coliseum at the Arizona State Fairgrounds until 2008. High-traffic

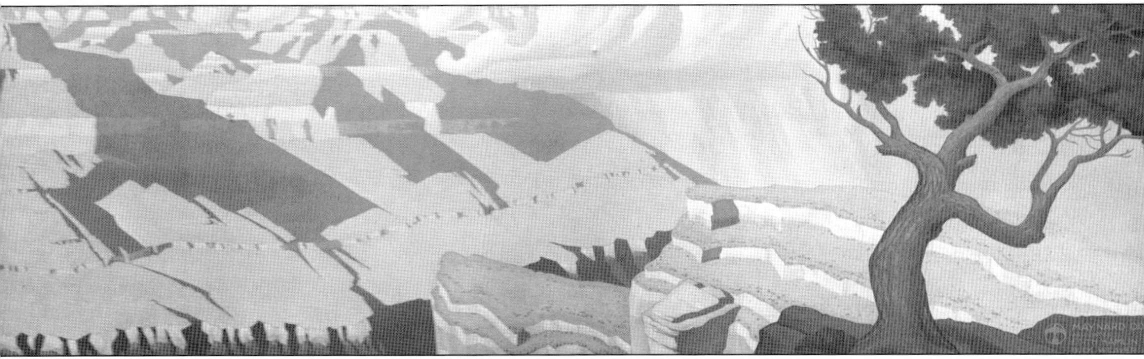

public spaces can take a toll on art. In the spirit of cooperation to save this rare treasure, the Arizona State Fair executed a 99-year lease with the Arizona Historical Society to care for the painting. It is now on display at the Arizona Historical Society Museum in Papago Park, Tempe, Arizona. (Courtesy of Arizona State Fair and Arizona Historical Society.)

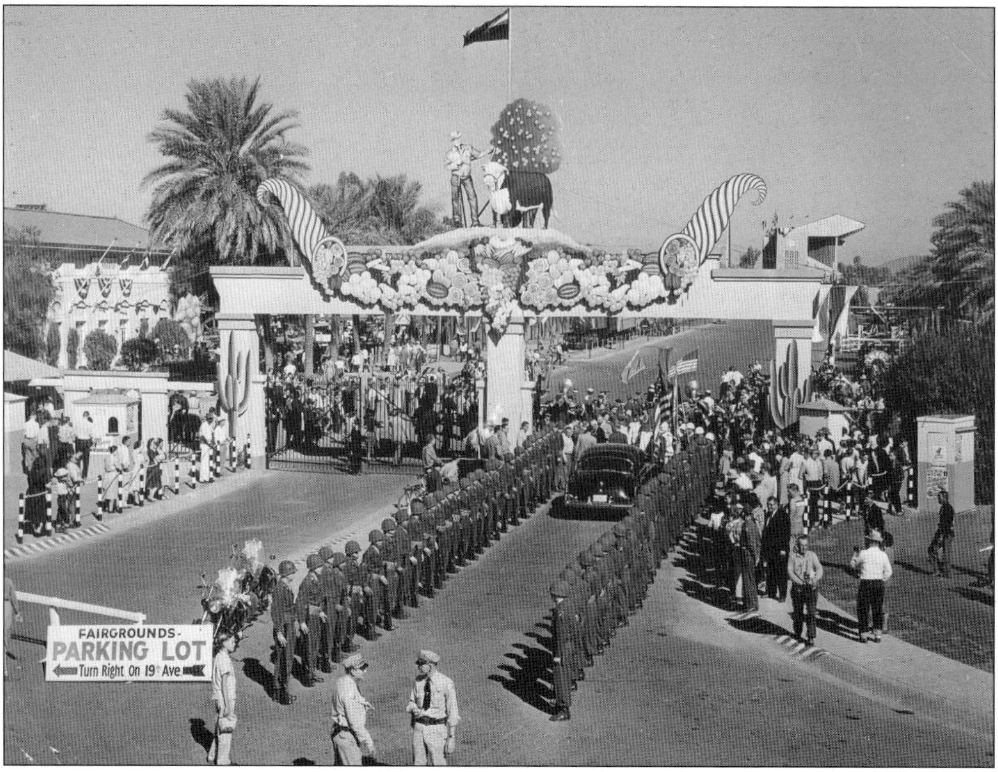

The opening-day pageantry of the Arizona State Fair in the years immediately following World War II is on display with a Military Honor Guard at the McDowell Road and Nineteenth Avenue gate. The 1919 Mining Building is shown on the left, and the B.B. Moeur Stadium is in the upper-right background. (Courtesy of the family archives of Paul F. Jones.)

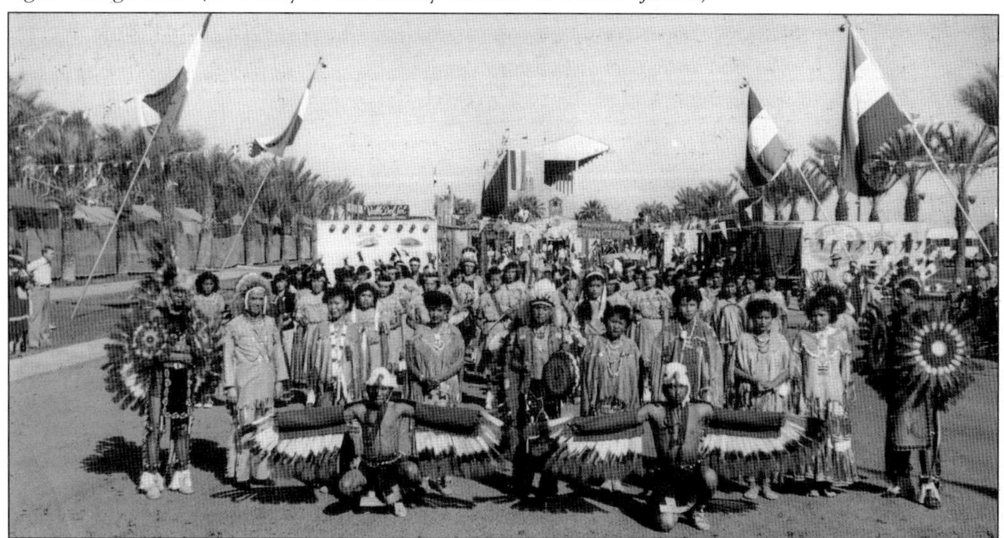

Arizona's Native American heritage has played a significant role in the state fairs. Here, tribal members and exhibitors in native dress are pictured on the main street. At one time, a Native American village was displayed on the grounds. The Valle Del Sol restaurant is pictured behind the tribal members. (Courtesy of the family archives of Paul F. Jones.)

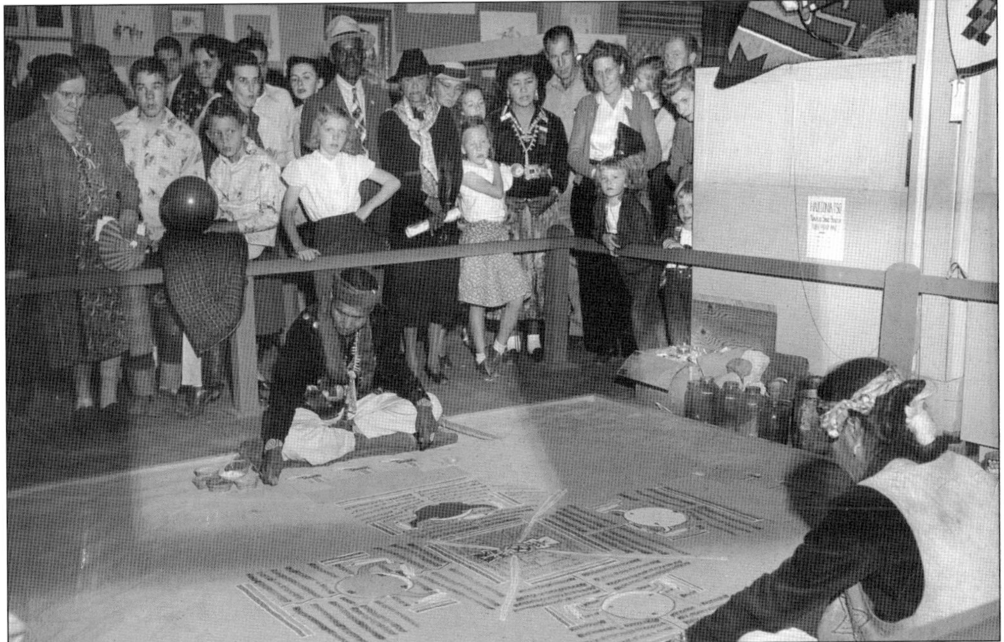

The Navajo Nation sand painter Hauegonia Tso, of Rock Point, Arizona, is depicted creating a meticulous painting. These "dry paintings" are symbolic of stories in Navajo culture and are a sacred entity. The paintings have healing power to center the recipient and restore orderly forces that give direction to their life. (Courtesy of the family archives of Paul F. Jones.)

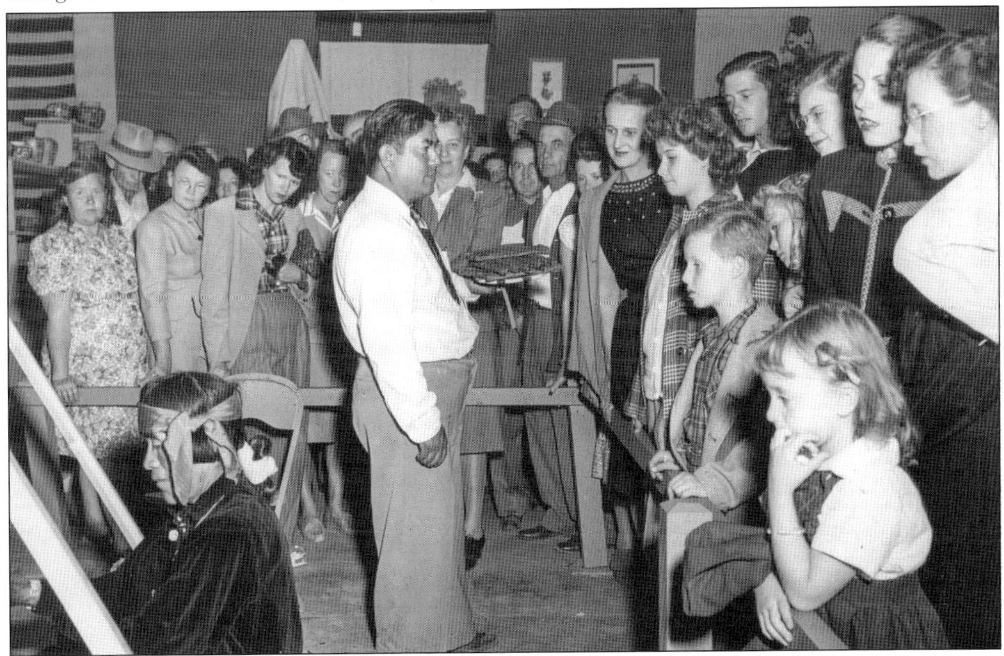

A weaver representing the Hopi Nation, Piki is shown at left presenting a display of his skills at the fair. Traditionally, weaving was done by men for hundreds of years. Another Hopi gentleman is serving bread made from corn and water to the crowd. These demonstrations were an enjoyable way to learn history. (Courtesy of the family archives of Paul F. Jones.)

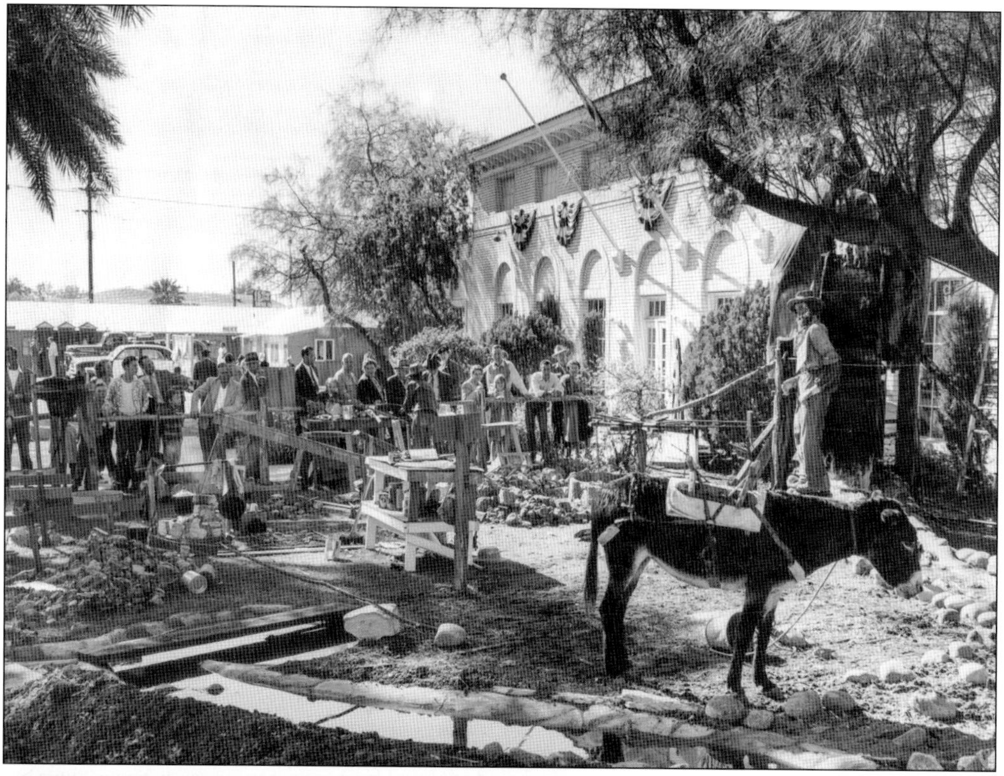

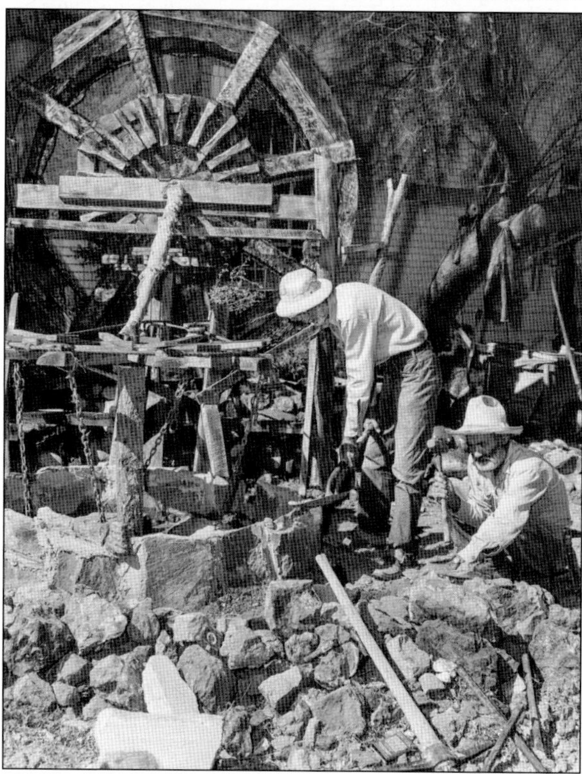

The riches of Arizona mines were the incentives that drew early settlers. The Mineral Museum, above, was dedicated in 1919, when mining provided much of the wealth in the state. The placid burro providing the power illustrates the ingenuity used to move and crush ore prior to the coming of electricity. (Courtesy of the family archives of Paul F. Jones.)

The prospectors mining for riches depict a typical mining site in early days. Gold was discovered along the Colorado River in 1862. Henry Wickenburg discovered gold at the Vulture Mine in 1863, near the city named for him. Copper has been a leading industry in the state since the late 1800s. (Courtesy of the family archives of Paul F. Jones.)

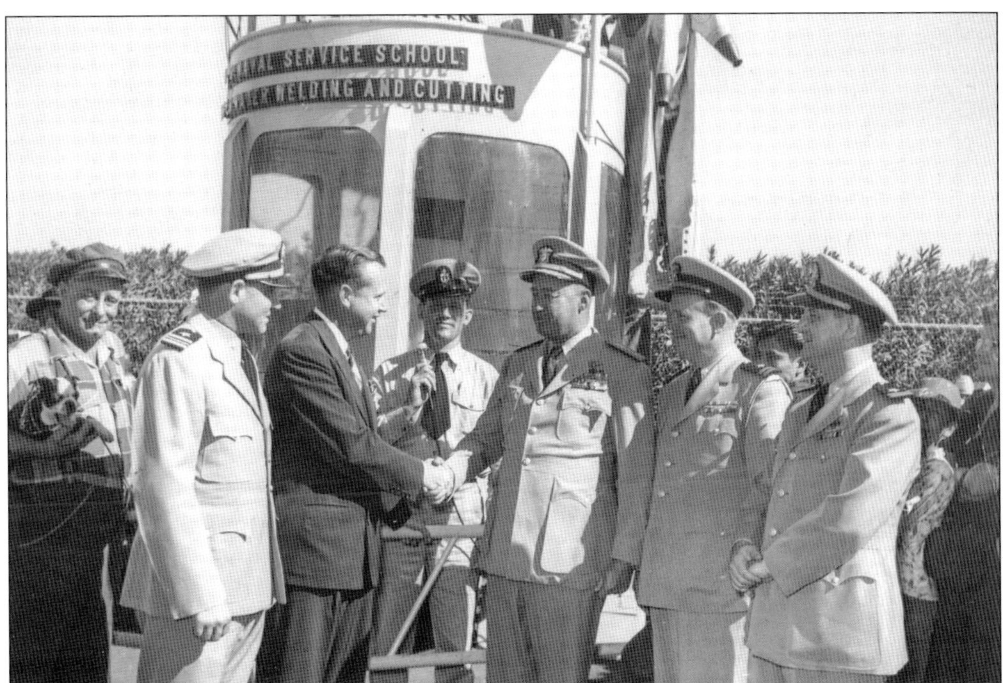

In the years after World War II, there was a great deal of curiosity among children and adults about items used by the armed services as related to the war. Admiral Joseph J. "Jocko" Clark and other officers opened this fair exhibition of the Naval Service School's underwater welding and cutting techniques. (Courtesy of the family archives of Paul F. Jones.)

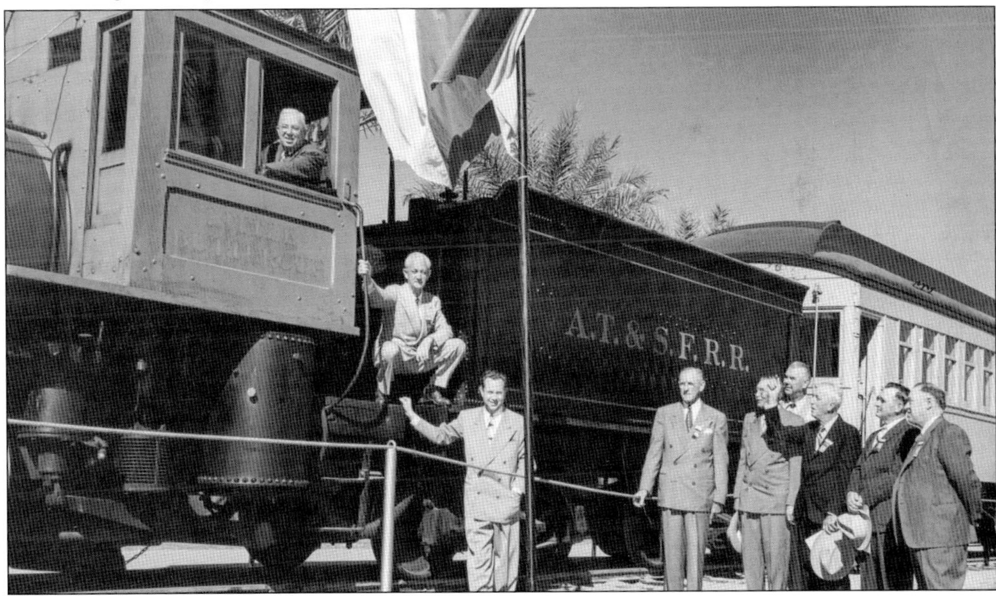

Little Buttercup, with Gov. Dan Garvey at the throttle, was an 1879 steam engine that became a movie star. The engine appeared in *Santa Fe*, the Columbia Pictures story of the Santa Fe Railroad. In addition to the state fair, the historic iron horse had appeared at the Chicago Railroad Fair and the San Bernardino, California, Orange Festival. (Courtesy of the family archives of Paul F. Jones.)

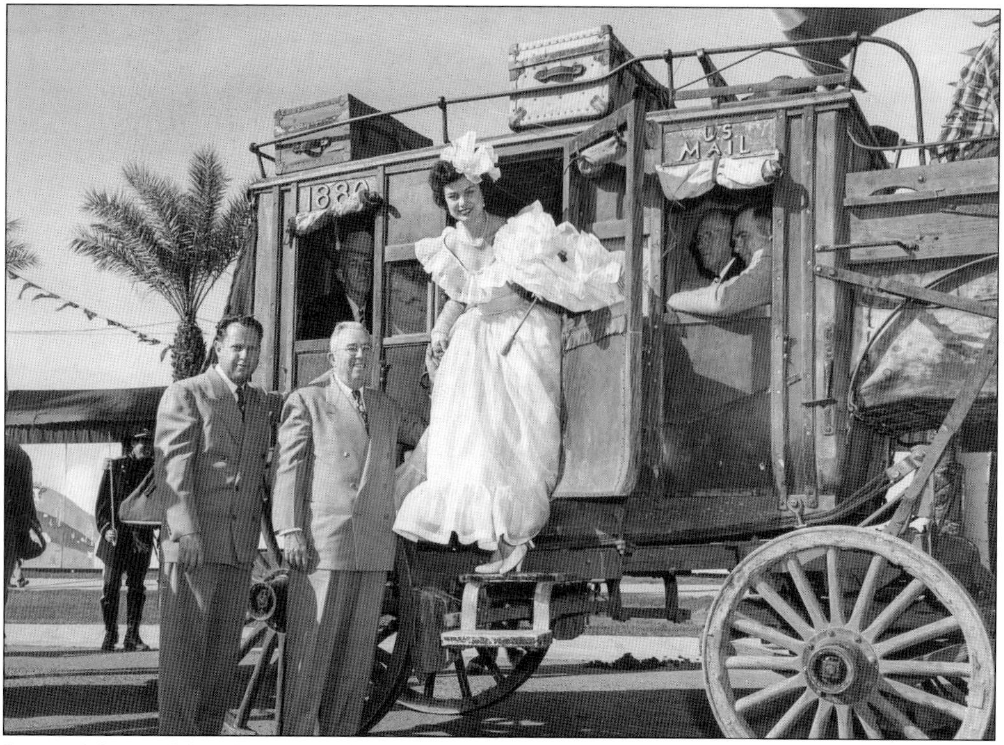

Jacque Mercer, Miss America of 1949, opened the Arizona State Fair that year. She was an Arizonan who grew up on a ranch near Litchfield Park. She is pictured above in costume with a parasol, alighting from a carriage. Holding her hand is Gov. Dan Garvey, and at far left is the secretary of the fair, Paul F. Jones. The photographer was Joey Starr, one of Arizona's best-known photographers during the 1940s and 1950s. The scene below depicts the old gate that adorned the fairgrounds on McDowell Road. It lasted 50 years prior to being replaced in 1961. (Both, courtesy of the family archives of Paul F. Jones.)

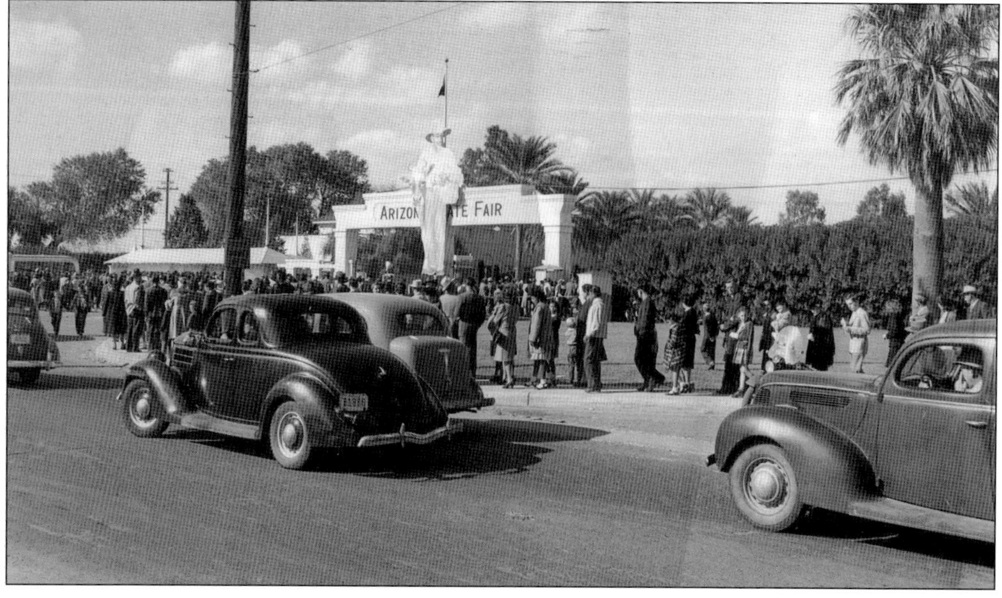

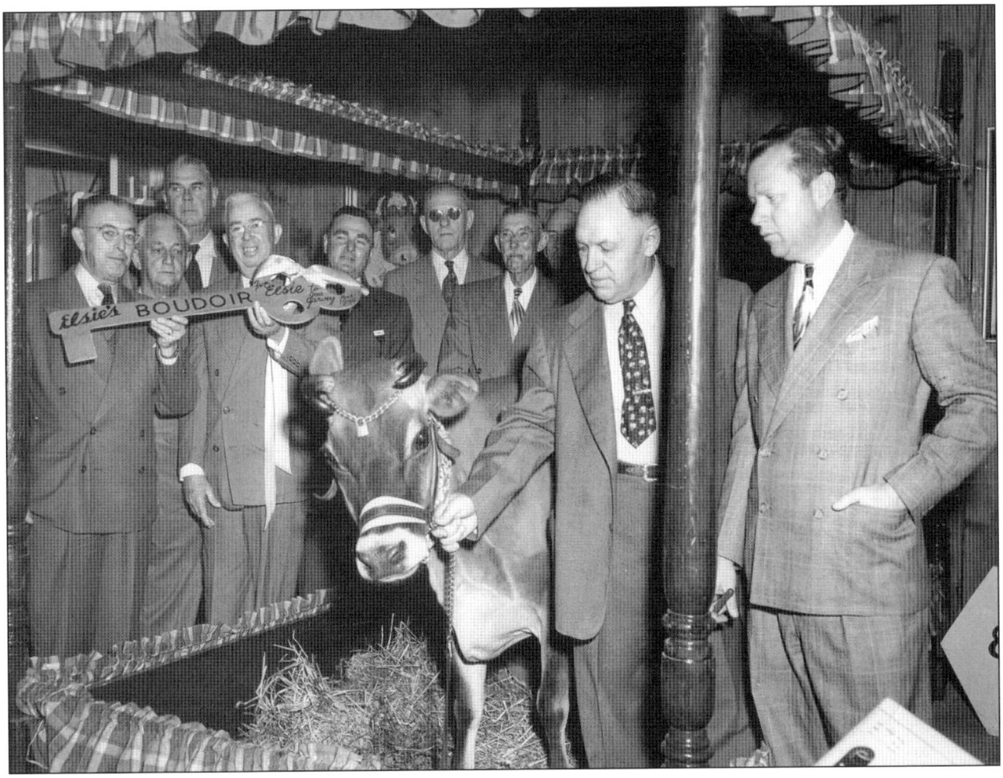

Elsie, the Borden cow, enchanted many generations of children. One of the most effective marketing tools ever created, Elsie started out as a cartoon that morphed into a real live cow when people continually asked to see her at the 1939 New York World's Fair. The real-life Jersey cow, Elsie had a fancy plaid boudoir when at the Arizona State Fair in 1948. Her admirers included Gov. Dan Garvey, holding the top end of the key, and a host of gentlemen callers. Cowgirl Jane Williams, pictured at right, remembers having a small model of Elsie as a memento. (Above, courtesy of the family archives of Paul F. Jones; right, courtesy of Jane Williams.)

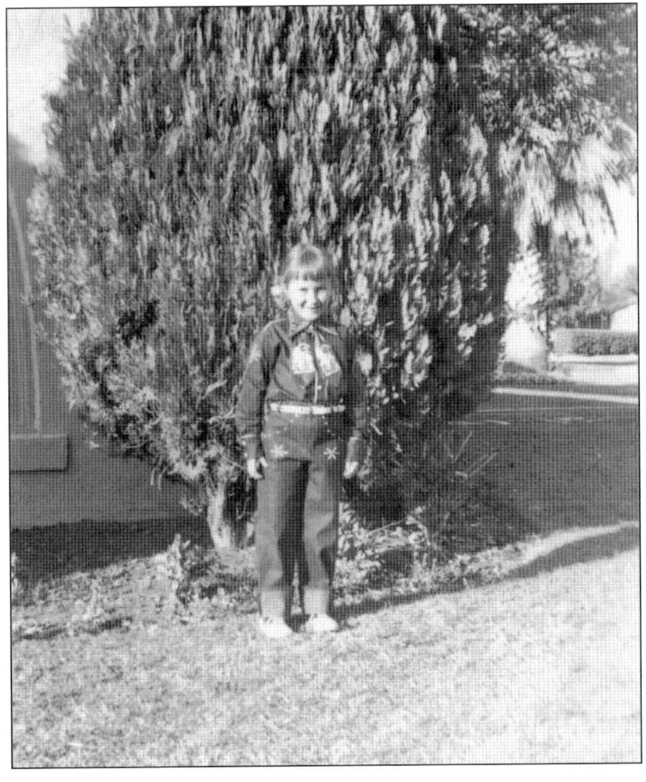

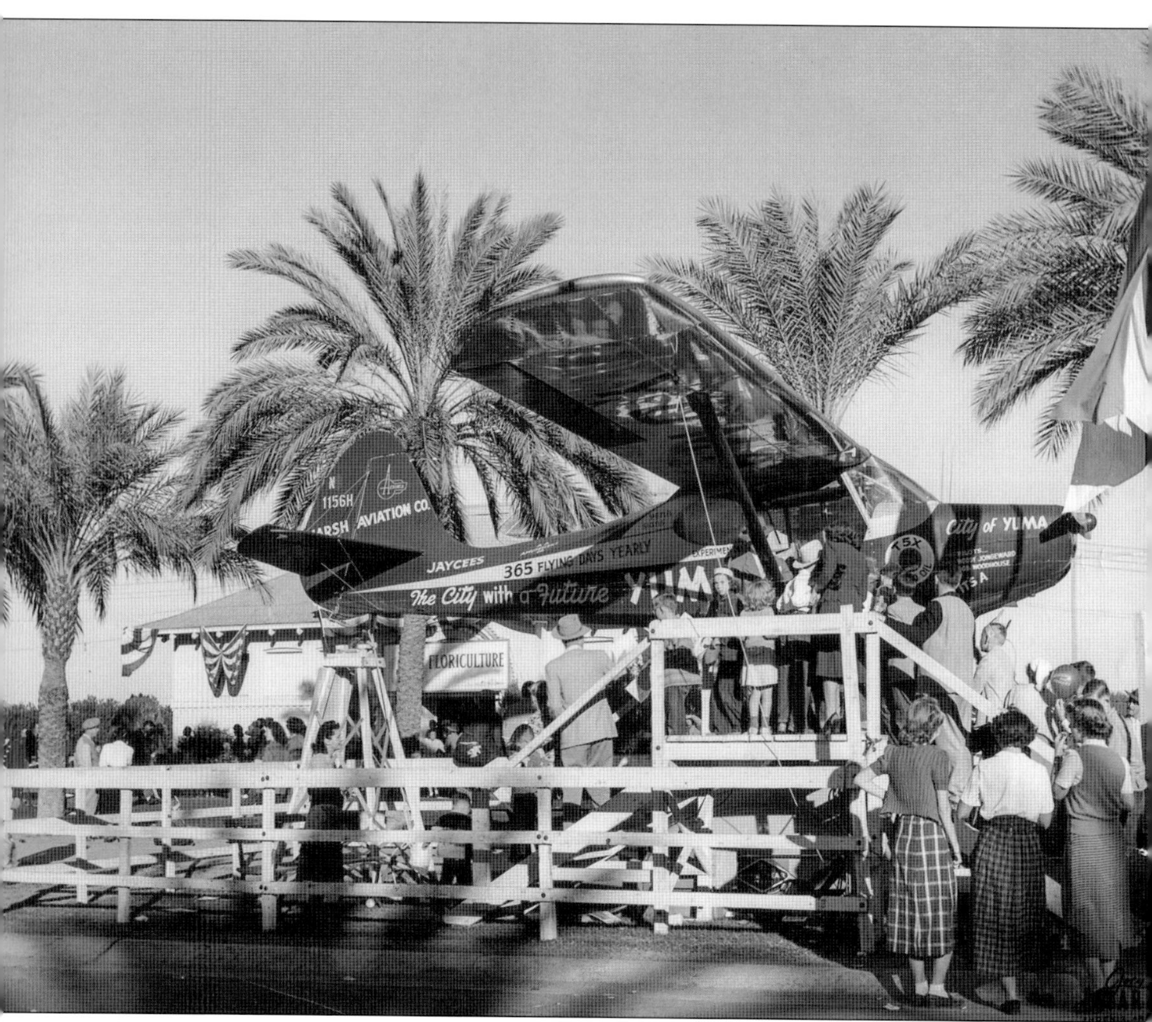

The city of Yuma, in southwestern Arizona, had an Army Air Forces pilot training base that closed after World War II ended. The entrepreneurial spirit of the city prompted a publicity stunt to promote the area's flying opportunities. In 1949, boosters purchased an Aeronca Sedan to try to break the continuous flying record of 42 days to illustrate Yuma's ideal flying weather. The goal was to be aloft 1,010 hours, or Ten-Ten for short, promoting Yuma as "the City with a Future" with year-round flying. The plane was modified with extra fuel tanks added to enable midair fueling. After two false starts, the *City of Yuma* took off on August 24, 1949, broke the record, and just kept on going, landing nearly 47 days later on October 10, 1949, or 10/10/1949. Pandemonium erupted in Yuma on a small scale similar to Lindberg's 1927 landing in Paris. (Courtesy of the family archives of Paul F. Jones.)

Four

Growth and Development

The 1950s introduced an era of prosperity and expansion, perhaps even greater than the immediate postwar years. Phoenix was attracting clean industries such as Motorola and, later, General Electric, which eventually became the third-largest employer in the state. Honeywell, Sperry Rand, and other technology and aerospace companies diversified the economy and brought residents eager to be part of this Western city. AiResearch Company, which left the fairgrounds after the war to return to California, established a new plant on the east side of the city.

The decade was notable for the fears projected during the Cold War, and duck-and-cover drills were practiced in schools. The leadership of the state was optimistic as new businesses and home building proliferated. Arizona prospered as the population expanded.

Shopping centers sprang up in what had been the outskirts as residential areas, and industrial parks boomed. The enterprises that had been in the original retail center of the city were opening second locations in other areas or abandoning downtown altogether. Commerce moved northward and high-rise edifices, such as Del Webb's Towne House in the Rosenzweig Center and the Executive Towers on West Clarendon at Central Avenue. A new, larger city hall was constructed in 1960, as well as a separate building on the same block of Jefferson Street for the expansive Council Chambers. Elegant apartments such as the Chateau de Ville on east Palm Lane and the Olympus on north Central Avenue at Maryland Avenue accommodated newcomers in this growth spurt.

The fairgrounds needed a large exhibit space to showcase the bounty and diversity of the state. A vast exhibit space for Phoenix had been needed and speculated about since the 1950s. In the early 1960s, legislation was passed to permit the proposed coliseum project to be constructed on state-owned land. At the state fairgrounds, the best racetrack in the West gave way to the new Veterans Memorial Coliseum.

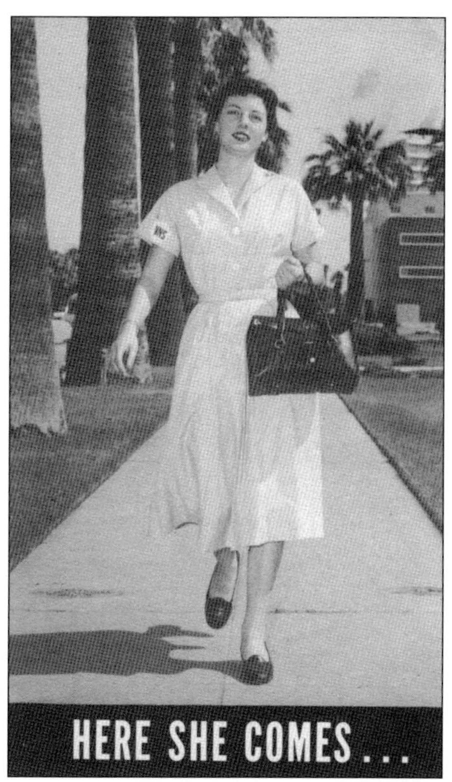

The history of one of the largest events currently held at the state fairgrounds dates back decades. Free nursing care by Visiting Nurse Associations was provided to individuals without access to health care. This photograph of a mid-century visiting nurse indicates the service was funded by the United Fund. (Courtesy of Volunteer Nonprofit Service Association, Inc.)

The Visiting Nurse Service Auxiliary (VNSA) was formed in Phoenix in 1949, when women saw a need to help the program. Auxiliary volunteers drove the nurses to visit patients. Volunteers also performed clerical duties, maintained equipment, supplies, a library, and conducted fundraising. Three student nurses are pictured with Anna Lochhead (right). (Courtesy of Volunteer Nonprofit Service Association, Inc.)

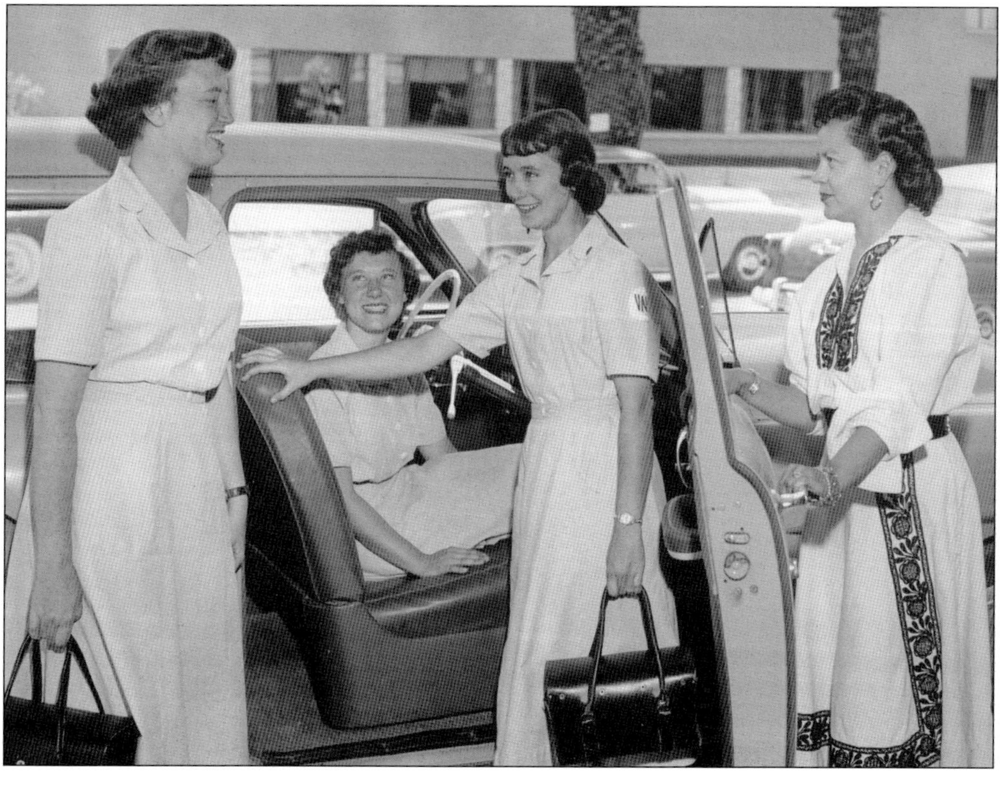

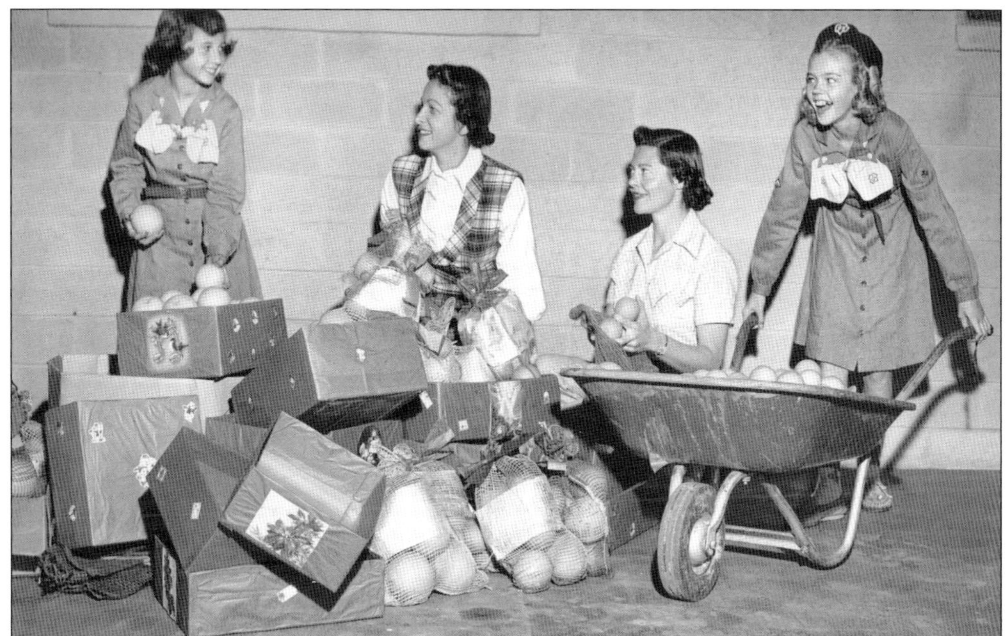

In addition to preparing supplies for visiting nurses and hosting parties for the Golden Gate Settlement House, auxiliary members created packages of fruit for sick patients. Pictured from left to right, Girl Scout Carol Shepherd helps auxiliary members Judy Wolf, Jane Keebler, and Scout Beverly Gabrelcik prepare bags of fruit to be distributed in 1952. (Courtesy of Volunteer Nonprofit Service Association, Inc.)

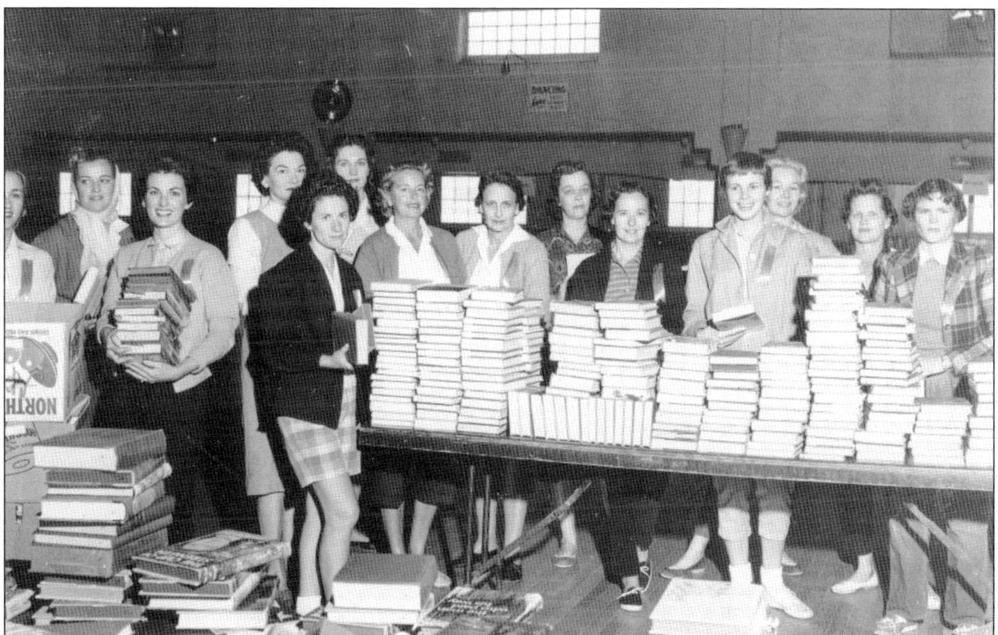

In the 1950s, the auxiliary created a used book sale to generate money for their charities. The first sale was at the Central Dryv Inn, a drive-in with carhops, located at 1001 North Central Avenue at Roosevelt Street. In 1959, the sale was held at the Mirador Ballroom, 3820 North Central Avenue, seen above. (Courtesy of Volunteer Nonprofit Service Association, Inc.)

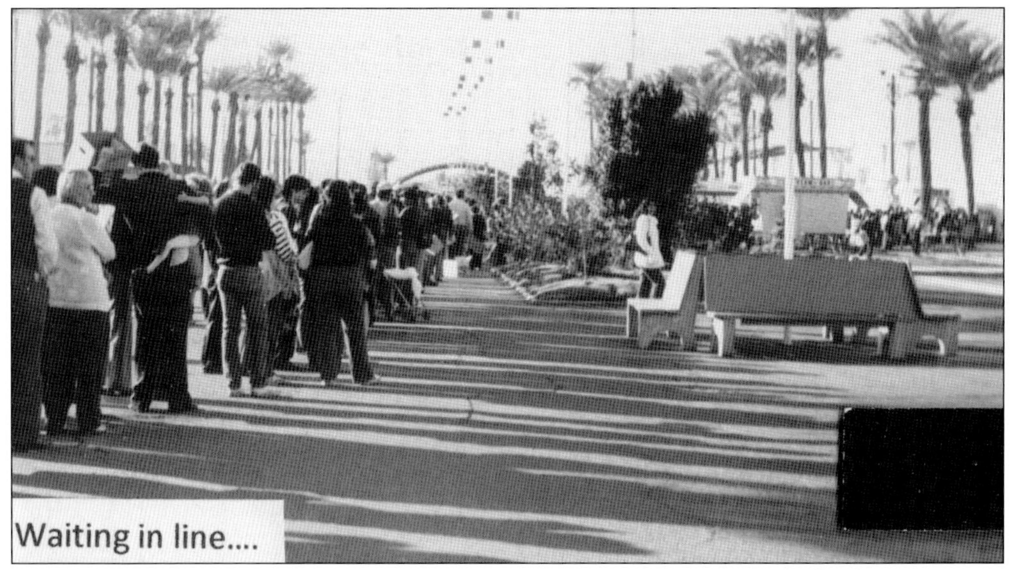

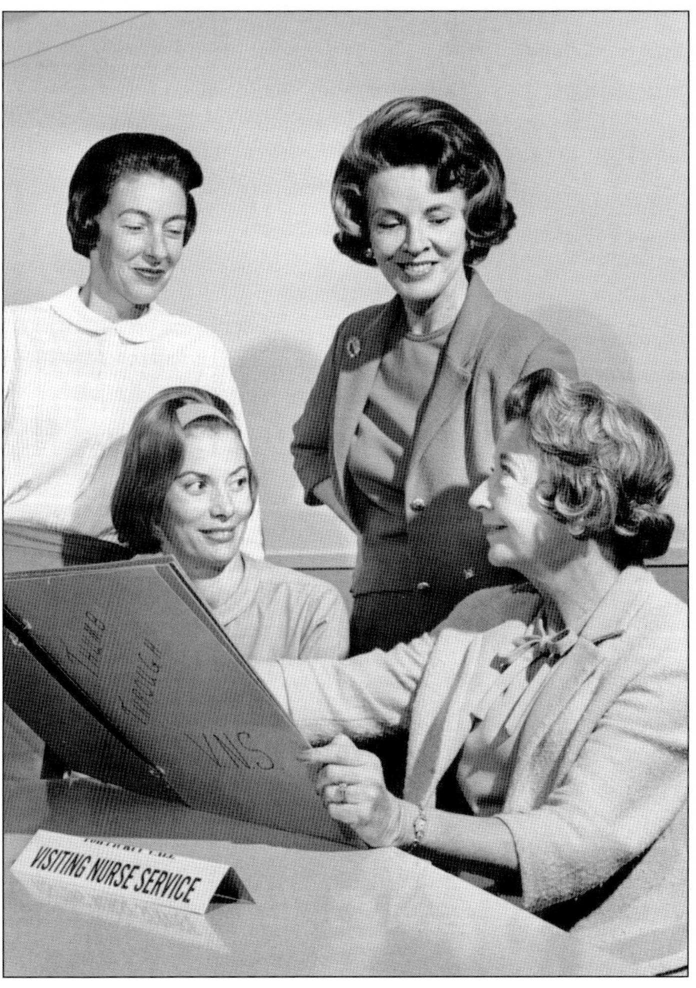

Hundreds of patrons are pictured waiting in line for the opening of the annual book sale at the fairgrounds. This tradition, now in its 60th year, began as a fundraiser for the nonprofit Visiting Nurse Service Auxiliary in 1957. In later years, the organization changed the name to Volunteer Nonprofit Service Association, Inc., (VNSA). The funds raised are directed to Literacy Volunteers of Maricopa County and Arizona Friends of Foster Children Foundation. Pictured left, members are, from left to right, (sitting) Jerre Penn, book sale chairman 1964–1965, and Peggy Hurley, founder of the VNSA; (standing) Jean Bush, past president VNSA 1960–1961, and Esther Wendel, VNSA president 1964–1965. (Both, courtesy of Volunteer Nonprofit Service Association, Inc.)

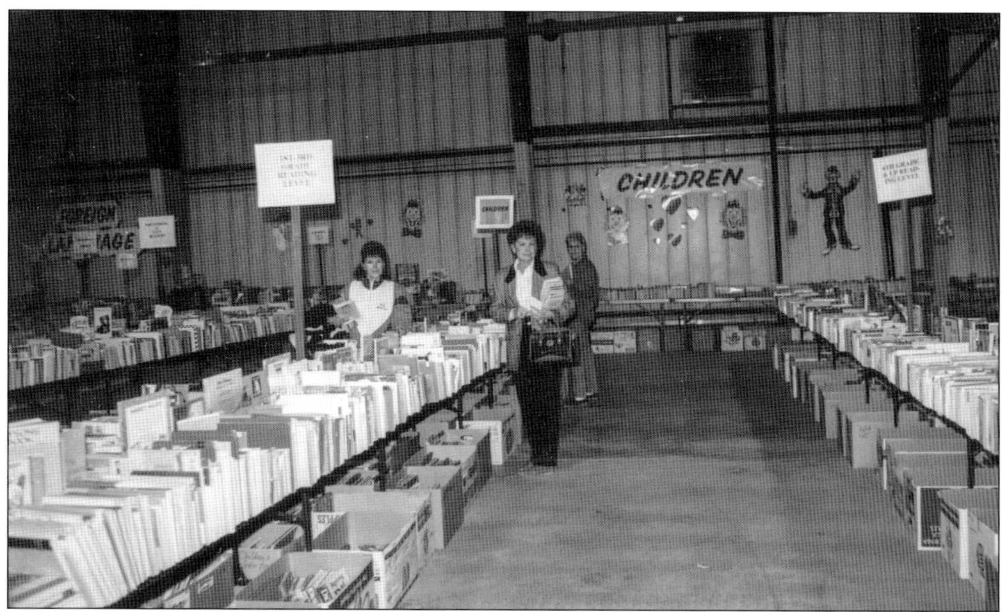

The thousands of donated books at the VNSA Book Sale are displayed on long tables in the Exhibit Building on the fairgrounds, above. The offerings have included autographed first editions, books from the Frank Sinatra collection, cookbooks, and magazines. The volunteer group has been assisted by many organizations, including Boy and Girl Scouts. Teamsters Locals Nos. 104 and 752 have partnered with VNSA almost since the beginning. In recent years, the VNSA has expanded to work with the Arizona Department of Corrections inmates to move books. The wise old owl mascot, Vanessa, below, is pictured at the 1992 sale. (Both, courtesy of Volunteer Nonprofit Service Association, Inc.)

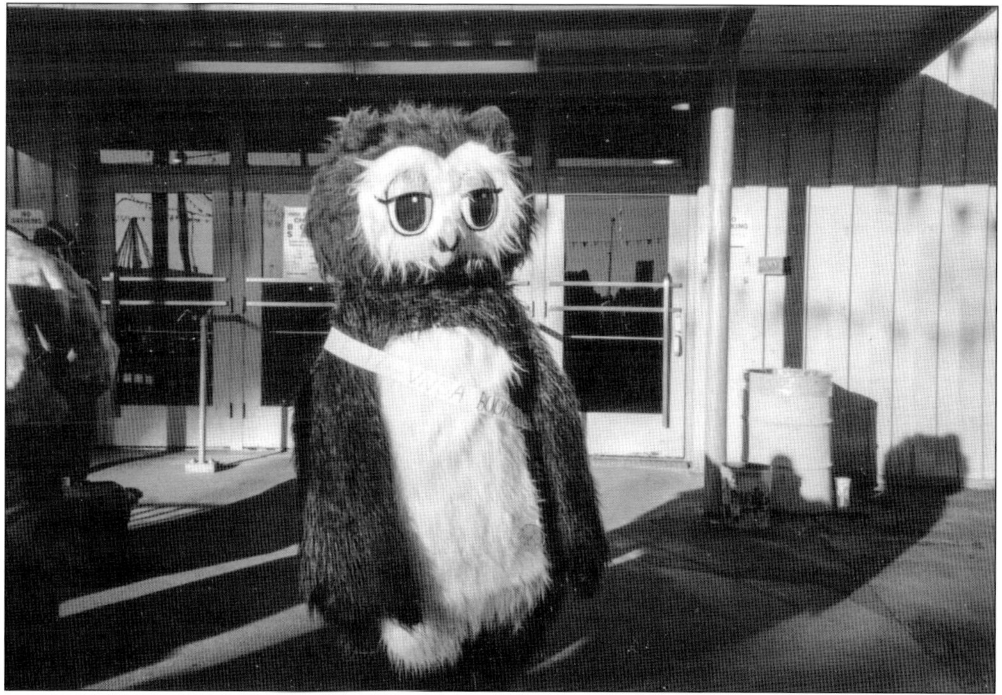

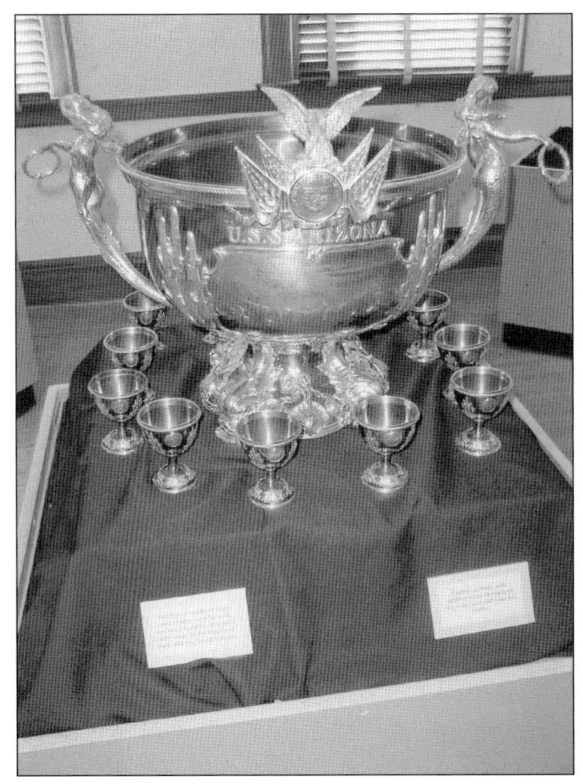

It was customary to create silver services for new battleships in the 20th century. The USS *Arizona* was commissioned in 1913. Schoolchildren raised pennies, and residents deposited money at banks. The copper mines contributed more than half the $9,000 total. To stimulate contributions, the service was displayed at the state fair in November 1916. Manufactured by Reed and Barton, the service was shown throughout the state, notably at the Phelps Dodge Mercantile Company in Bisbee. The copper-clad punch bowl is at left, and the goblets are below. The ship was christened in June 1915, with the traditional champagne and also a copper-embellished bottle filled with the first water over the Roosevelt Dam spillway. (Both, photographs by D. Taylor Arrazola, courtesy of the Arizona Capitol Museum.)

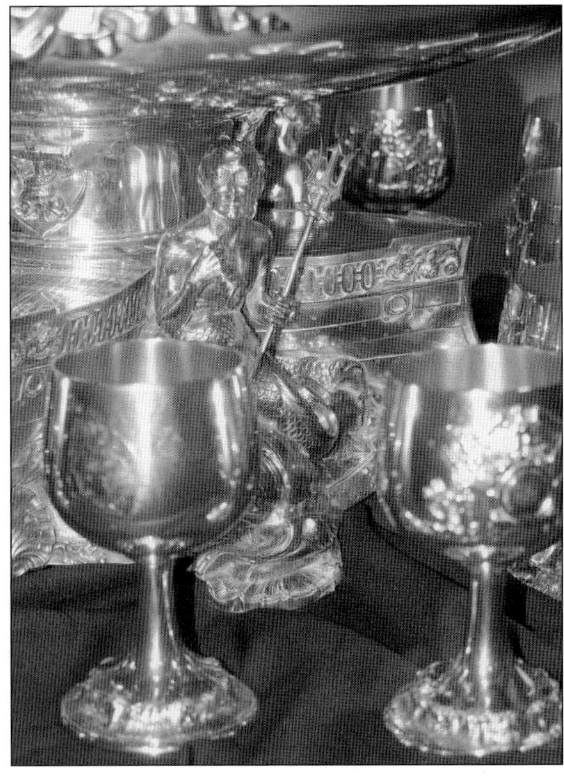

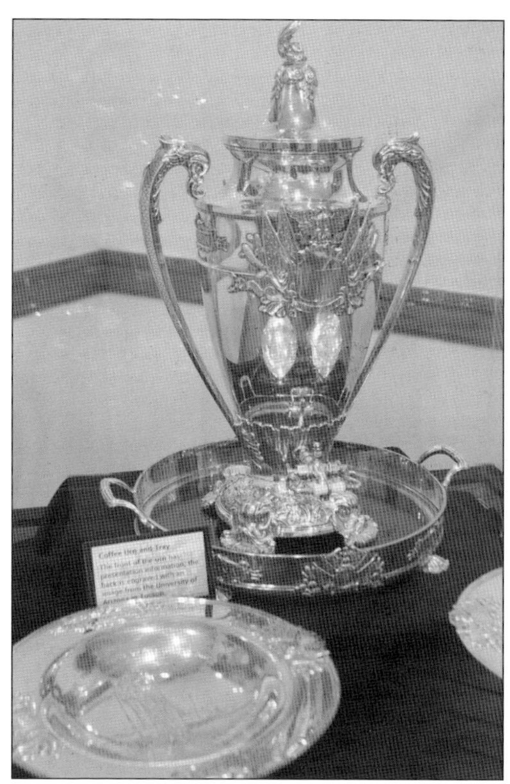

The coffee urn for the silver service, pictured at right, was decorated with Arizona scenes. The entire service was removed from the USS *Arizona* prior to preparing it for action in the Pacific. The battleship was sunk at Pearl Harbor in 1941 and is a national memorial. The service, described as "one of the finest in service in the Navy," was returned to Arizona at the request of Gov. Howard Pyle in the early 1950s. It was displayed for several years at the Arizona State Fair and was later found stored under the B.B. Moeur Stadium. The Arizona Copper Miner statuette, shown below, was also returned to Arizona in 1999, after being located in the Naval Historical Center in Washington, DC. (Both, photographs by D. Taylor Arrazola, courtesy of the Arizona Capitol Museum.)

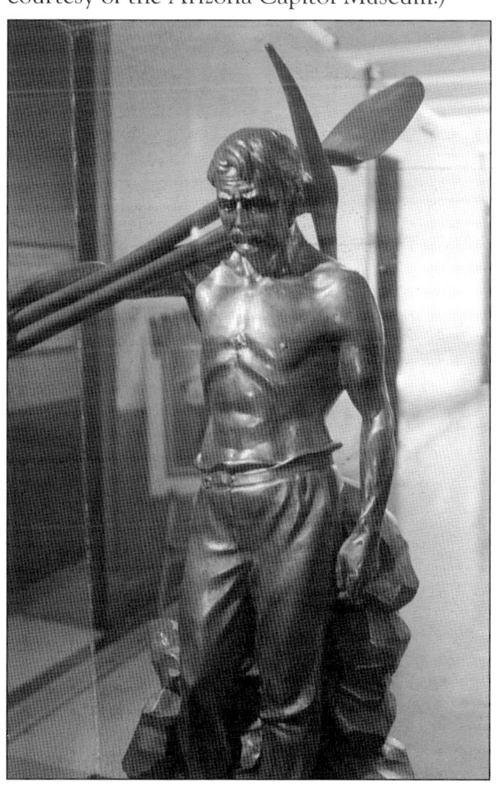

DON'T MISS THIS

RUMMAGE SALE

OF THE

Junior League

OF PHOENIX

at 313 NORTH CENTRAL

(Just North of Van Buren)

Sat. October 9th, and Mon., Tuesday and Wednesday October 11th, 12th and 13th

from 9 A.M. to 5 P.M.—Saturday Nite till 9 P.M.

BETTER THAN EVER RUMMAGE

CLEAN • SIZED • SELECTED

—SUPER QUALITY—

The Junior League Rummage Sale at the fairgrounds has changed from its early beginnings. What became the Junior League was founded in 1930, as the Welfare League of Phoenix. The league promoted volunteerism among women to support the Public School Welfare Fund amid a deepening Depression. Over the last eight decades, community projects have changed as needs evolved. Susan Carpenter Kelly, the Junior League president from 1951 to 1953, is pictured below assisting Scouts on a project. The early rummage sales were held in the old Standard Oil Building at 313 North Central Avenue, which is the present location of the Westin Phoenix Downtown Hotel. (Both, courtesy of the Phoenix Junior League.)

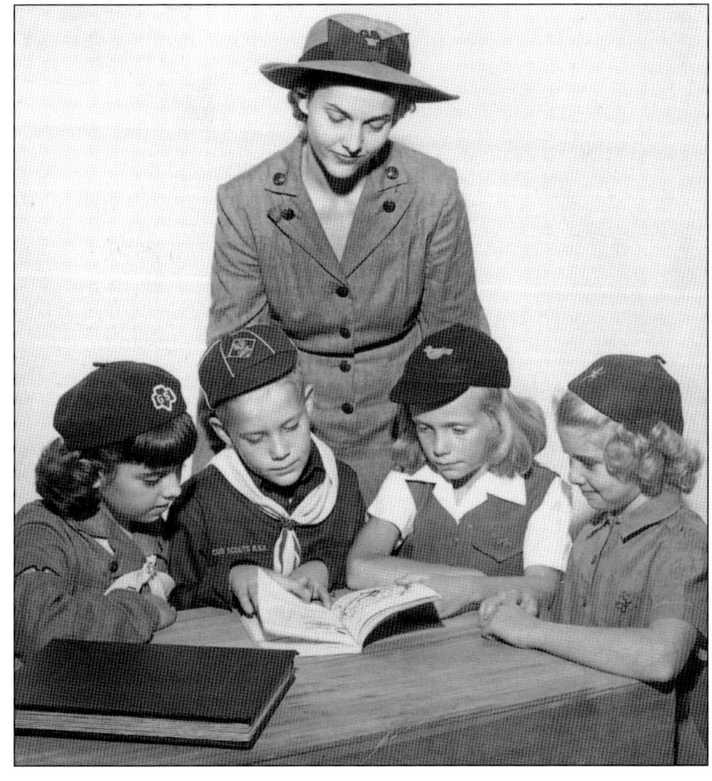

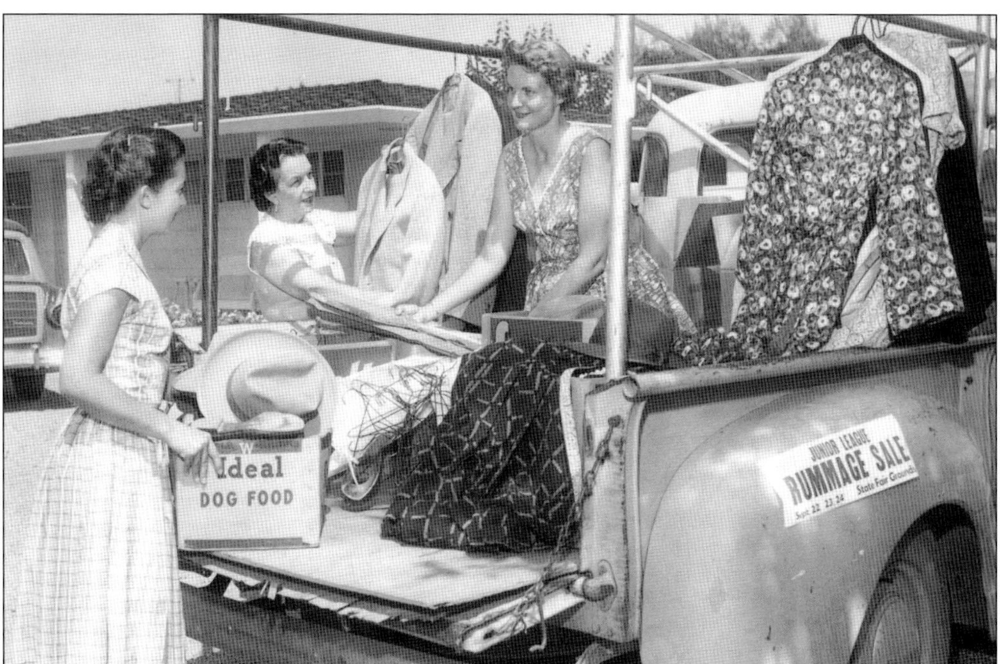

Volunteers at the 1955 rummage sale, pictured above, were filling a truck with donated items to take to the 19th annual sale, the earliest one held on the fairgrounds. The highlight of the sale was an auction of 22 new and used cars donated by valley automobile dealers. Billboards advertising the sale were donated by local companies. The Junior League volunteers worked all year and expected to gross a tidy amount for their service projects but this sale far exceeded expectations. From 1954 to 1955, the Junior League donated a portion of the revenue from the sale to the Arizona State Fair. (Both, courtesy of the Phoenix Junior League.)

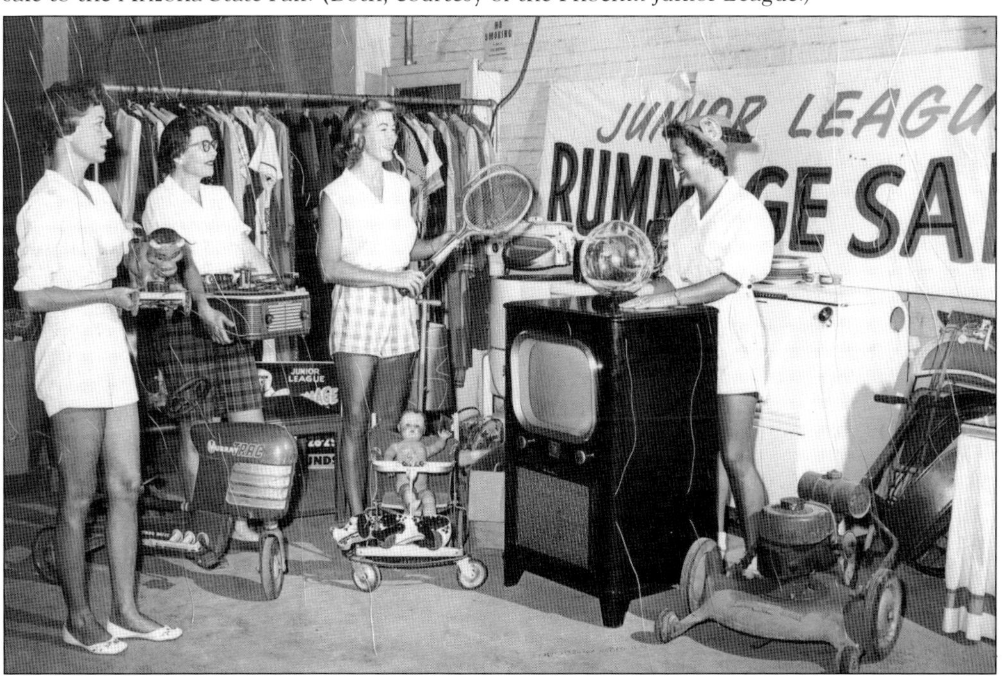

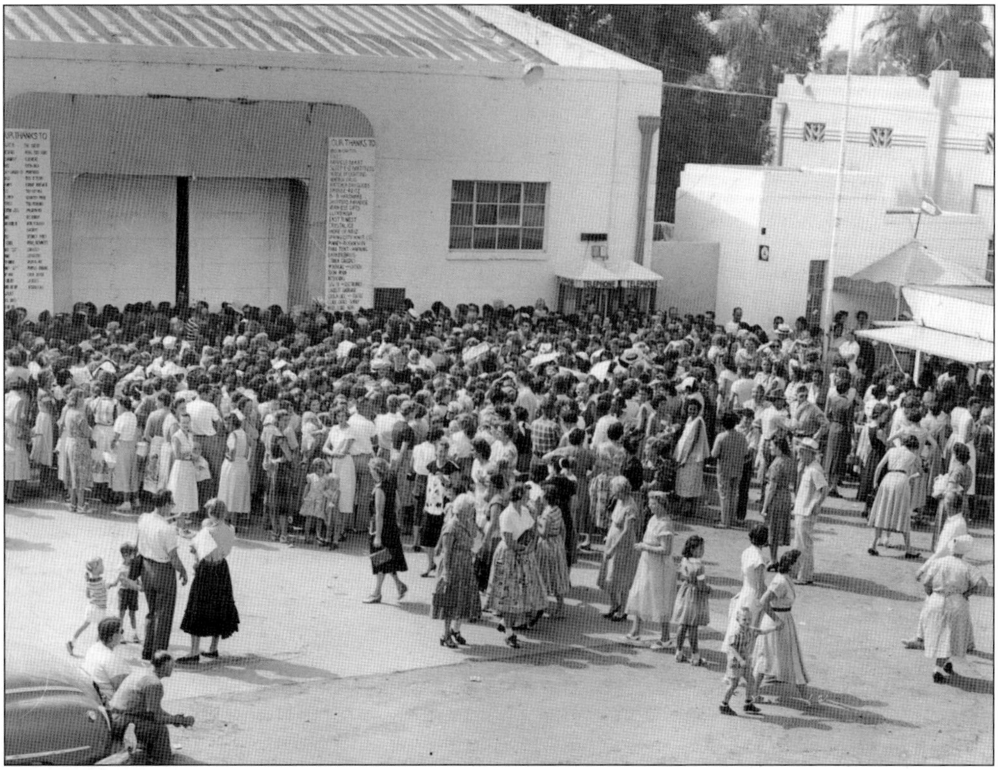

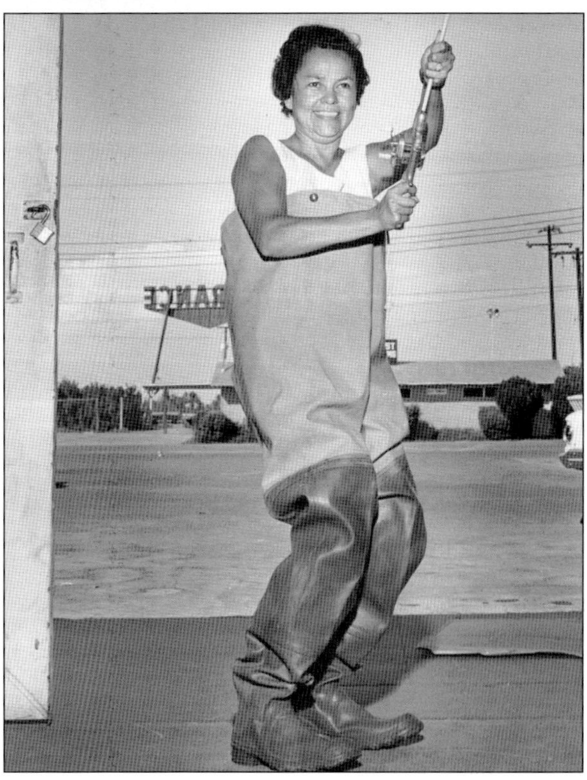

The Junior League Rummage Sale has been a tradition for decades at the state fairgrounds. Pictured above, large crowds gathered for hours prior to the 1956 sale in order to have one of the first opportunities to go through the offerings. The eagerly awaited mid-century sales were comprised of furniture, toys, sporting goods, lawn equipment, and furniture. The considerable profits have gone toward aiding the various charities chosen by the league. Volunteering was fun when it came time to hold the annual sale at the fairgrounds. Shown at left, member Anna Lochhead was demonstrating her expertise with high waders and a fishing pole. (Both, courtesy of the Phoenix Junior League.)

The Junior League volunteers worked hard to make every sale better than the previous one. Pictured in the Lakin garage sorting donations, from left to right are Mary Ellen McGeorge, Patricia Martin, and Maxine Lakin. Note the diversity of items. The annual sales provided support for dental clinics, opportunities for the blind, historic preservation, and many other causes benefiting Phoenicians. The perennial rummage sale guard was Phoenix Police lieutenant Bernard J. Dunn. Looking like an old-fashioned turn-of-the-century cop, he was dressed for cold weather in a donated trench coat displaying a living room lamp at one of the mid-century sales. (Both, courtesy of the Phoenix Junior League.)

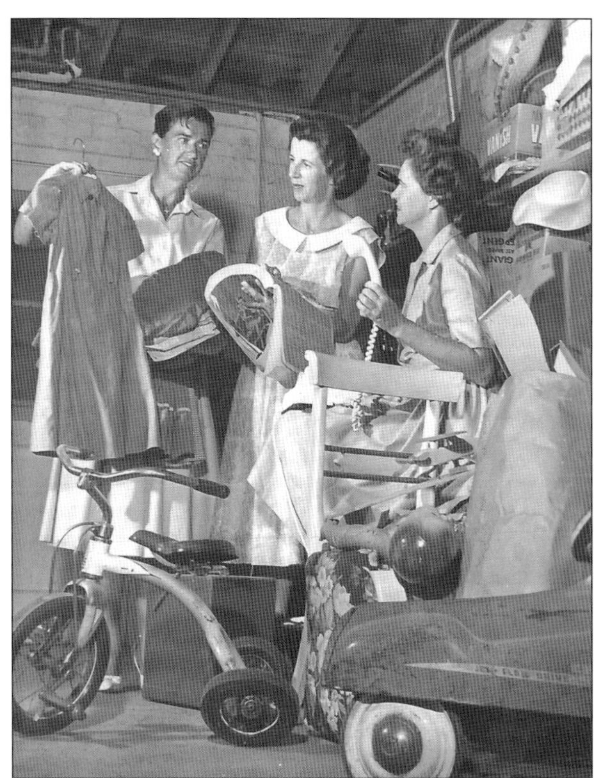

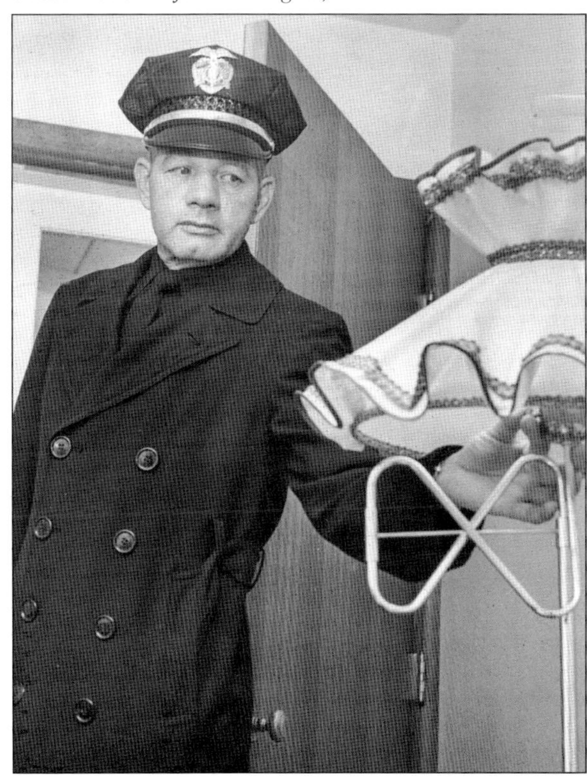

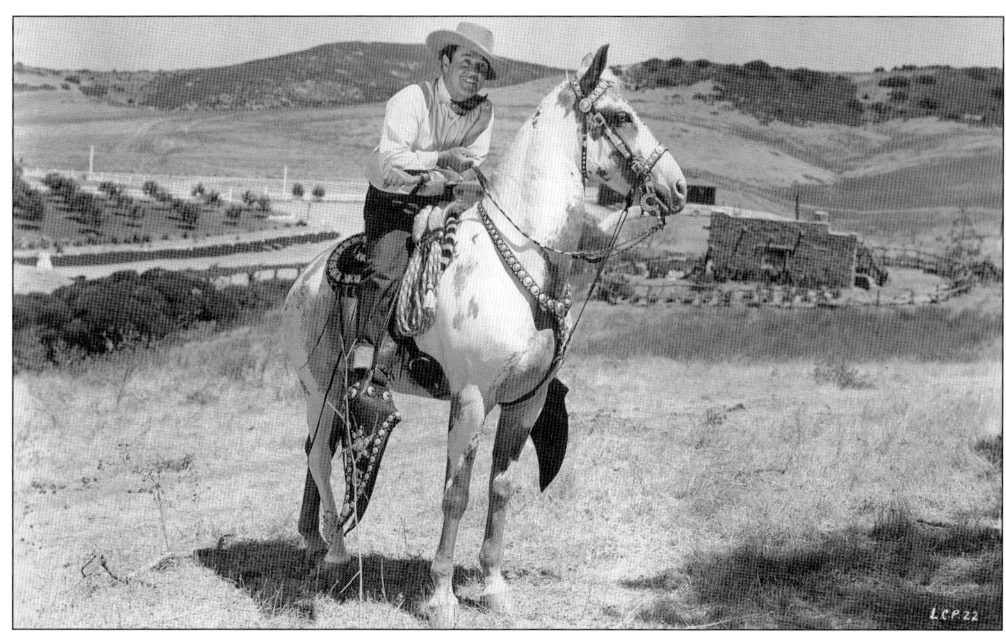

Leo Carrillo, above, was a talented movie actor from 1927 through the 1950s. He is best known today for his portrayal of Pancho, the sidekick of the Cisco Kid, televised from 1950 to 1956. *The Cisco Kid* was created by O'Henry, the pen name of William Sidney Porter, in a 1907 story, titled the *The Caballero's Way*. Cisco was originally a desperado, but Cisco and Pancho were portrayed as modern Robin Hoods on television. Carrillo's Diamond Cluster Supreme Parade Saddle, designed around 1960, by Edward H. Bohlin (1895–1980) was formerly displayed at the state fair. It is now on exhibit at Western Spirit: Scottsdale's Museum of the West. Carrillo was active in preservation and conservation. His historic ranch is now a city park in Carlsbad, California. (Above, courtesy of the Carrillo Ranch Archives, City of Carlsbad, California; below, courtesy of the Arizona State Fair and Loren Anderson Photography.)

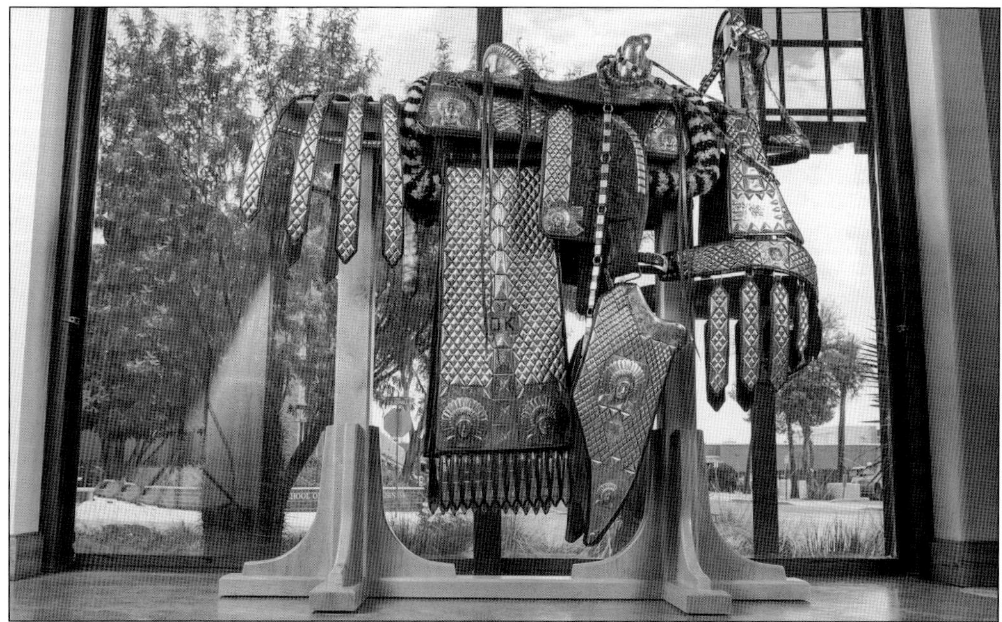

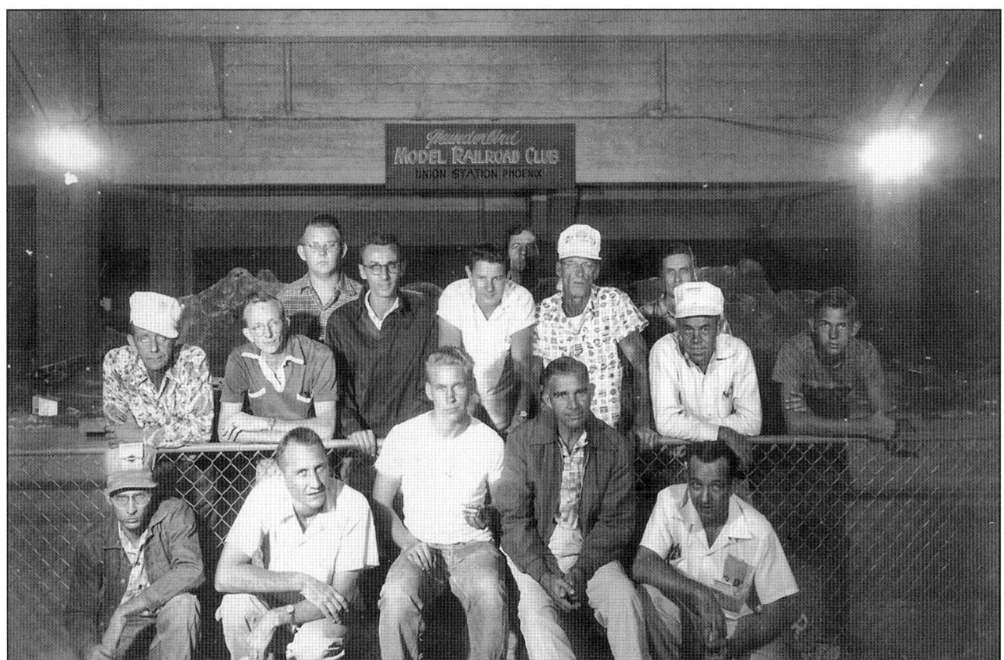

The Thunderbird Model Railroad Club, shown above, operated a scale model layout for the Arizona State Fair from 1953 through 1960. The club moved to Union Station in 1960 and remained there until the downtown train station closed eight years later. They were invited back to the fair and now have the entire railroad installed under the north part of B.B. Moeur Stadium. The members are very proud of what they have accomplished and continue to meet every Tuesday evening. The track, below, is designed to allow the club members to interact with the viewing public at fair time. (Both, courtesy of the Thunderbird Model Railroad Club, Archives.)

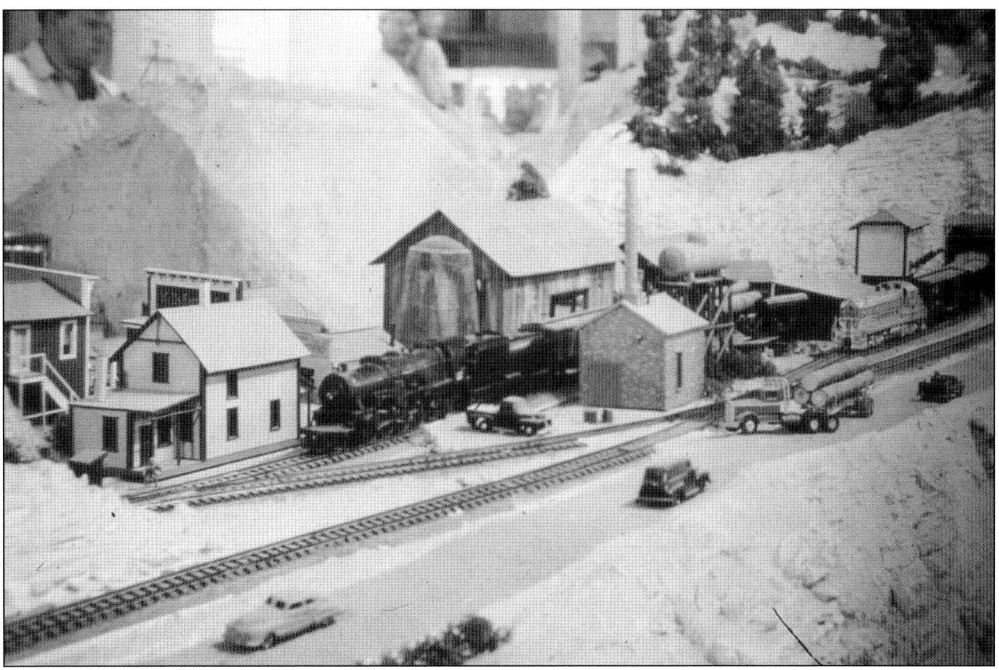

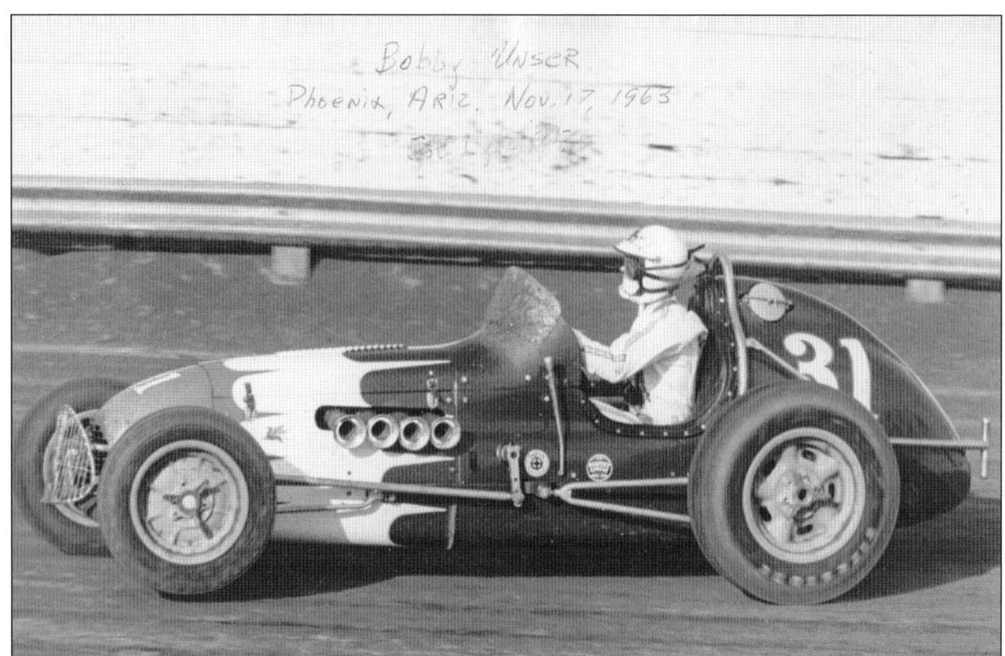

The Bobby Ball Memorial Race was a fixture at the fairgrounds beginning in the 1950s. In 1957, Jimmy Bryan won his second victory in the annual race. Bobby Unser, pictured on November 17, 1963, took 9th place in the 14th annual race that was won by Rodger Ward on the one-mile track. (Courtesy of Mel Martin.)

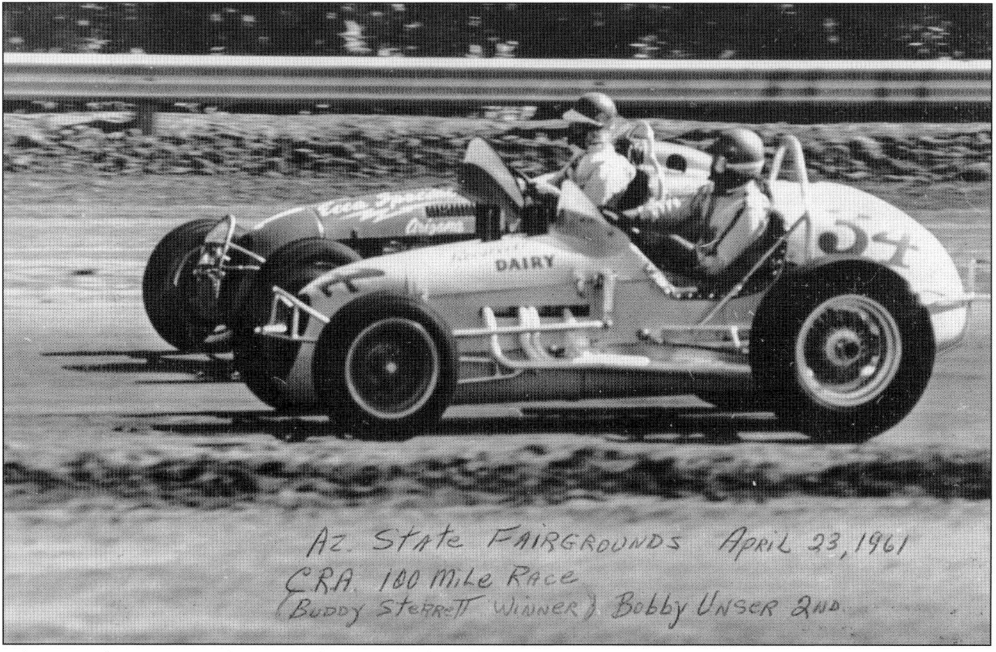

This April 23, 1961, photograph is from the Champion Racing Association 100-mile race at the Arizona State Fairgrounds. Bobby Unser in the dark No. 1 car came in second. The white No. 34 car in the foreground was driven by Don Barnes. Buddy Sterrett was the winner of the race. (Courtesy of Mel Martin.)

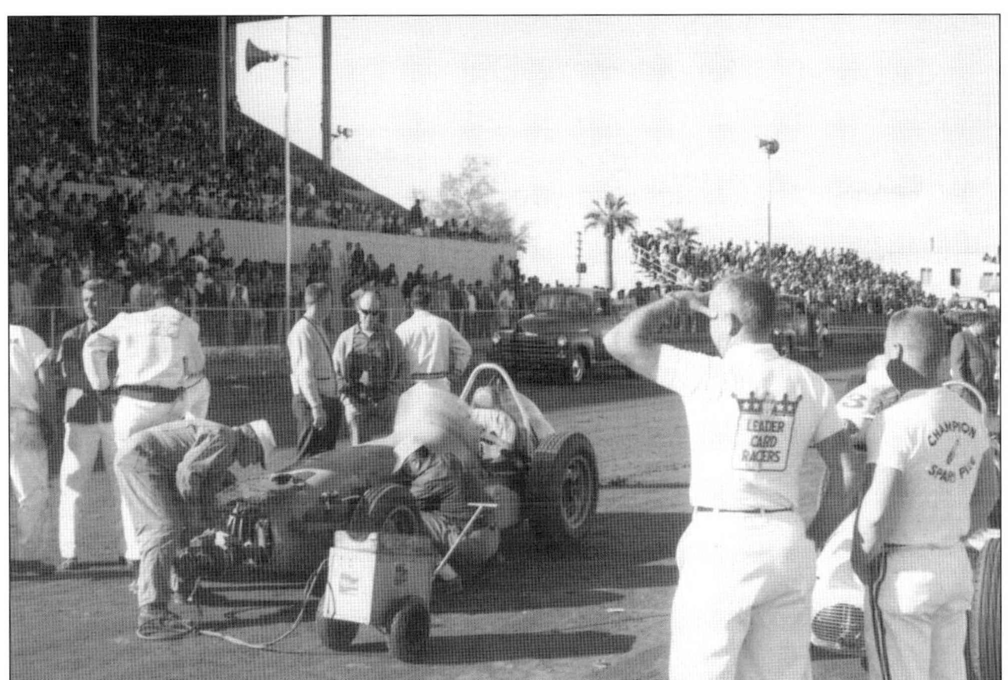

The Bobby Ball Memorial Race, sponsored by the US Auto Club (USAC), took place on the fairgrounds on November 18, 1962. The reverse of the photograph above reads as follows: "Left of the first pickup truck is where Elmer George went into the people." George lost control, rammed the guard rail, and the car broke through a chain-link fence and landed upside down. 22 spectators were injured. George, an experienced driver, survived the crash. Whether it was for the car races or the rodeo, young boys were always willing to climb over the fence, or sneak under a tent, to get a closer view, as seen at right. (Above, courtesy of Derek Horn; right, courtesy of the Markow family archives.)

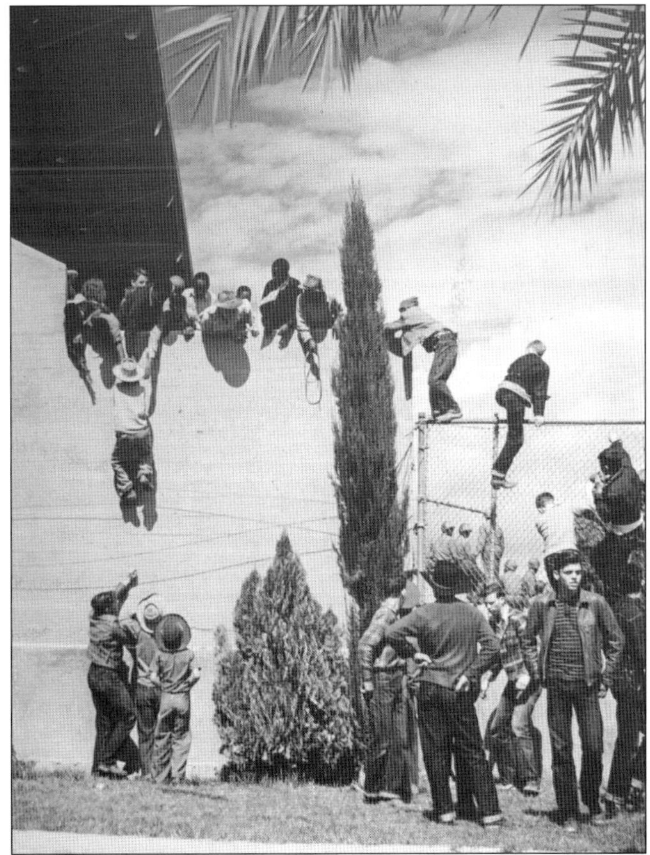

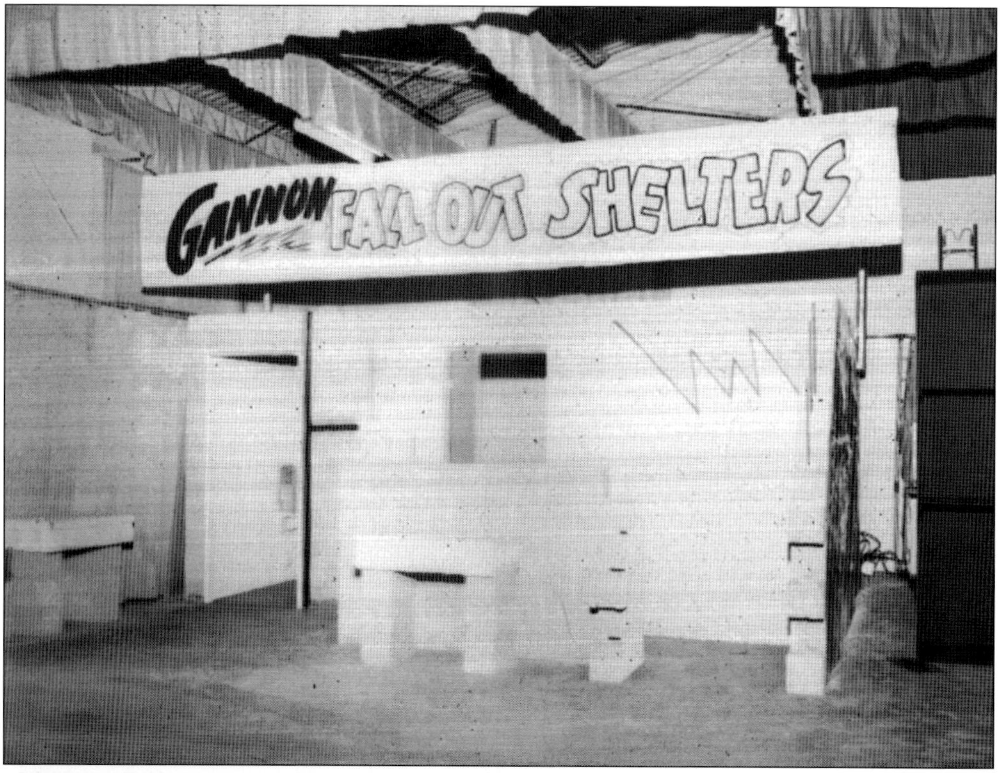

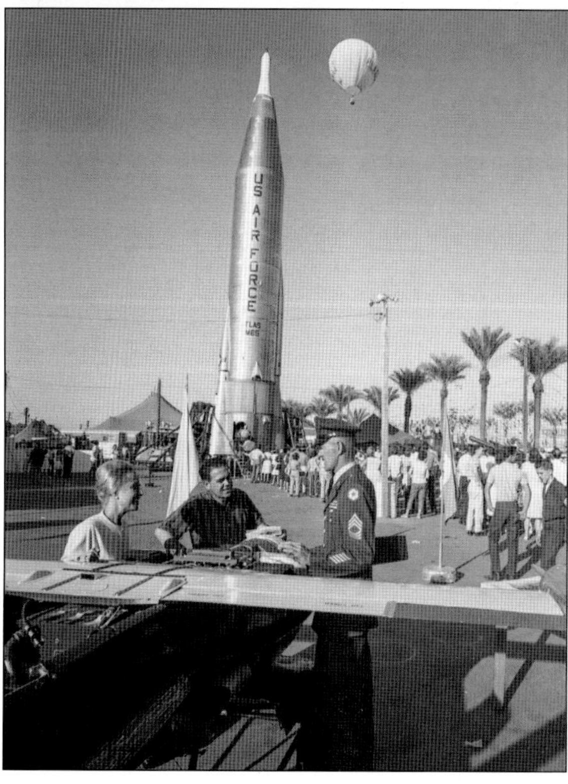

The Cold War was icy as the Berlin Wall went up on August 13, 1961. Pres. John Kennedy suggested in October that Americans take safety precautions. By November 1961, a fallout shelter was on display at the state fair. Backyards were the ideal spot for the shelters. The atmosphere of the times induced many to buy. By 1962, the country was experiencing the Cuban Missile Crisis. President Kennedy, to the relief of millions on October 28, 1962, had persuaded the Soviet Union that it was in their best interest to remove their missiles from Cuba. In a display of readiness, a US Atlas missile was an attraction at the 1962 fair, pictured at left. (Above, courtesy of the Markow family archives; left, courtesy of the Herb and Dorothy McLaughlin Collection, Arizona State University Libraries.)

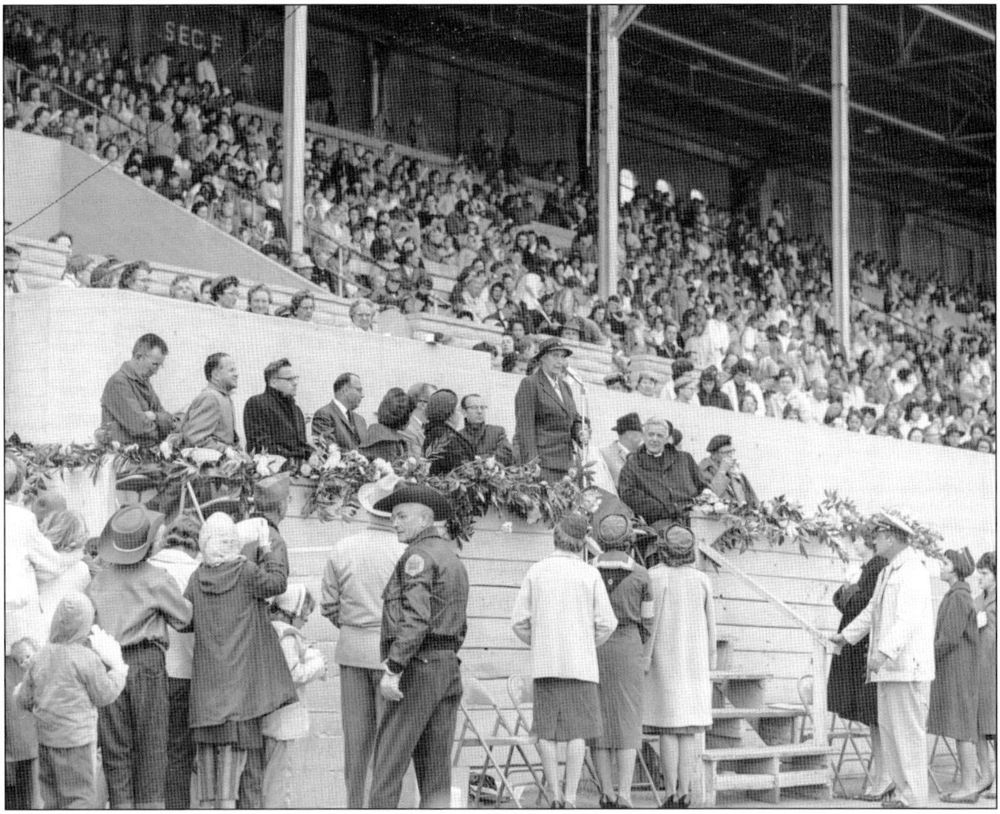

The fairgrounds was the site of a Golden Years Pageant representing 50 years of Scouting in the United States and an early celebration of statehood for Arizona on Saturday, January 13, 1962. Lady Olave Baden-Powell, the world chief guide, was honored by hundreds of Scouts. The 10,000-person audience remembered the date as "the day it snowed in Phoenix." Snow is a rare event for the desert city. Decades later, scouting was still a major force in Arizona. Preservation activist and author G.G. George, pictured at right, was presented with the Girl Scouts Arizona's Women of Achievement Political Leader Award in 1993. (Above, courtesy of the Girl Scouts, Arizona, Cactus-Pine Council; right, courtesy of the author.)

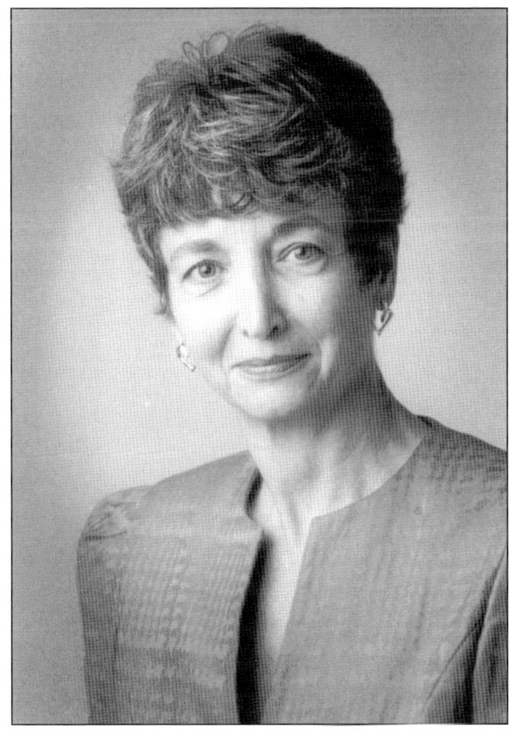

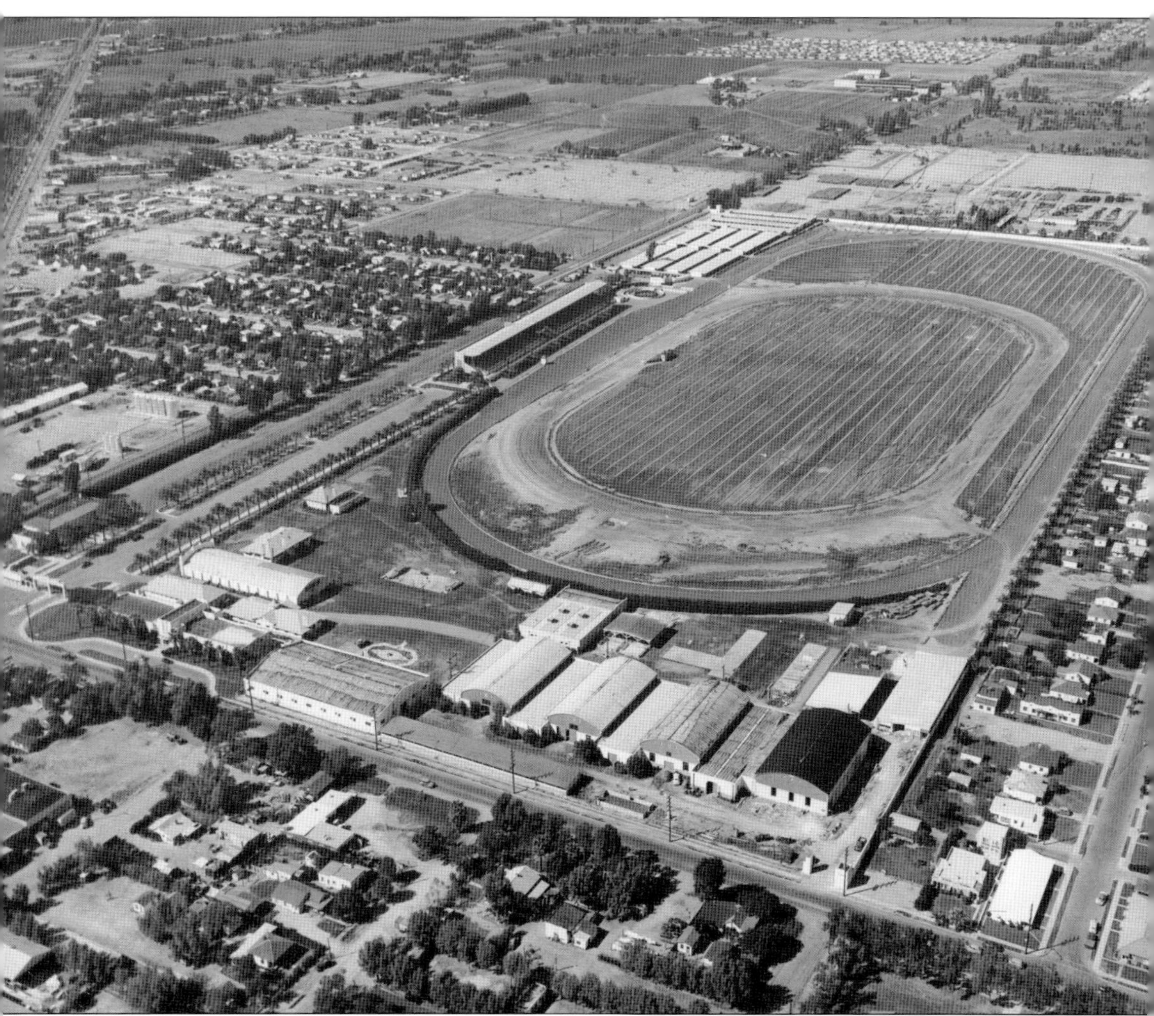

Phoenix needed a large exhibition venue in the 1950s. This aerial photograph was given to Paul F. Jones, secretary of the fair commission. There is the following scrawled note in the grassy infield by Paul Turnbow, a *Phoenix Gazette* reporter: "To Paul Jones – build your new fairgrounds here." The Arizona State Planning and Building Commission began to study sites for the relocation of the fairgrounds. The 1957 study by architects stated, "After careful consideration of all factors it was determined that the State-owned land in Papago Park was the most suitable for a new state fairgrounds." The study included a Preliminary Proposed Master Plan that looked toward the future when a site would be needed that was twice the size of the current fairgrounds. The Papago Park plan was shelved, and the area formerly occupied by the racetrack and infield became the location of the new coliseum in 1965. (Courtesy of the family archives of Paul F. Jones.)

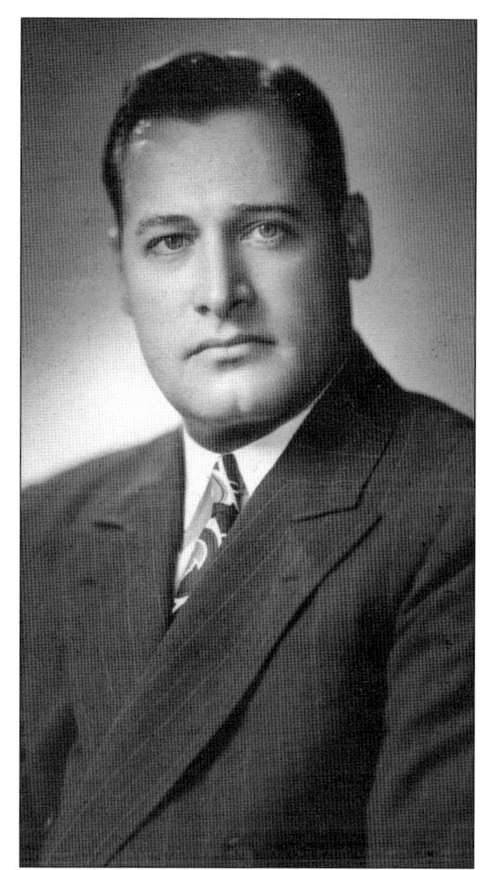

John J. Dickmann, president of Manhattan-Dickman Construction Company, pictured at right, was responsible for many public buildings during Arizona's mid-century growth spurt. The Veterans Memorial Coliseum, built in 1965, is among the best known. The coliseum is notable for many factors, like its seemingly round shape but with a roof that resembles a parabola. The design by Phoenix firm Lescher and Mahoney, in conjunction with Place and Place of Tucson, Arizona, was innovative engineering. Leslie J. Mahoney said it was his favorite building to design. The concrete floor and bleachers of the coliseum were being constructed in the photograph below. The grandstand, Moeur Stadium, built by the Works Progress Administration (WPA), is pictured in the background. (Both, courtesy of Marilyn Dickmann Barrows.)

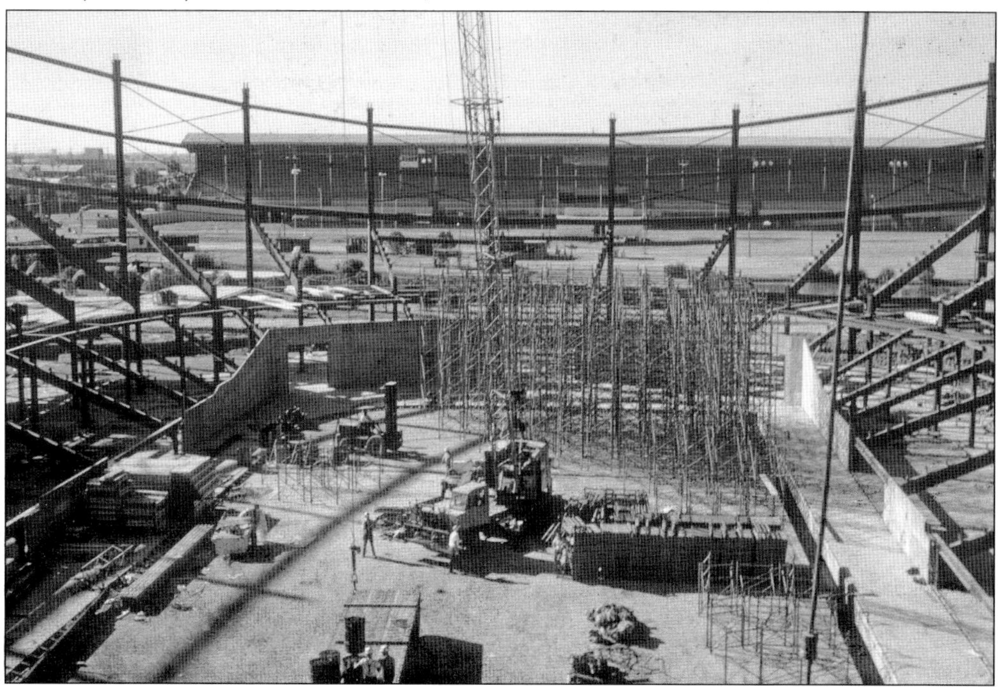

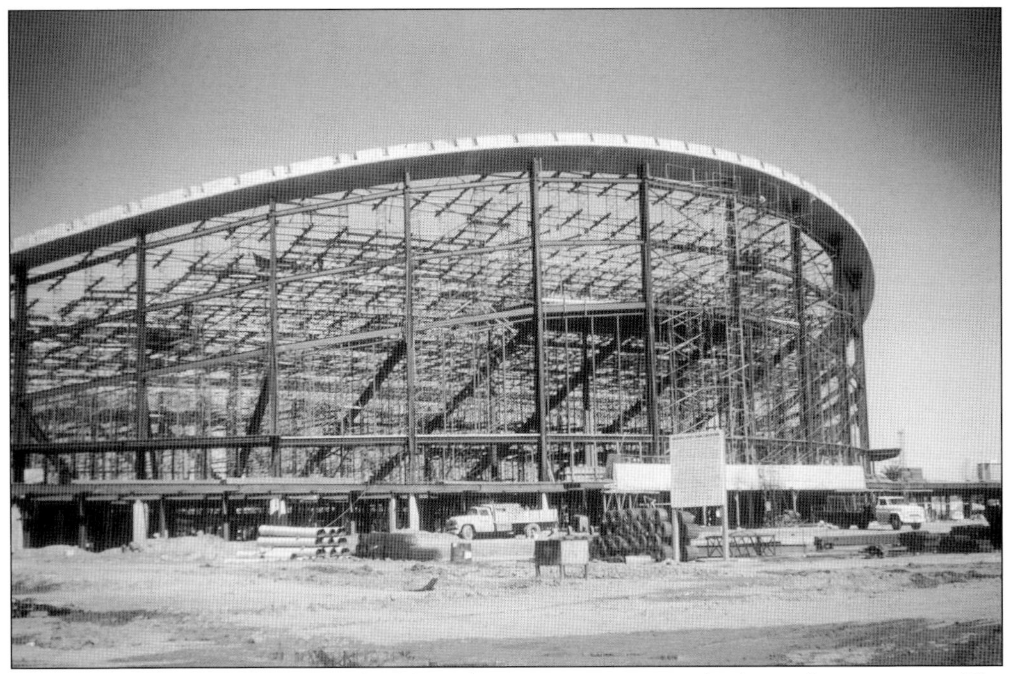

The round steel skeleton framework of the coliseum is seen in an early phase of construction. The roof is circular with a diameter of 367 feet. The periphery of the roof is a 12-foot-wide concrete ring beam supported by steel columns spanning a column free interior of 119,500 square feet. Steel cables were strung across the roof, forming a grid pattern of 10-foot squares, like a gigantic fishing net. Erection of the cables and roof panels was handled by Reliance Truck Company, which devised the square steel spreader to put the precast panels in place. (Both, courtesy of Marilyn Dickmann Barrows.)

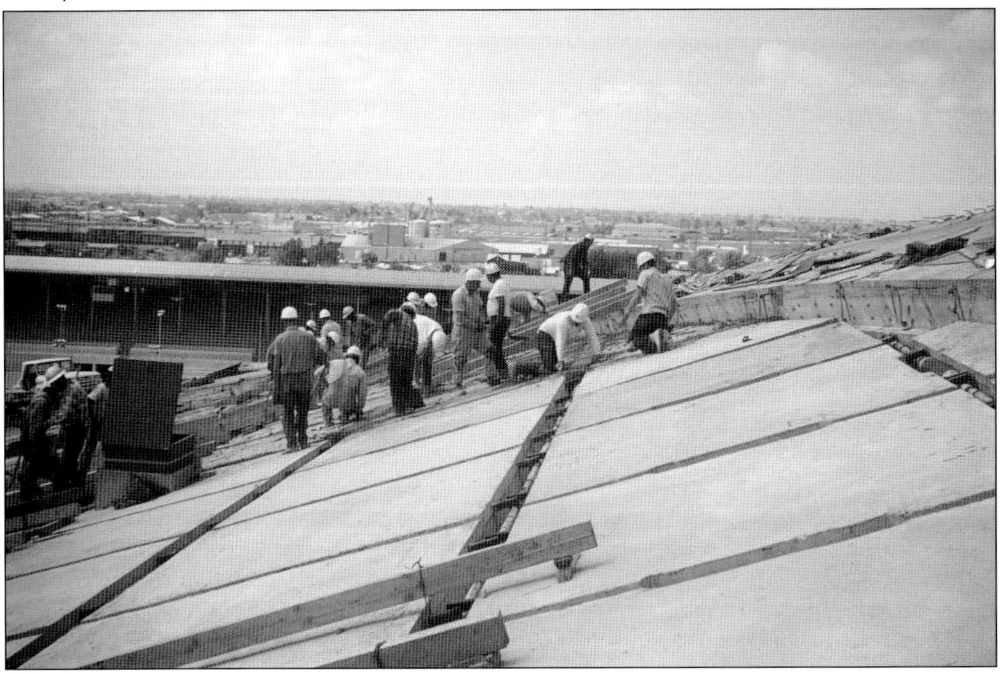

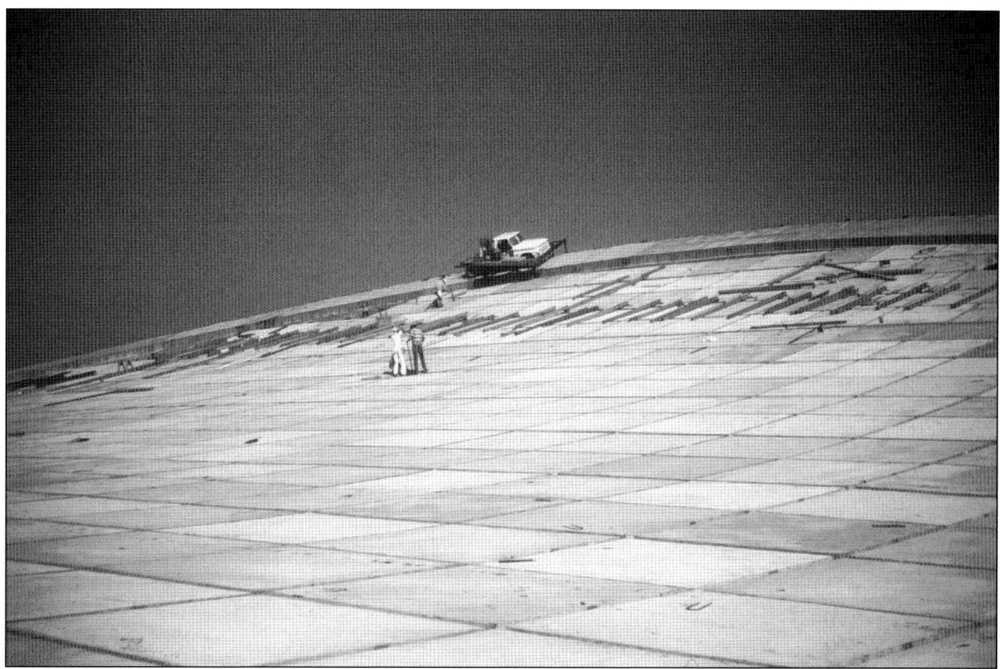

The wide concrete ring beam was used as a road for four trucks, one in each quadrant, when hydraulic jacks were used to tighten the cables. The trucks were fitted with steel outriggers that carried platforms for jacks and workmen. Note the curvature of the concrete panels above. Two 50-ton cranes were braced with lattice towers to hoist each of the 1,050 precast panels to the rooftop. Each panel weighing 3,400 pounds was carefully dropped into place, and then the cables were tightened by workers on the roof. The circular saddle-type roof was believed to be the world's largest of its type when completed. (Both, courtesy of Marilyn Dickmann Barrows.)

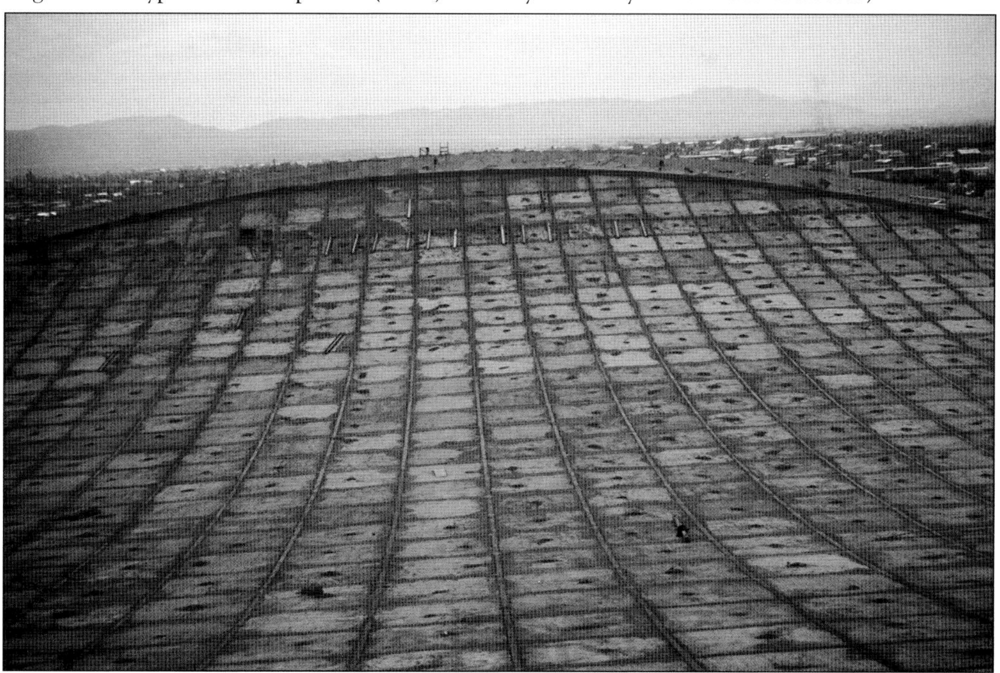

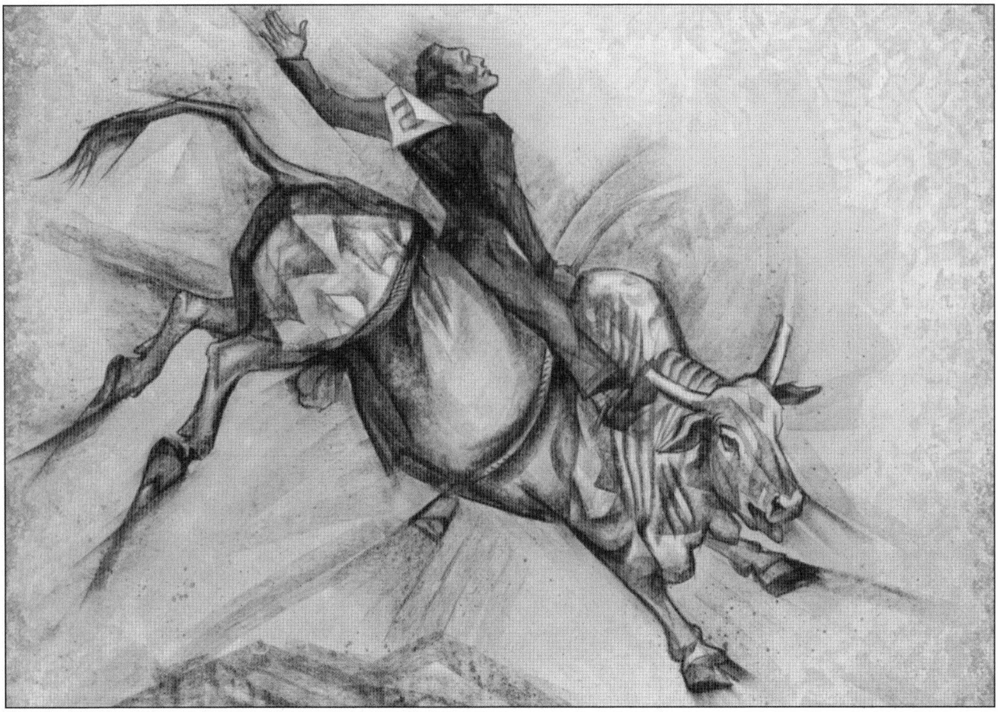

Paul Coze was a French American anthropologist enamored with the romance of the West who became an authority on Native Americans. A cofounder of the Scouts de France, he served as editor of the *Scouts* magazine. He moved to the United States in 1938 and, thereafter, to Phoenix, becoming one of the preeminent mid-century Arizona artists. His work includes many public art commissions, including murals evoking rodeos and Southwestern culture in the Veterans Memorial Coliseum, above and below. Coze was a rodeo aficionado and drew different interpretations of Native Americans, beauty queens, scenes of bucking broncs, steer bulldogging, and other rodeo events inside the structure. (Both, courtesy of Edward Jensen.)

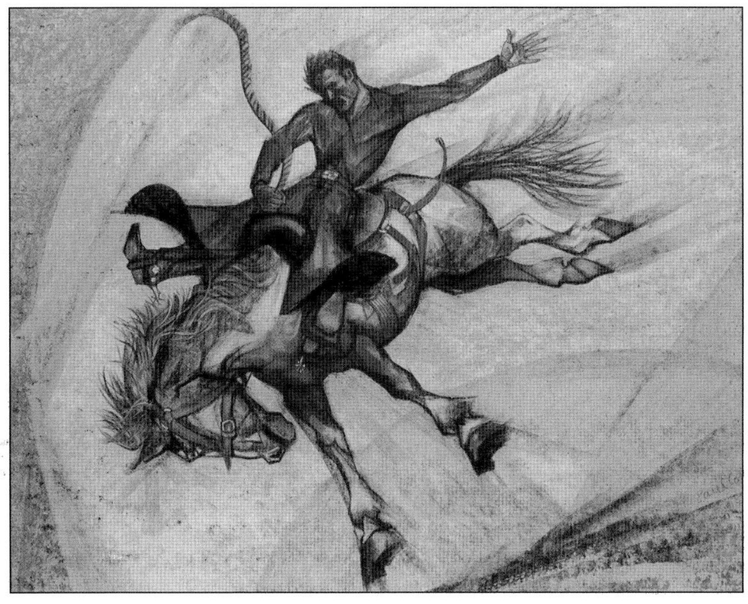

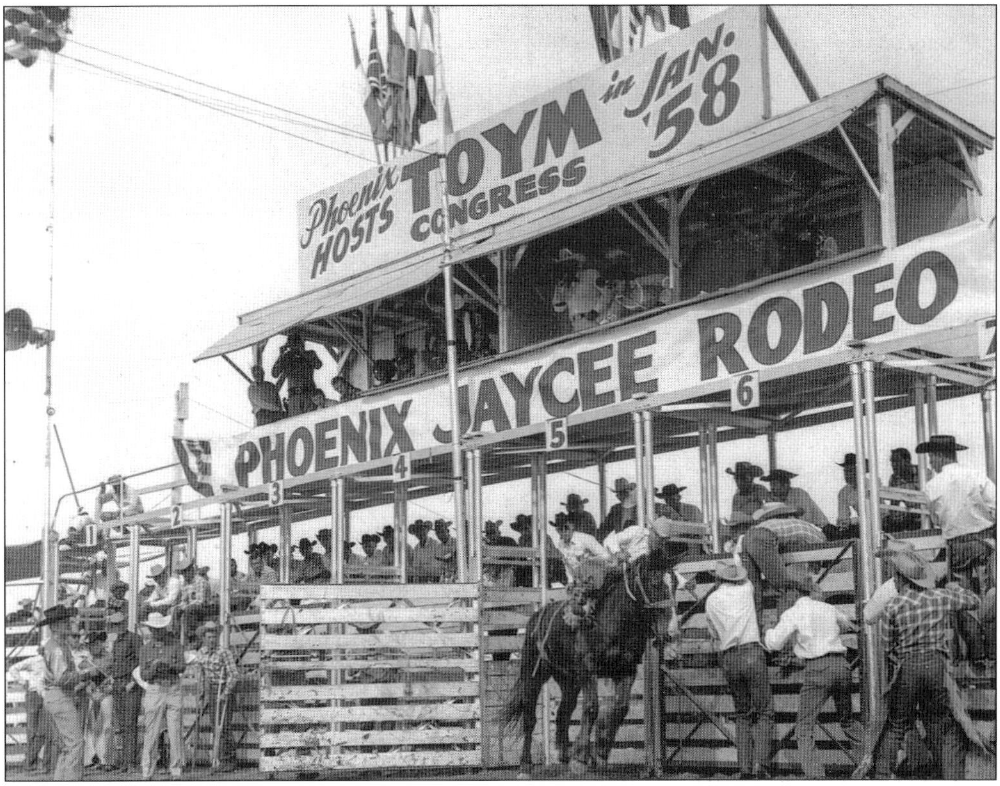

The mid-1960s brought an end to the Phoenix Jaycees rodeos that were held outside on the grassy lawn at the fairgrounds. After the new Veterans Memorial Coliseum was opened in 1965, the Western spectacle of the Jaycees rodeo moved inside; however, the enthusiasm, pomp, and ceremony of the opening night of the rodeo, shown below, continued undiminished. The Jaycees' hand-built wooden corrals had given way to steel corrals and other modern touches for the coliseum. The coliseum was large enough to accommodate ice shows, basketball, hockey, football, political figures, superstar concerts, and many other events in air-conditioned comfort. (Both, courtesy of the Phoenix Jaycees.)

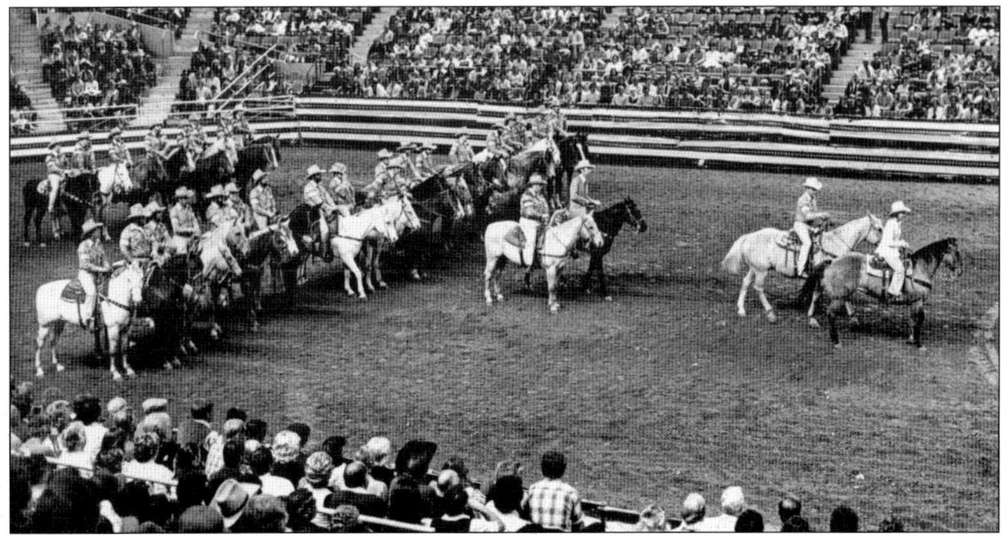

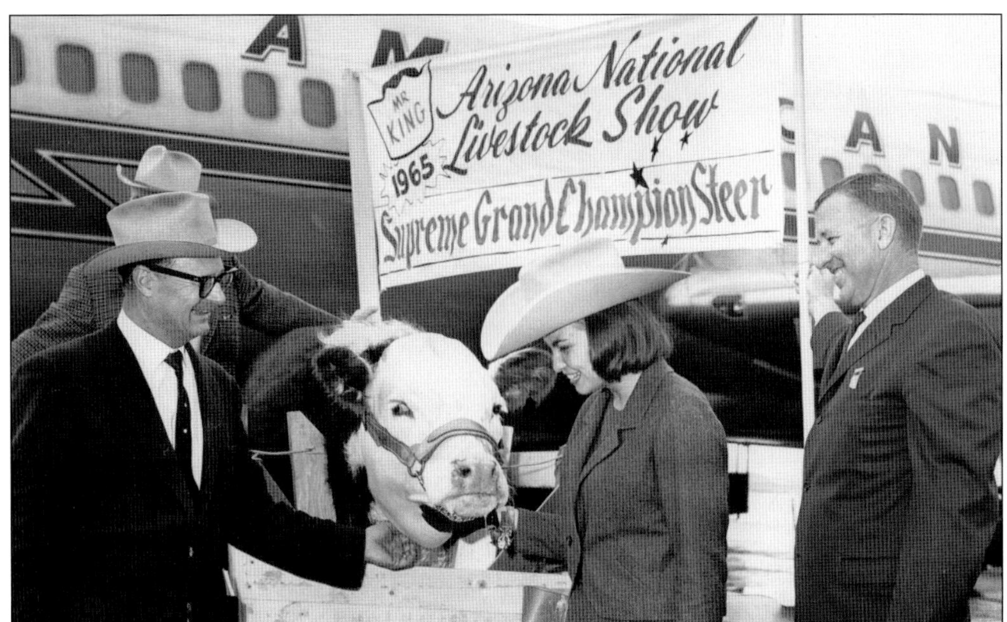

Vonda Kay VanDyke, representing Arizona, was crowned Miss America of 1965. She is at Sky Harbor Airport by an American Airlines plane, with Lee TePoel, manager of the Arizona National Livestock Show (ANLS), above left. The show's Supreme Grand Champion Steer, named Mr. King, is in the convertible, and Dr. Bart Cardon, president of the ANLS, is at right. (Courtesy of the Arizona National Livestock Show.)

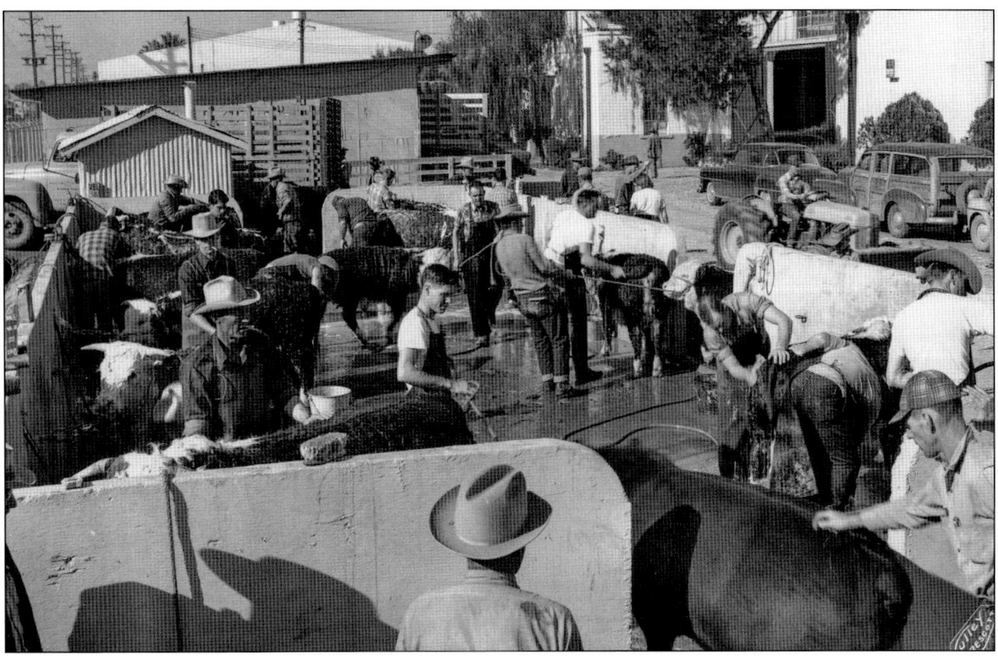

The prosperous 1950s brought both young and mature cowmen to the "wash rack," an area to wash and groom their entrants in the various classes. In those years, the ANLS was ranked third of the top shows in the country. Note the woodie station wagon in front of the cattle barns. (Courtesy of the Arizona National Livestock Show.)

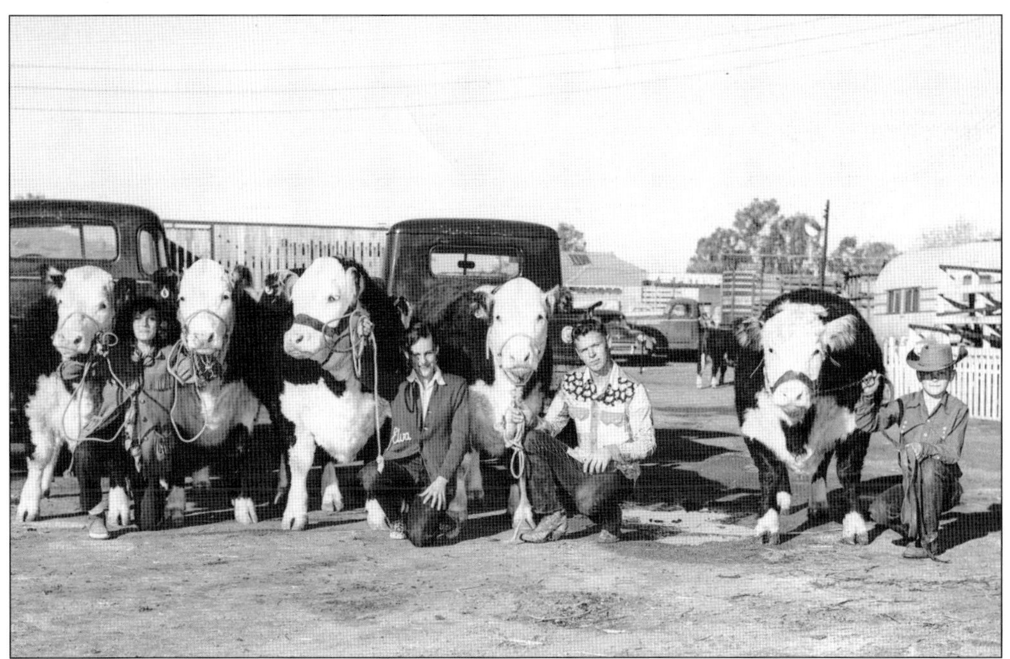

The groomed white-face Herefords have exited the wash rack, have been dried, and are on their way to the show ring. The 4-H members and Future Farmers of America are proud of their animals. The cowgirl on the left is showing two entries. The cowboy on the right is careful to keep his entry out of the water on the ground. (Courtesy of the Arizona National Livestock Show.)

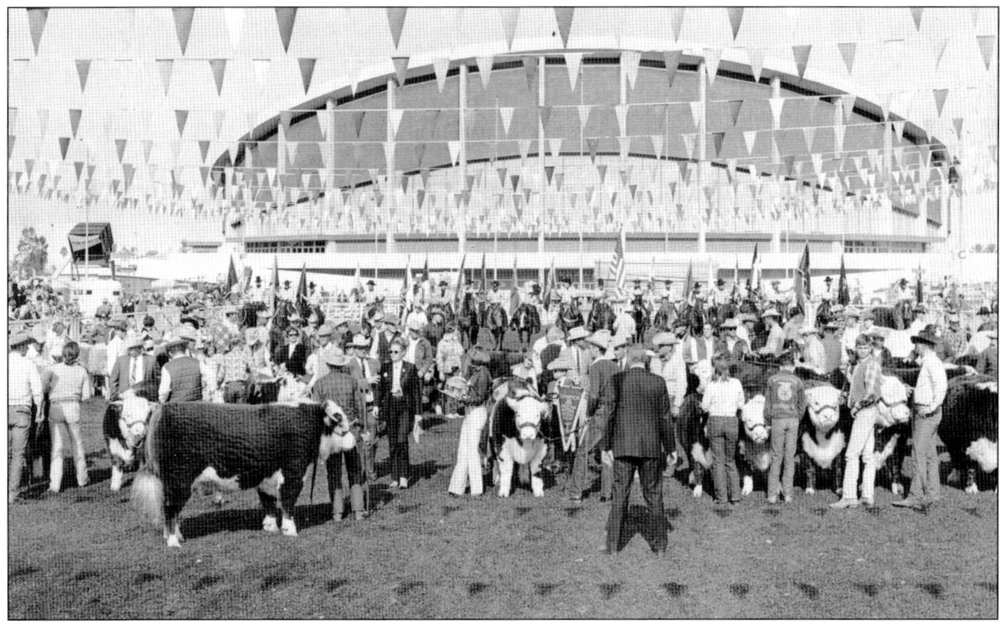

This festive scene depicts the parade of champions in front of the coliseum in 1968. John Wayne presented the trophies and gave autographs. Herefords, Angus, Charolais, Brahma, Shorthorn, Brangus, and a few Texas Longhorns were exhibited. The Wickenburg Gold Shirt Gang made the grand entry on horseback with flags flying. (Courtesy of the Arizona National Livestock Show.)

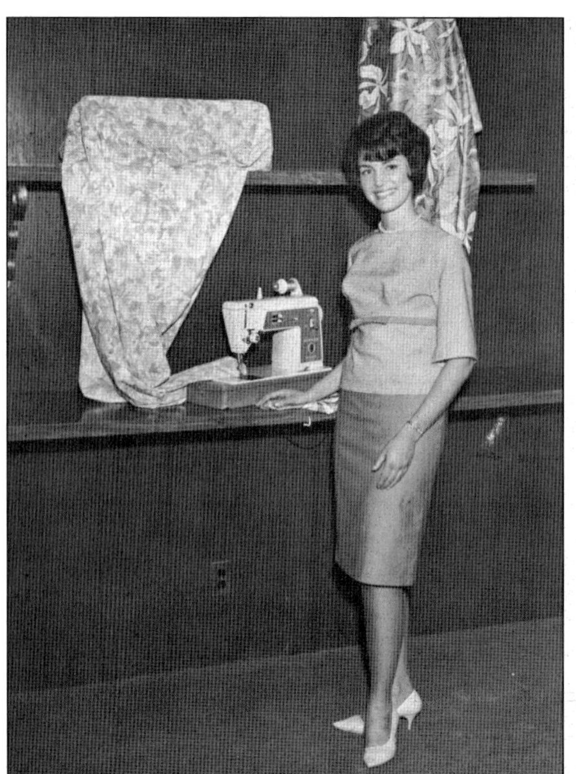

The Arizona Cotton Growers Association and the Phoenix Cotton Wives annually chose a woman as fashion and goodwill ambassadress for the cotton industry. Pictured is Pamela Arle, named the Arizona Maid of Cotton in 1966–1967. The winner would appear at the fair and also represented Arizona in the National Cotton Contest. (Courtesy of the Arizona Cotton Growers Association.)

F.G. Hardwick won a $500 prize for growing the first bale of the season at the second territorial fair in 1885. Experiments eventually produced Pima cotton for which Arizona became famous. The judges for the 1961 Cotton Week Poster Contest are pictured with the winning entry by Alice Hanna. (Courtesy of Picture the Past Antiques.)

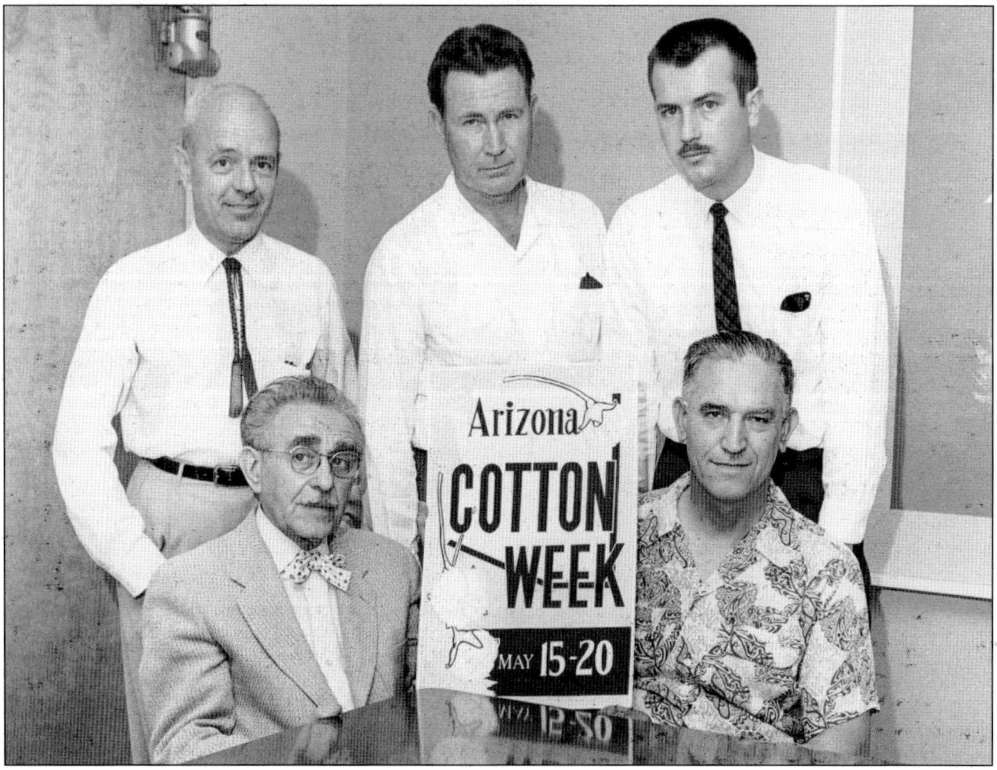

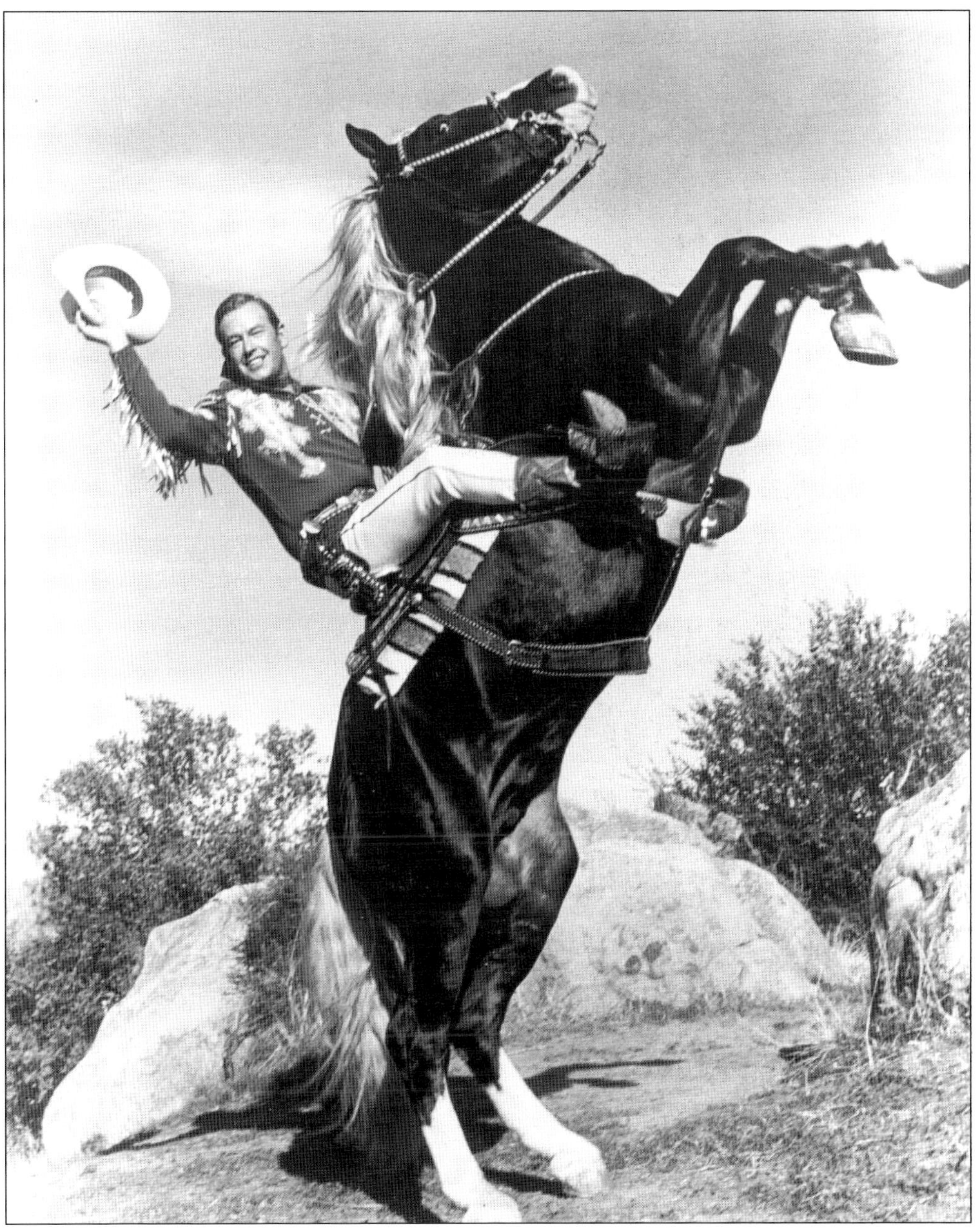

Arizona cowboy icon Rex Allen was born in Willcox, Arizona. Living on a ranch for his early life, he played the guitar and was a natural horseman. He migrated to Phoenix in 1938, after graduating from Willcox High School. Phoenix was beginning to boom again in the late 1930s, and Rex found enjoyable work on the radio. Through his singing and guitar playing, he had connected with Jack Williams, an announcer on KOY Radio, who featured the talented musician on his live shows. California was a golden magnet for many in Depression-era Arizona, and Rex found work in Hollywood. He appeared in many movies as the "Arizona Cowboy" and earned a star on the Hollywood Walk of Fame. Rex, pictured on the "Wonder Horse," KoKo, appeared as host of the state fair many times in the 1960s and 1970s. (Courtesy of the Rex Allen Arizona Cowboy Museum.)

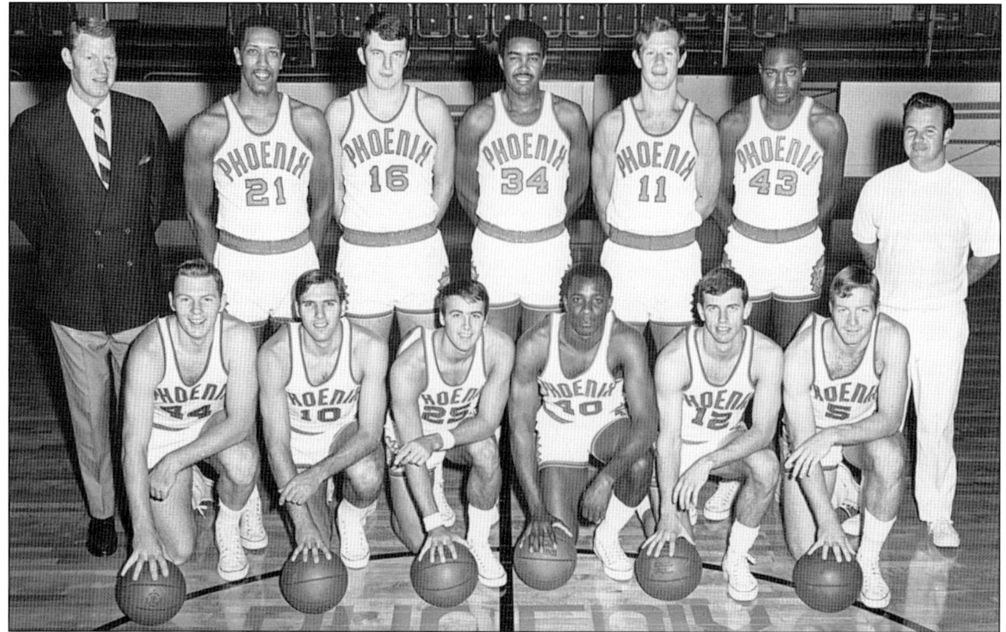

The lineup of the 1968–1969 Phoenix Suns' first season roster is posing for a photograph at center court. Included in the photograph are coach John Graham "Red" Kerr and trainer Joe Proski. The team played all home games in the Veterans Memorial Coliseum, which came to be known alliteratively as "the Madhouse on McDowell." The photograph below was taken at a 1971–1972 home game in the coliseum. Neal Walk (No. 41) is on the left. Center Cornelius "Connie" Hawkins (No. 42) is hovering over the ball. Clem Haskins (No. 11), the guard on the far right, is in action against his former team, the Chicago Bulls. (Both, courtesy of the Phoenix Suns.)

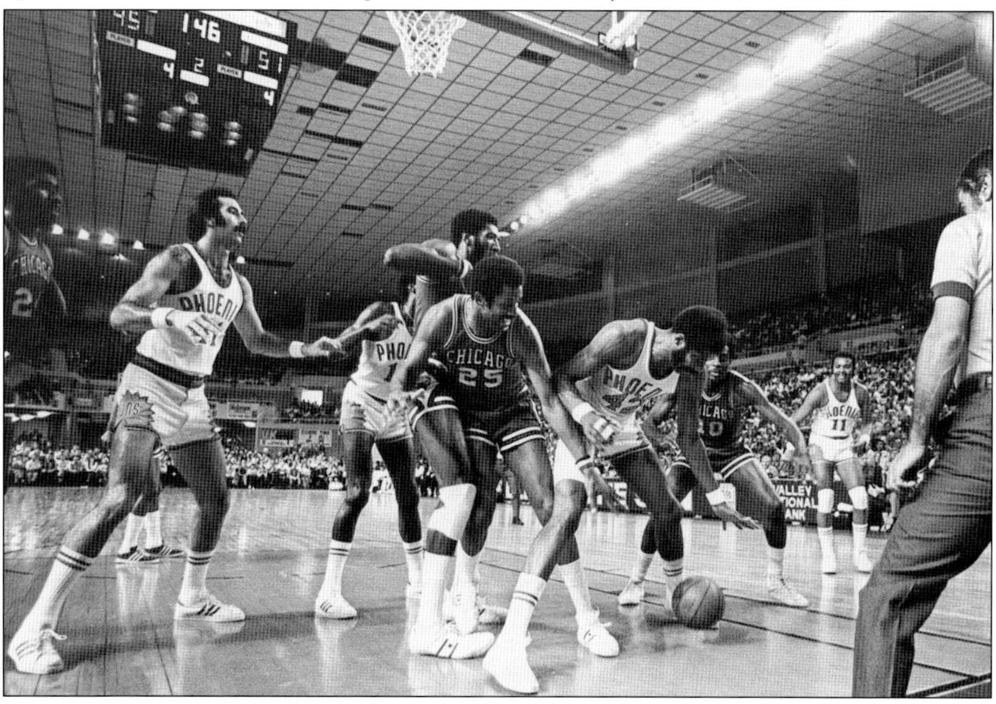

This home game, pictured at right, depicts Alvan Adams in action. The official Getty Images caption for this photograph reads as follows: "Alvan Adams (No. 33) of the Phoenix Suns drives to the basket against the Golden State Warriors during the 1977 Season at the Veterans Memorial Coliseum in Phoenix, Arizona." Alvan, originally from Oklahoma, was called the "OK Kid." He played his entire career with the Suns. Dick Van Arsdale (No. 5), of the Phoenix Suns, below, makes a move to the basket during a game played in 1970 at the Veterans Memorial Coliseum in Phoenix, Arizona. He played shooting guard. Dick was often called the "Original Sun." He was later joined on the Suns team by his identical twin brother, Tom Van Arsdale. (Both, courtesy of the Phoenix Suns and Getty Images.)

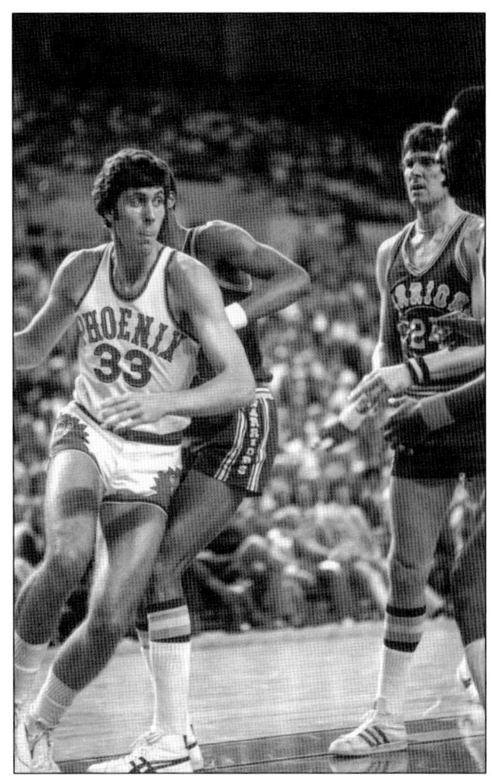

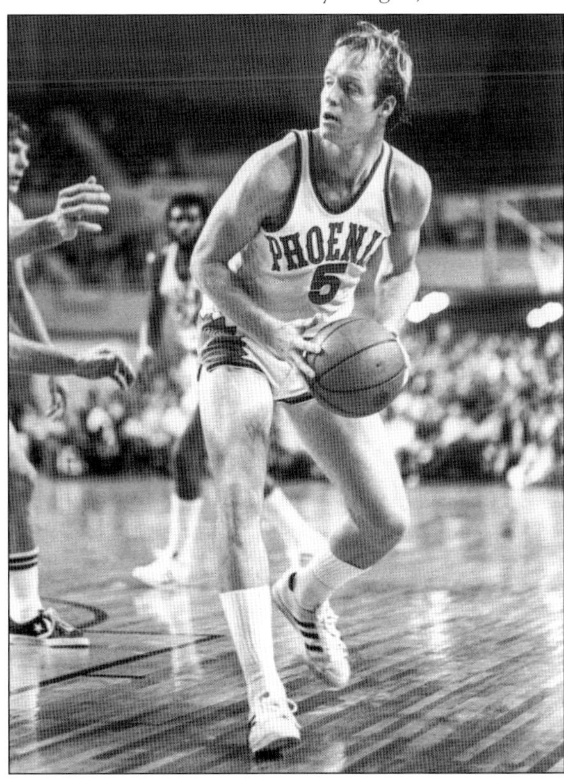

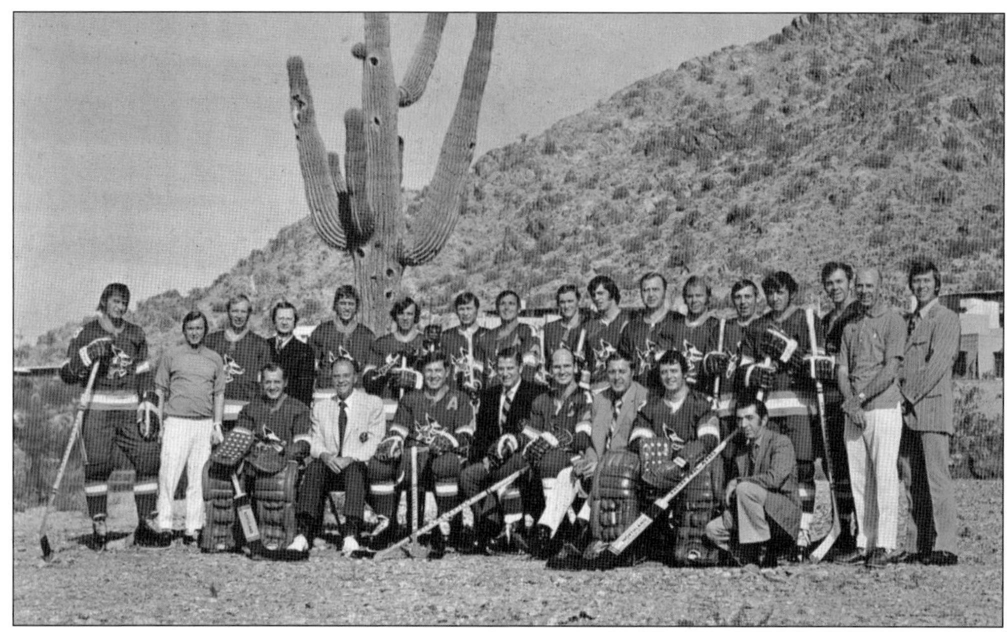

The Phoenix Roadrunners were a professional team in the World Hockey Association that utilized the Veterans Memorial Coliseum for their home games. In the photograph above, the entire team, including management, publicist, and trainers, assembled in full game regalia near Camelback Mountain to graphically illustrate that there was indeed hockey played in the desert. The Roadrunners had the largest booster club in the league. The management team also organized a hockey school to train future player prospects. Pictured below are, from left to right, player Scott Beaudion, commentator Michale Lenard, potential player Peter Bjelopetrovich, J.C. Minough, potential player Rohny Click, and team captain Al McLeod. (Above, courtesy of Bob Liddington; below, courtesy of Rohny Click.)

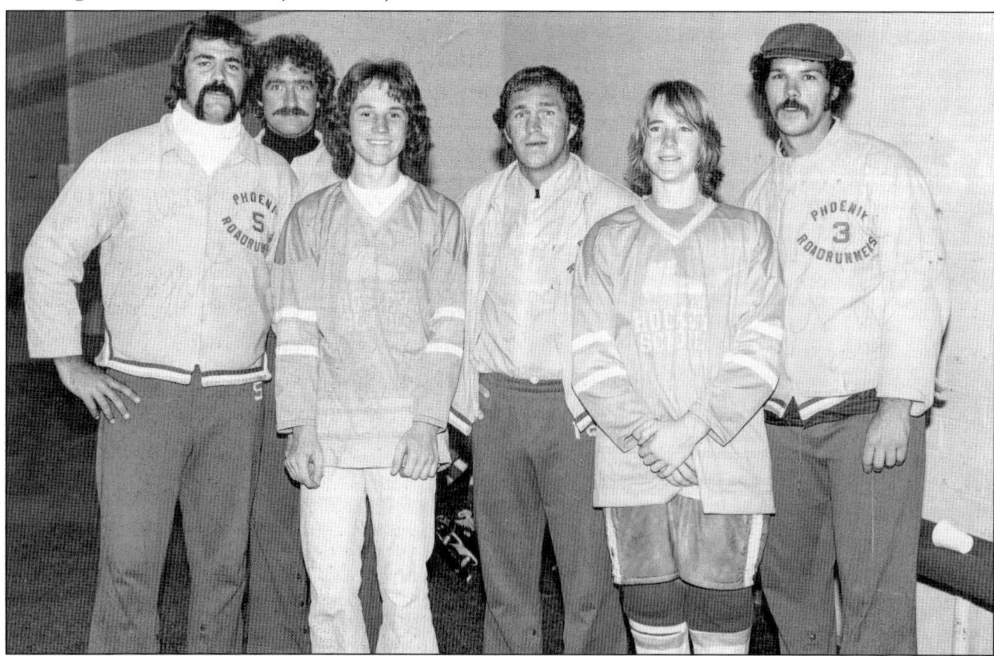

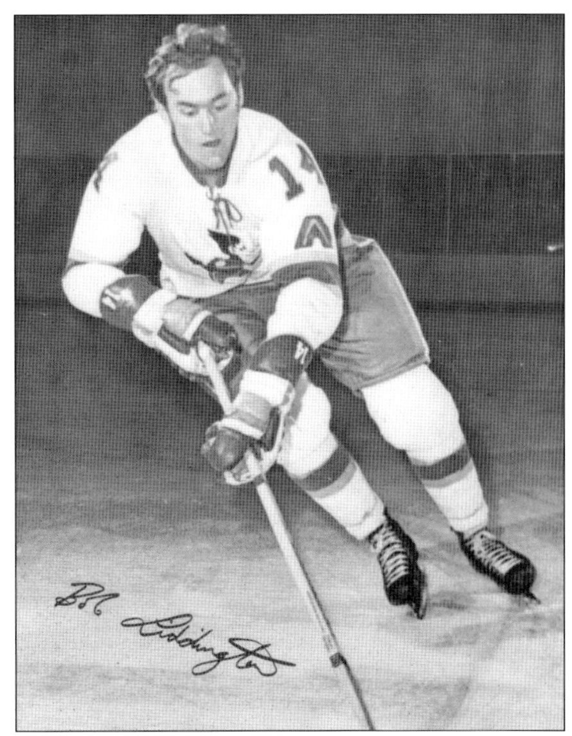

Bob Liddington, a former member of the Phoenix Roadrunners Hockey team, remembers that when the Jaycees rodeos were utilizing the coliseum, the team could not practice there. The players would put on their uniforms at the coliseum, travel in groups all the way to the Arcadia Ice Arena at Tower Plaza, practice there, and then travel back to the coliseum to shower and change into street clothes. The shot below shows how frantic, fast, and exciting the Roadrunners games were for the fans. Bob Liddington (No. 14) was in action against the Salt Lake Golden Eagles goalie in the vintage face mask. (Both, courtesy of Bob Liddington.)

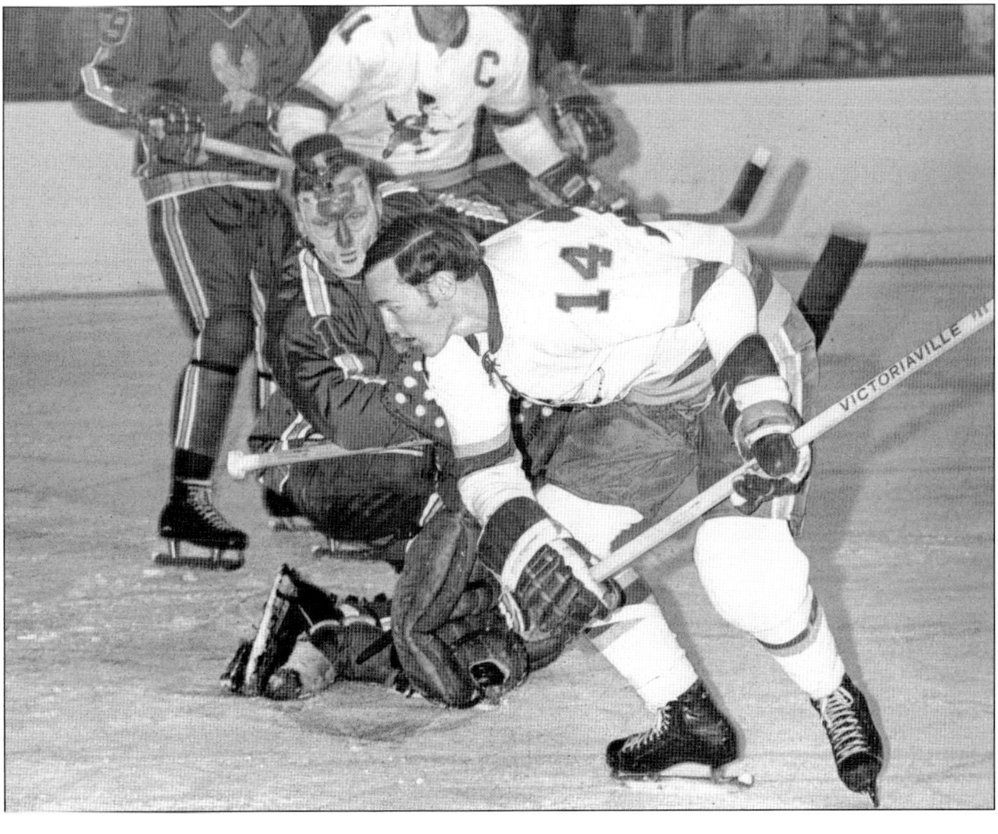

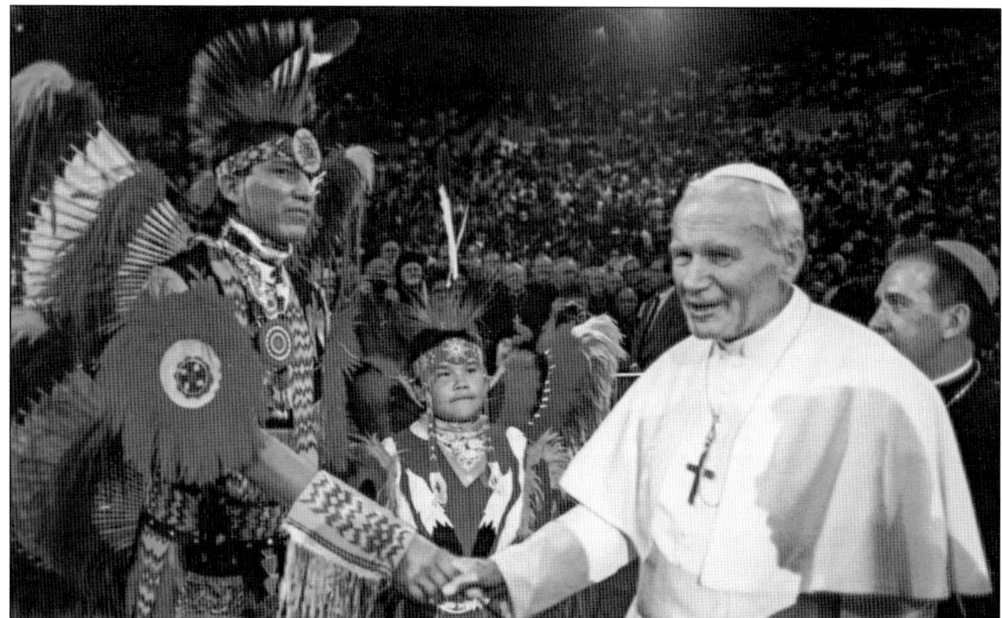

On September 14, 1987, Pope John Paul II visited Phoenix to bring greetings of joy and peace to the people of the city and the great Southwest. His entourage traveled south on Central Avenue as thousands lined the street to view him. Children presented flowers to him at numerous stops. (Courtesy of the Roman Catholic Diocese of Phoenix Archives.)

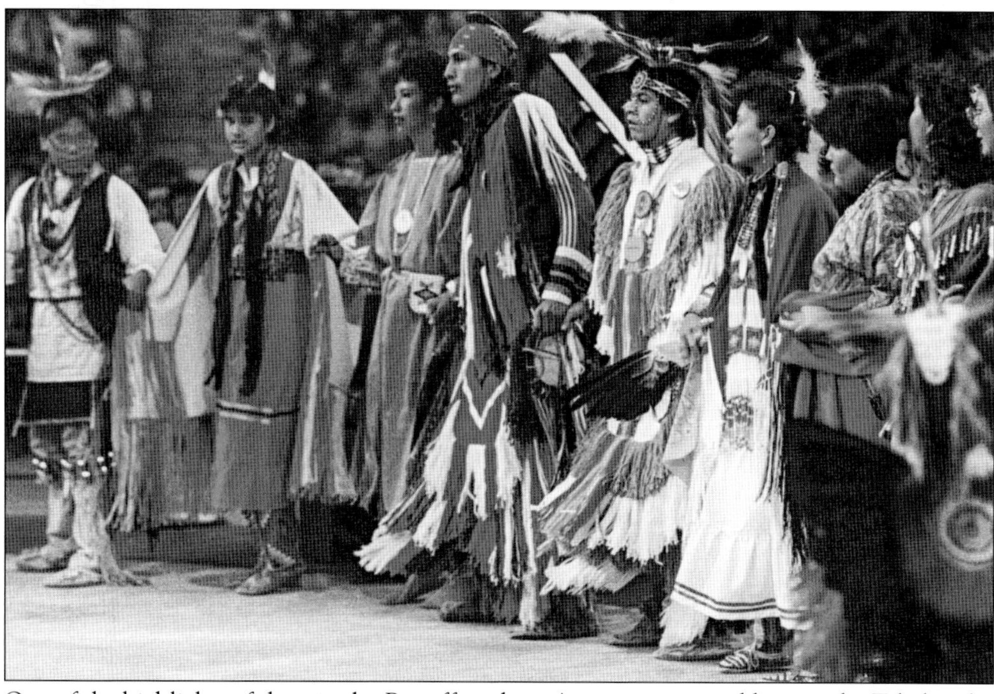

One of the highlights of the trip the Pontiff made to Arizona was an address to the Tekakwitha Conference in the coliseum. The conference was a gathering of Catholic members of the Native American community. Pope John Paul II received an eagle feather as a symbol of peace, love, and respect. (Courtesy of the Roman Catholic Diocese of Phoenix Archives.)

Arizona governor Rose Mofford is shown in the Veterans Memorial Coliseum on November 2, 1989, with Mother Teresa of Calcutta, winner of the Nobel Peace Prize. Governor Mofford honored Mother Teresa's request to build a refuge for the homeless. Mother Teresa became a Catholic saint on September 4, 2016. (Courtesy of the Roman Catholic Diocese of Phoenix Archives.)

A very different Paul Coze mural from those found in the coliseum was created for Phoenix City Council Chambers, pictured. The mosaic depicts the history of the Salt River Valley from the Hohokam to the present. When the council chambers were remodeled, the mural was moved to St. Mary's High School. (Photograph by Edward Jensen, courtesy of St. Mary's Catholic High School.)

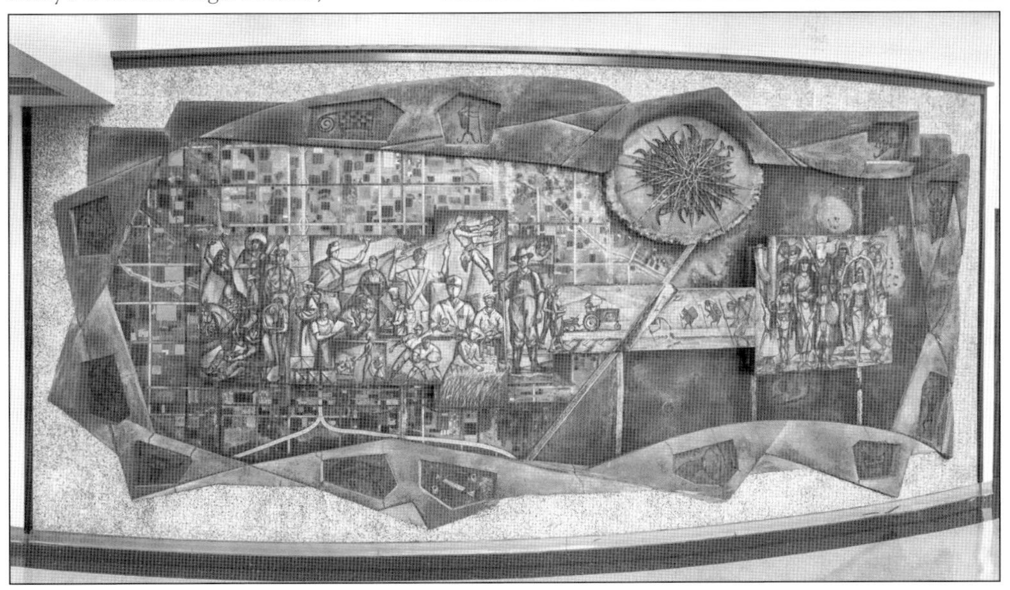

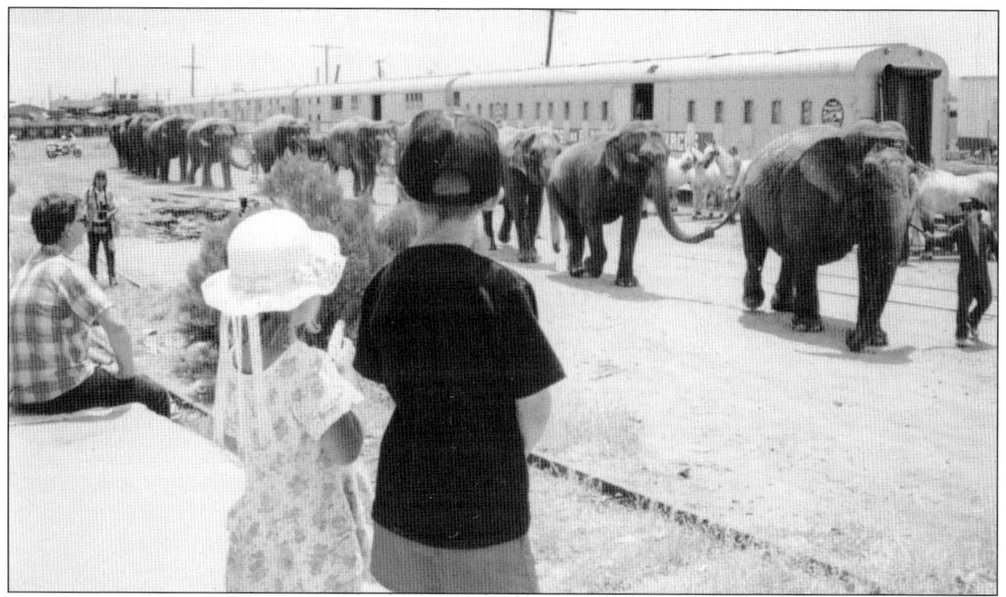

For decades, Ringling Bros. and Barnum & Bailey Circus offloaded the numerous performing animals from the circus train at Union Station downtown. In the intense, dusty heat of summer, elephants and other animals paraded from downtown, turned north on Fifteenth Avenue, and then to the fairgrounds. Students from the Phoenix Elementary School District No. 1, Monterey Park School, once had a special experience. At Dr. Ruth Ann Marston's request, they were allowed to wash the road dust off the elephants at the fairgrounds. The students had studied how to care for various animals. Circus officials gave permission and supervised the procedure, pictured below. (Both, courtesy of Jacqueline Radke.)

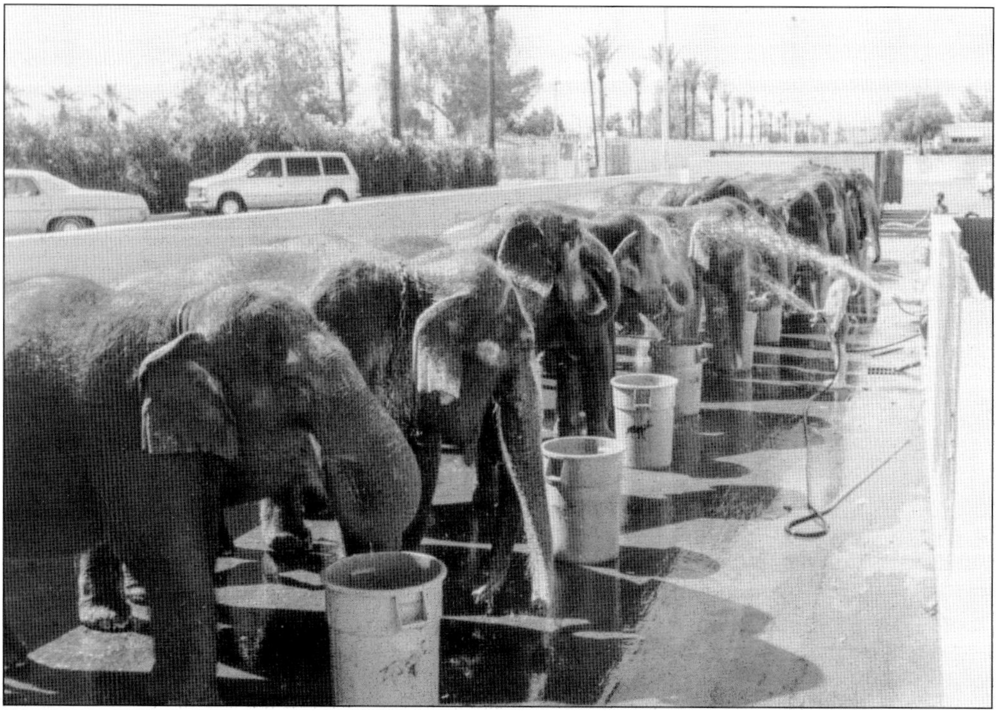

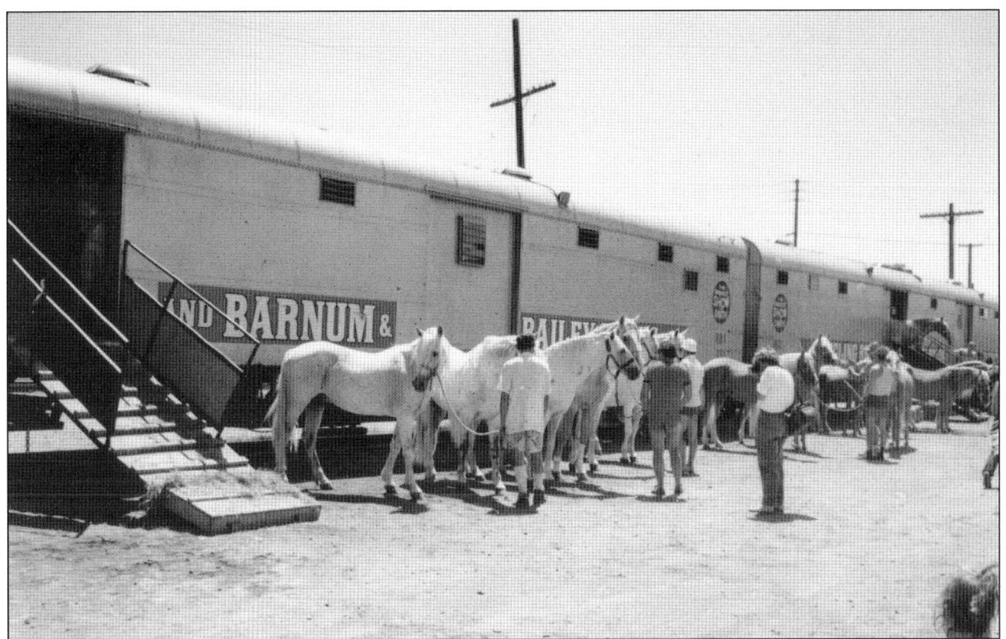

Other colorful, exotic circus animals made the trek to perform at the fairgrounds, as well. The white horses, so beloved in performance with their stunt riders, were lined up in formation, as were other animals. The route led under freeway overpasses and down verdant neighborhood streets, lined with palms in the F.Q. Story Historic District. Pictured below, camels are being gently led through scenes reminiscent of the desert atmosphere of their land of origin. The caged lions and tigers were trucked to the fairgrounds from Union Station when the circus came to town. (Both, courtesy of Jacqueline Radke.)

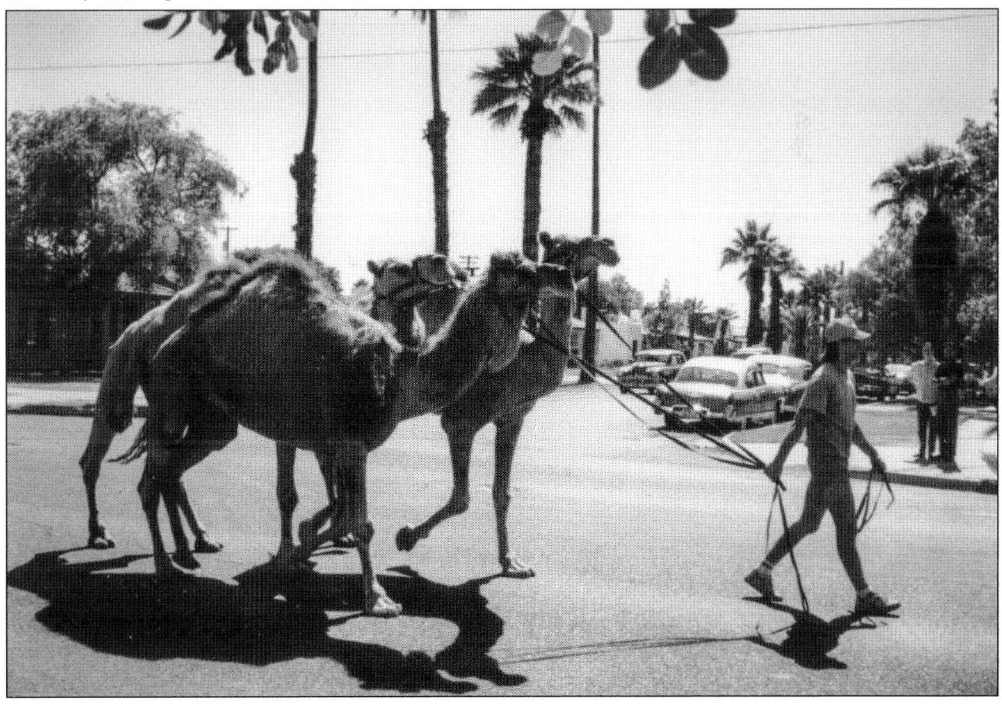

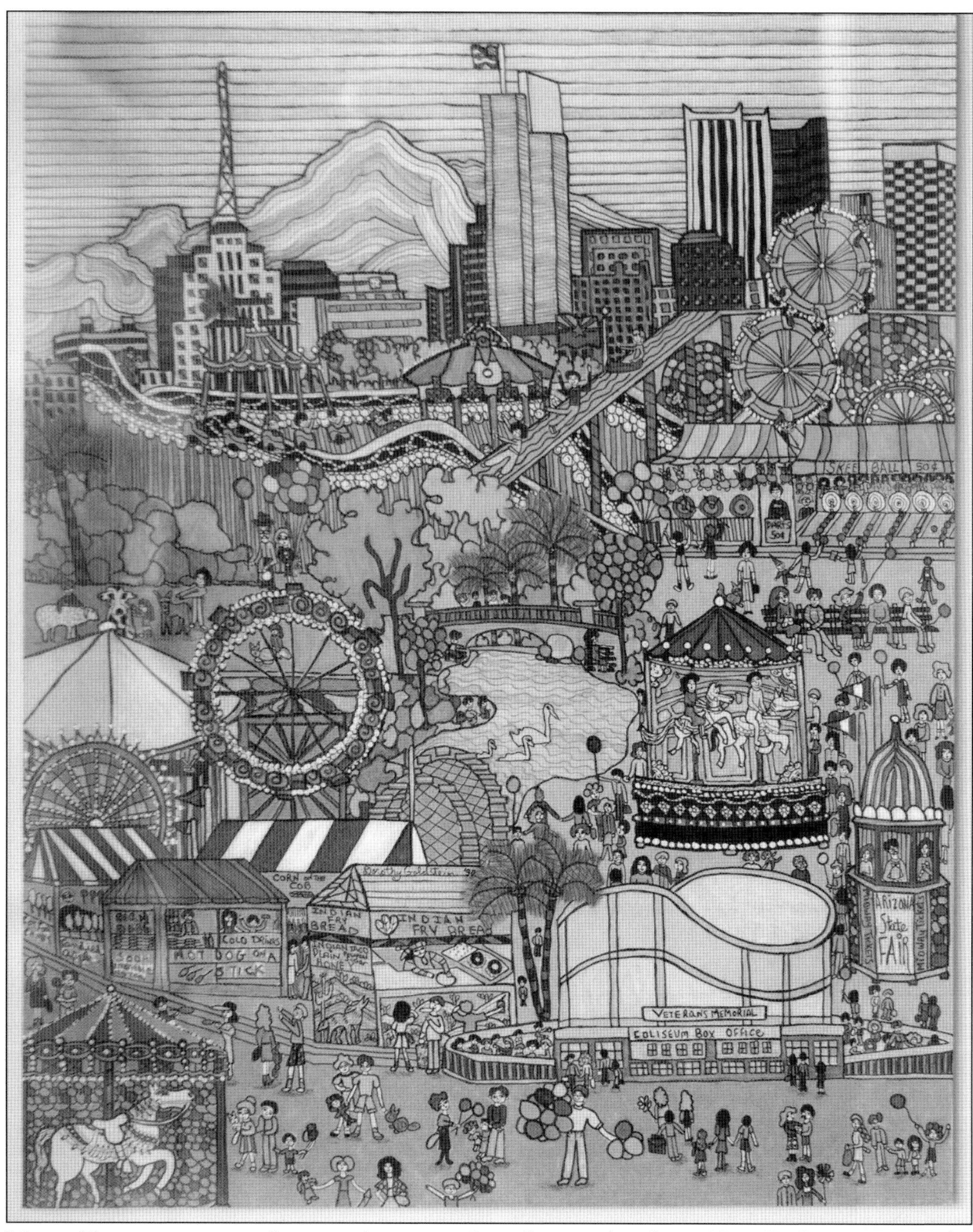

Metro Phoenix prizes its historical roots and modern technology. New York artist Dorothy Goldstein, living and painting in Phoenix, revels in art that captures a significant moment in time in her community. This award-winning depiction of the Arizona State Fair in the foreground, with city and mountain backdrop in the distance, captures the enthusiasm and excitement of the fair. The special report of the state fair commission for 1915–1916, in relation to the condition commented, "The State Fair Grounds are ideal for the purpose intended and with consistent landscape gardening, which has been started under plans obtained from the landscape gardening department of the University of Arizona, will soon be one of the most beautiful parks in the State. The plant is in better general condition than ever before and compares favorably with that of any in the West." (Courtesy of Dorothy Goldstein.)

Five

Into the Millennium

While state fairs take place annually, other events happen only once in a lifetime. Hurricane Katrina battered the US Gulf Coast on August 29, 2005. The Arizona State Fair staff was instructed by Gov. Janet Napolitano to prepare shelter in the Veterans Memorial Coliseum for thousands of evacuees. The coliseum became a mini-city for "Operation Good Neighbor." The result was a hugely successful rescue effort.

Nearly a decade later, it was a building on the fairgrounds itself that needed rescuing. In 2014, there were plans to demolish the historic 1938 WPA building. The populace was awakened when historian Vincent Murray notified his contact list of the imminent destruction of the building. That information flamed into front-page news as the preservation community learned that some thought the building had outlived its usefulness and should be torn down. A state budget gave no hint of plans to eliminate a building that was eligible for the National Register of Historic Places.

In July 2014, in anticipation of the proposed demolition, one large steel casement window on the north side of the WPA building was removed for preservation purposes. Phoenix mayor Greg Stanton and the city council then stationed police around the fairgrounds to halt further demolition.

This was a clarion call for preservation activists and statewide organizations. It provided an opportunity for them to work with the fairgrounds administration and fair board to help preserve not only the WPA Administration Building, but to also lend support and cooperation toward the restoration of all historic buildings on the grounds. In this latest demonstration of the good neighbor policy, the city, surrounding historic districts, and community members pulled together to donate money and resources to help stabilize the building.

The threatened demolition of the WPA building was the catalyst for telling the larger story of the lasting public works projects of the New Deal heritage on the fairgrounds. It has made people aware of the vast history gathered in one place and has provided the opportunity to retain the fairgrounds for future generations.

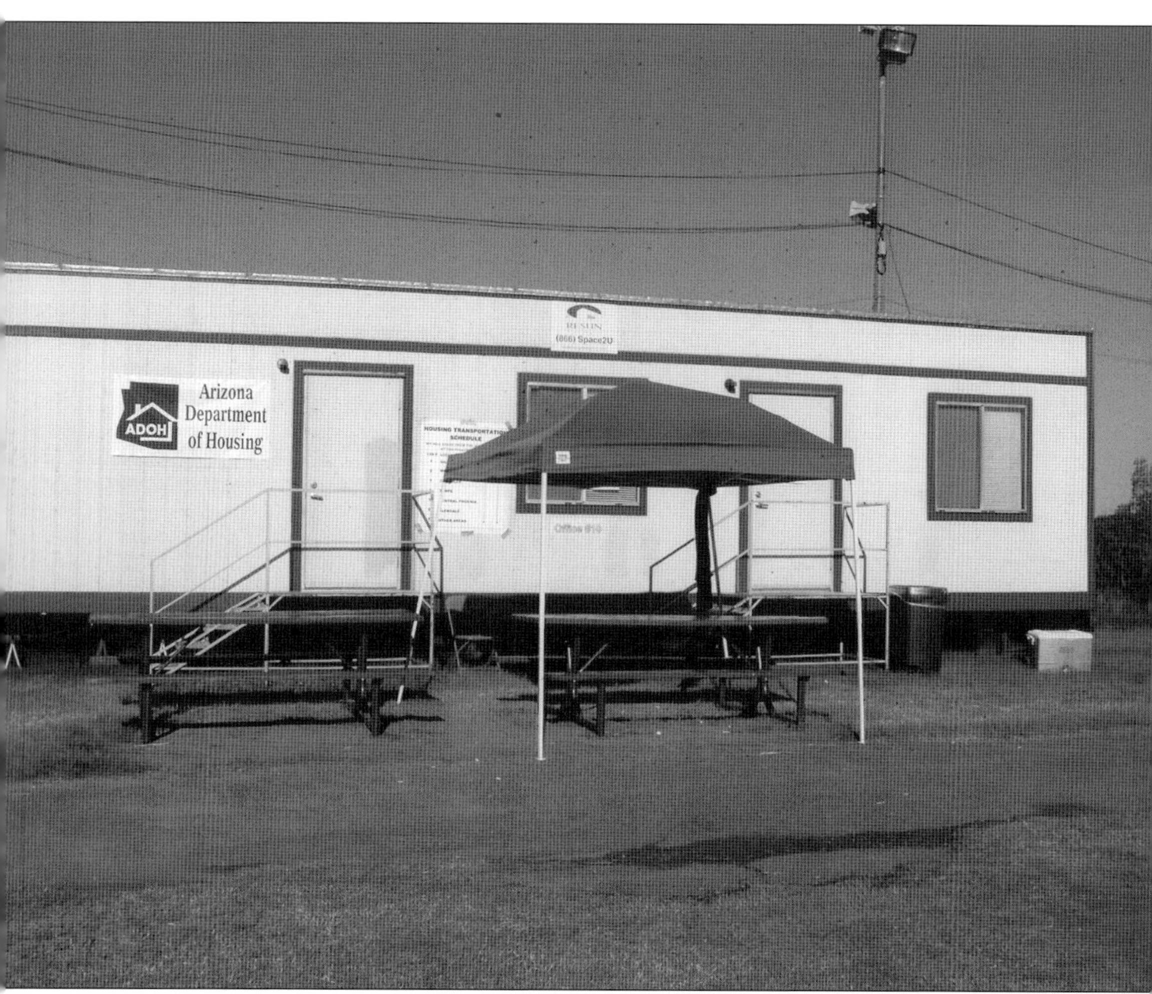

All of the entities caring for the Hurricane Katrina evacuees on the fairgrounds were directed by the Incident Command Team, which was given 48 hours to activate the rescue effort. The team directed fairgrounds employees and facilitated the Red Cross; Salvation Army; St. Vincent de Paul Services; AARP; Arizona Humane Society; city and state agencies, such as the Department of Economic Security; Phoenix Police and Fire; and hundreds of volunteers into a unified team. While the mini-city at the fairgrounds could shelter the evacuees, the demand for permanent housing arose as some were unable to return to former homes. The Arizona Department of Housing, pictured above, was on the fairgrounds to help find long-term housing. Job fairs were held for those able to work. The elderly were offered resources. A woman arriving in a wheelchair held out her arms to one of the nurses for a hug and to thank her. The nurse replied, "We've been waiting for you." The people of Arizona were honored and happy to help. (Courtesy of Arizona Department of Housing.)

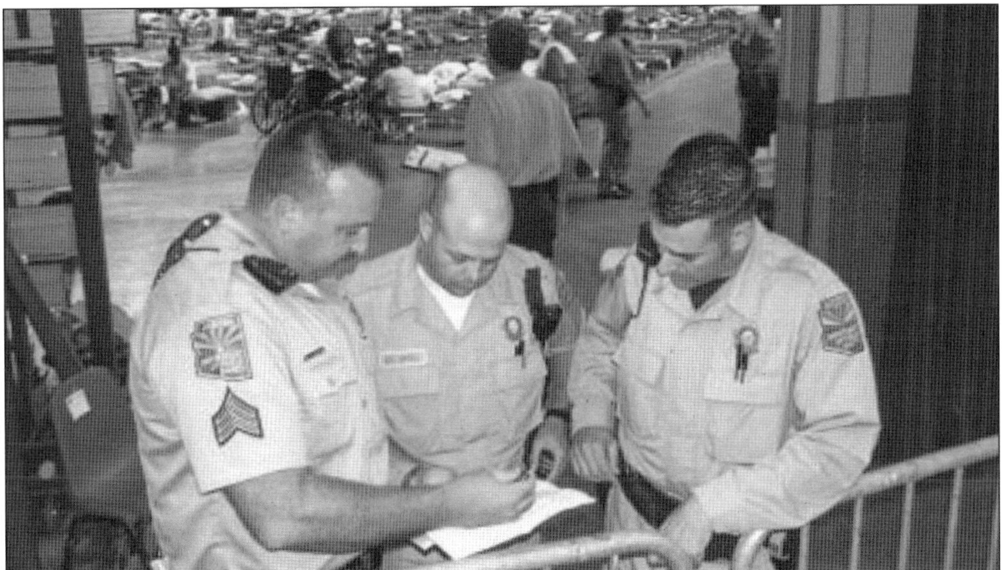

Arizona Department of Public Safety officers maintained a safe and secure haven in the Veterans Memorial Coliseum during Operation Good Neighbor. A medical clinic was established on the fairgrounds to furnish medical help for those affected by this traumatic experience. Psychological and psychiatric support teams, as well as stress management teams, went to work. Hospital teams and many volunteers brought supplies. A pharmacy was set up to service the needs of the rescued individuals. Many were put on flights only with thc clothes on their back. Evacuees were issued an identification badge, and even though all records were kept manually, it was highly organized. Any items carried in were checked on arrival to insure safety for everyone inside the coliseum. (Both, courtesy of Arizona Department of Public Safety.)

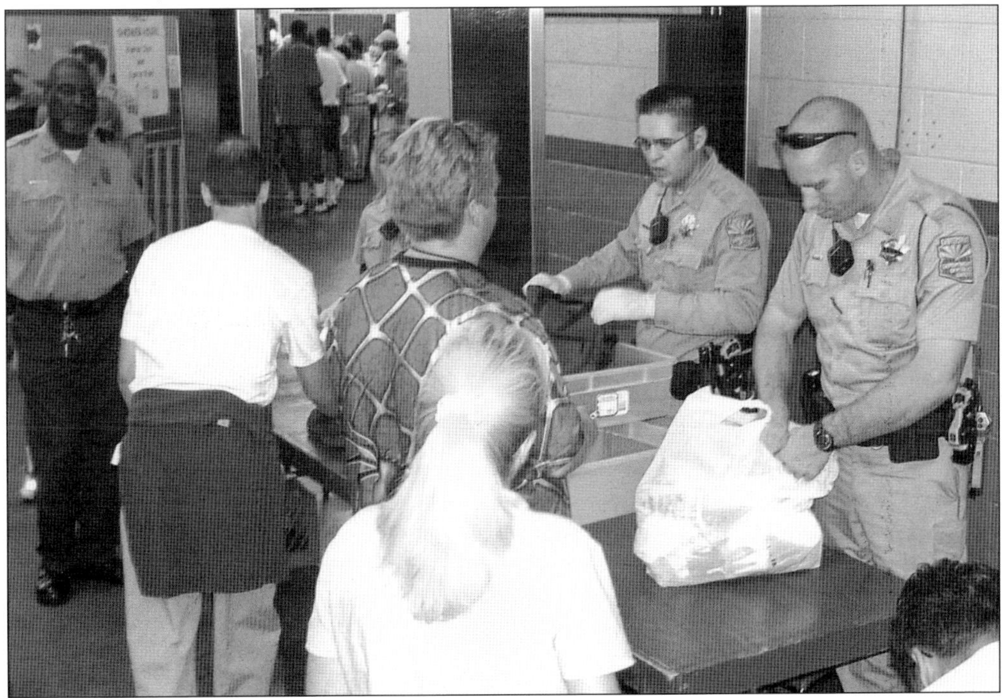

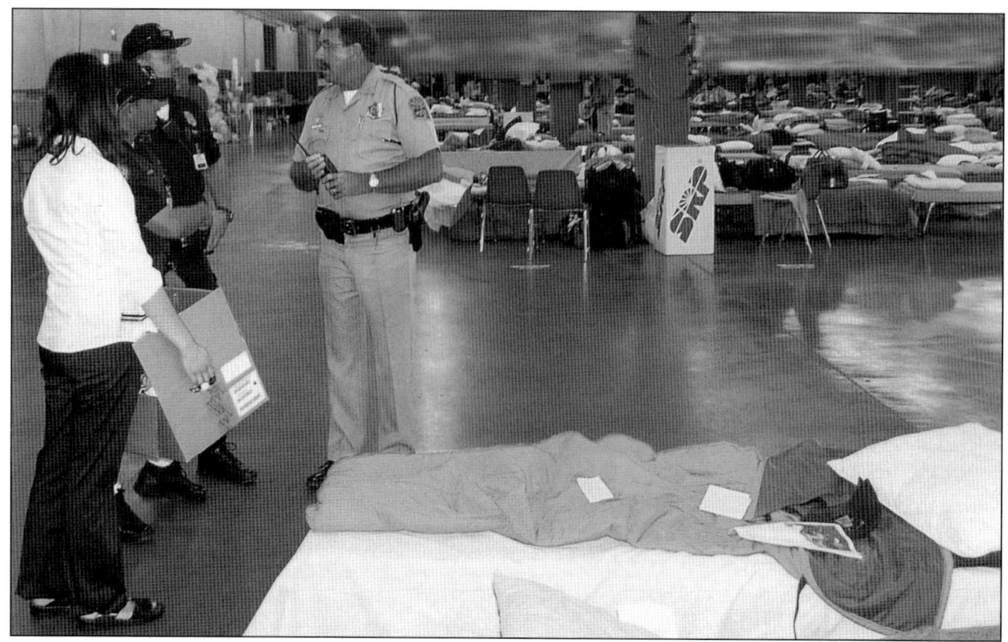

Department of Public Safety (DPS) commander Bob Halliday, pictured above, who supervised all police activity during Operation Good Neighbor, said, "The evacuees wanted to feel safe again and the police presence in the coliseum really helped in that regard." The DPS publication *Digest* referred to the event as "an historic law enforcement mission." There was free health care, clothes, and food as most evacuees brought no money with them, just what they could carry of their most precious belongings. With all his belongings in a plastic bag, an individual arrived with his dog. Veterinarians and vet techs were on site. The evacuees could relax once inside the coliseum and release the tension many had been under since being rescued from the flooded areas. They left behind a frightening experience and fled to safety, where everyone was treated with respect. (Both, courtesy of Arizona Department of Public Safety.)

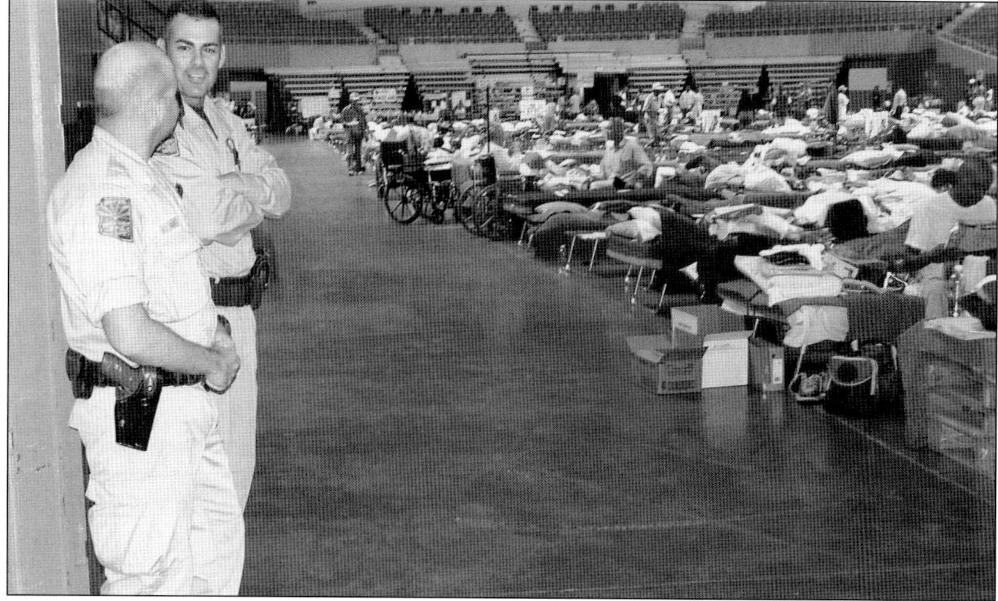

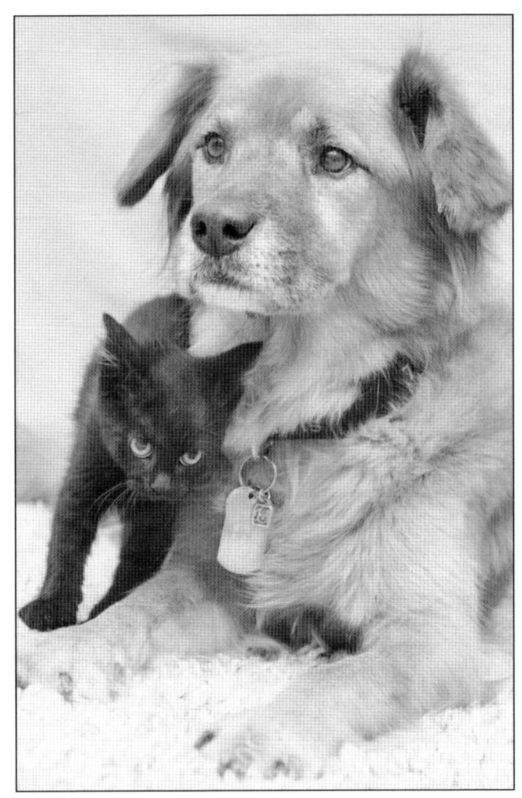

One of the touching stories to come from the devastating Katrina episode concerned a rescued dog. Volunteers and professionals from the Arizona Humane Society went to New Orleans to help animal victims of the tragedy. Boots, a golden retriever mix, was found in a field with badly injured paws. Many pets were brought to Phoenix to heal, and like many humans who came here to recover, some never left. Boots found a loving home in Arizona. He and his owner have volunteered at the Arizona Humane Society, helping to socialize kittens with other species and making them more adoptable. Boots became a "kitten nanny," according to the volunteers. (Both, courtesy of the Arizona Humane Society.)

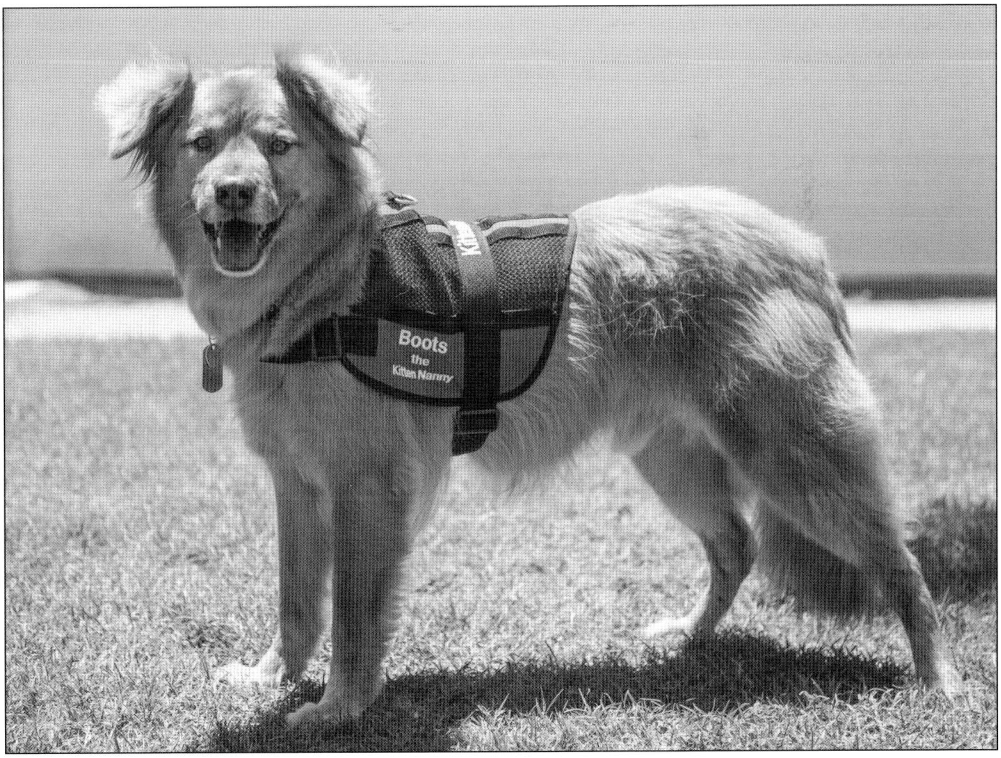

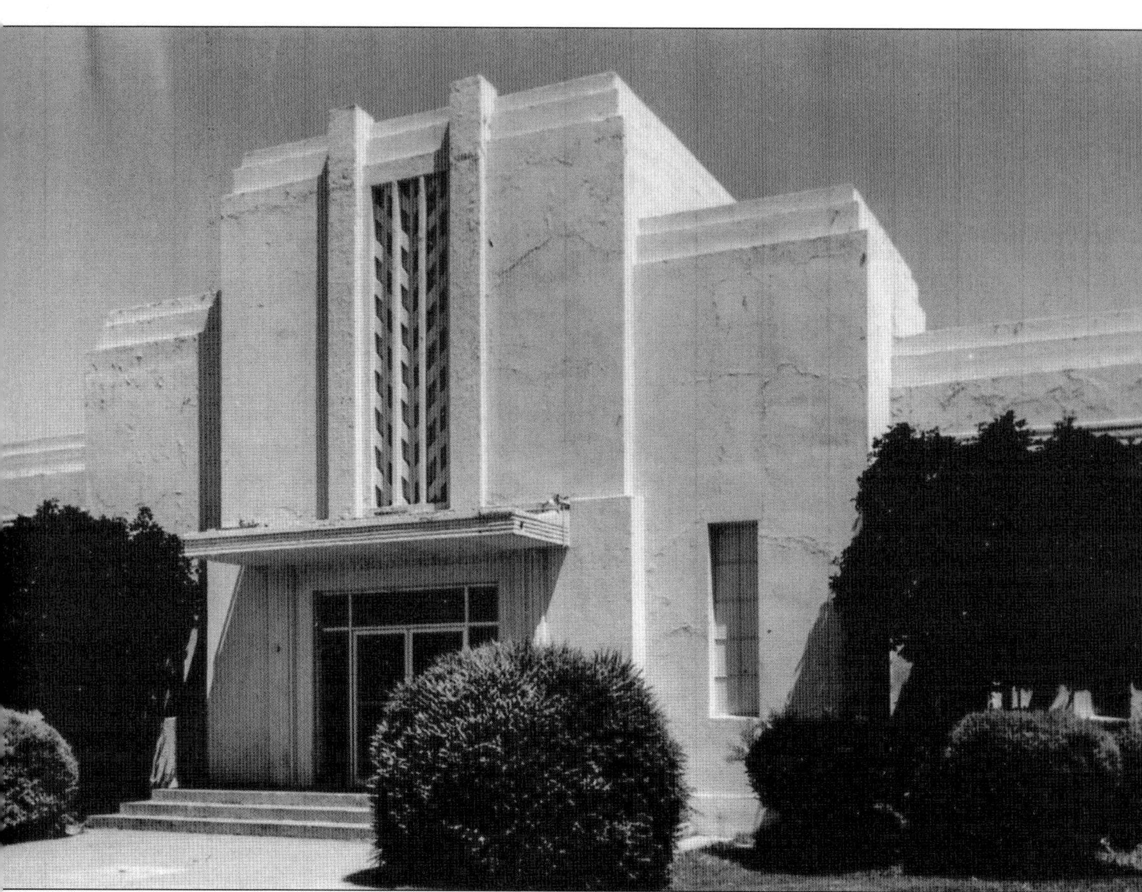

The WPA building, one of the most iconic buildings on the fairgrounds, is pictured in 1982. A Market and Economic Feasibility Analysis Growth Plan was prepared for the fair in 2008. In 2014, an attempt was made to begin implementing that plan by demolishing this building. An item for asphalt was inserted into the 2014 state budget that passed without revealing the plan, which was to destroy a historic structure to provide vendor space. State representatives Lela Alston and John Kavanagh decided that transparency was needed and brought the item to light. Beatrice Moore and Preserve Phoenix, led by attorney Jennifer Boucek, brought a suit to halt the demolition. The suit stated that the fair did not properly maintain or document a significant historic building under its jurisdiction and alleged violations of Arizona's Open Meeting Laws. A temporary restraining order was granted. (Courtesy of Encanto Citizens Association.)

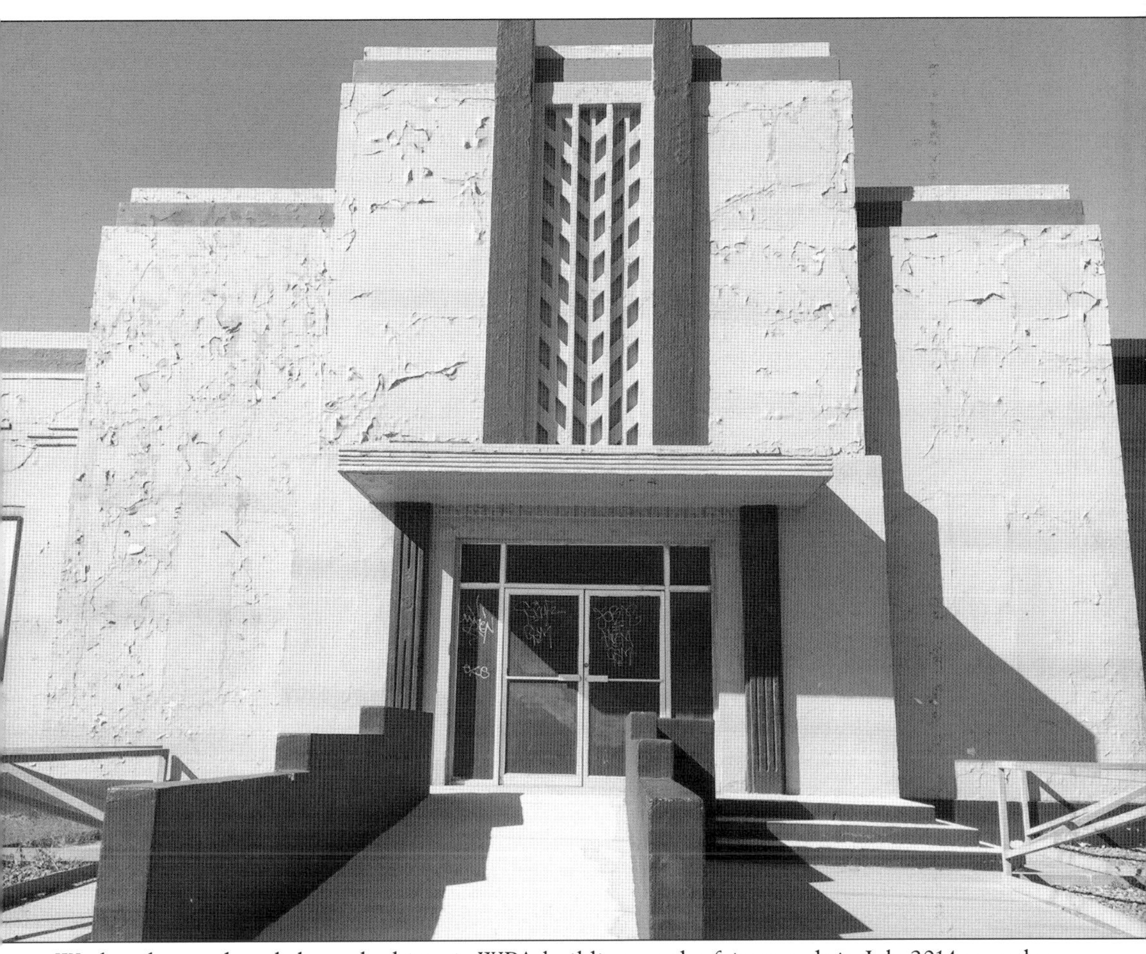

Workers began demolishing the historic WPA building on the fairgrounds in July 2014 to make room for vendor space. The City of Phoenix intended to preserve the 1938 building and immediately issued a stop-work order, as the fair had not received a demolition permit. On July 16, with the building in imminent danger of demolition, the Phoenix Historic Preservation Commission voted to establish a historic preservation overlay for the fairgrounds, opposed by the fair administrators. Interested parties formed the Arizona State Fairgrounds Stakeholders Group, led by Jim McPherson of the Arizona Preservation Foundation. The group focused on preserving the WPA building for adaptive reuse. It evolved into a group that wanted to preserve, revitalize, and enhance the entire fairgrounds. The stakeholders consisted of state legislators, nearby residents, preservation professionals, artists, interior designers, a former Phoenix planning director, representatives from the state fair, and historic preservation officers from the city and state. (Courtesy of Phil Allsopp.)

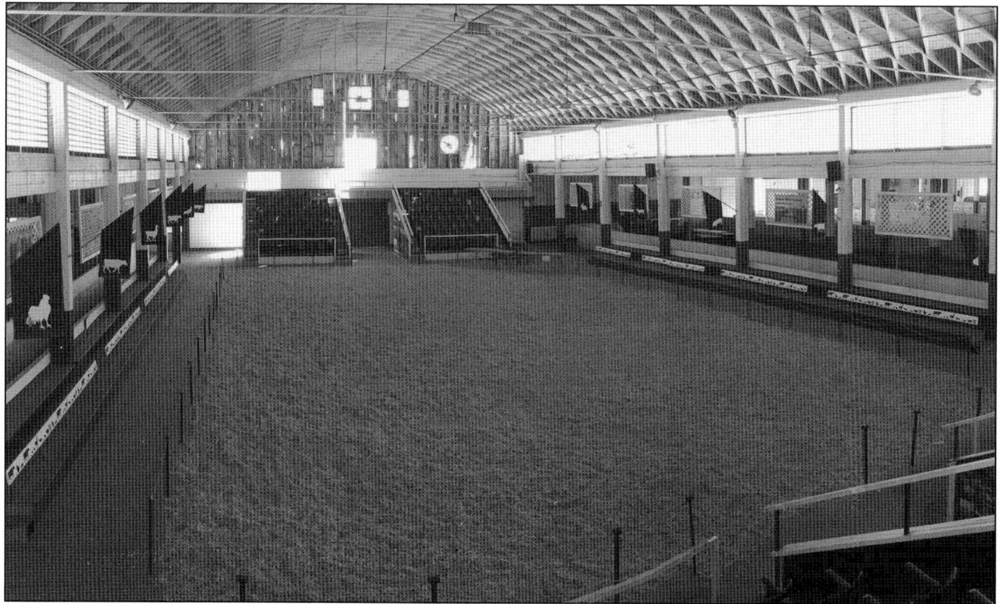

To further enhance the building knowledge the stakeholders group was amassing, team member Dr. Lauren Allsopp worked in the spring of 2015 with students from her historic preservation class at Arizona State University to write historic structure reports about the buildings on the fairgrounds, such as the cattle barns. Each report delved into a building's history and described materials used in its construction. The focus was an assessment of current conditions with recommendations and priorities for maintenance and upkeep. The reports were presented to an audience at the end of class. Some of the findings have been utilized by the fairgrounds staff. (Above, courtesy of Phil Allsopp; below, courtesy of Lauren Allsopp.)

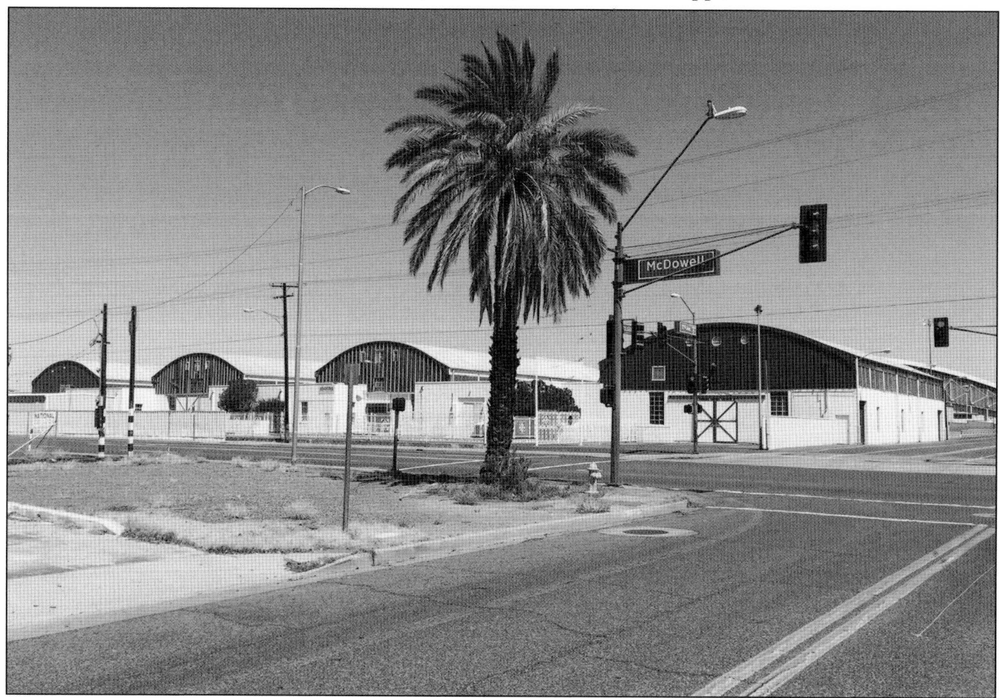

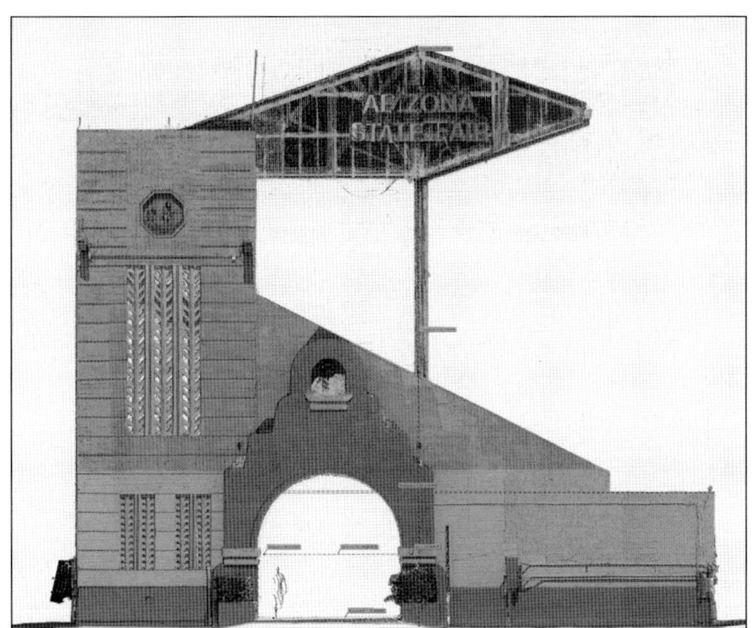

Laser scanning technology is used for capturing the features of structures in detail. The process creates point clouds, which are often hundreds of millions of points in three-dimensional space, as seen here. When the stakeholders group learned that the original blueprints for the WPA building existed, but none for B.B. Moeur Stadium, they raised money to have the structure professionally scanned for posterity. Features such as walls, floors, columns, and doors can be extracted from point clouds to create drawings and 3-D models of structures. The information can be used to direct the repair of vintage or historic buildings more accurately than blueprints created from traditional measured surveys. This process produces Historic American Building Survey–quality blueprints that will be housed in the Library of Congress. (Both, courtesy of Phil Allsopp; laser scanning by Paul Tice and ToPa3D team, Lauren Allsopp, PhD, and Phil Allsopp, DArch, RIBA and Smart Pad Living, LLC.)

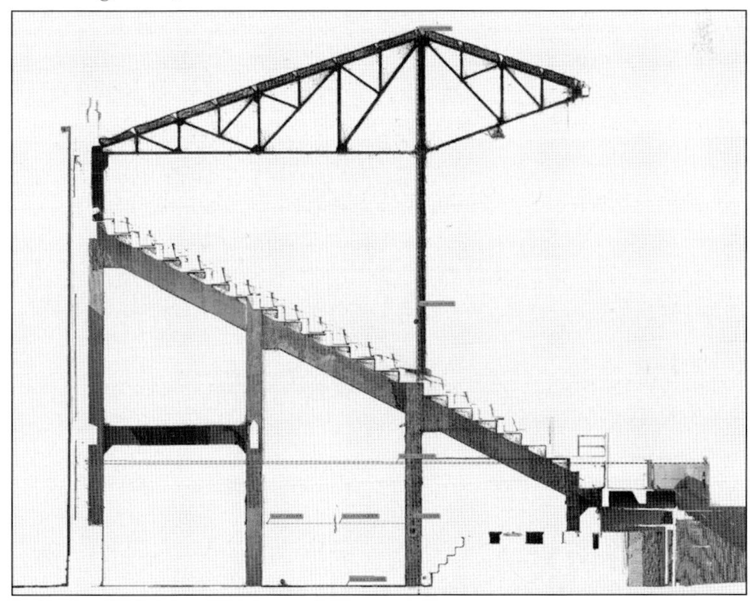

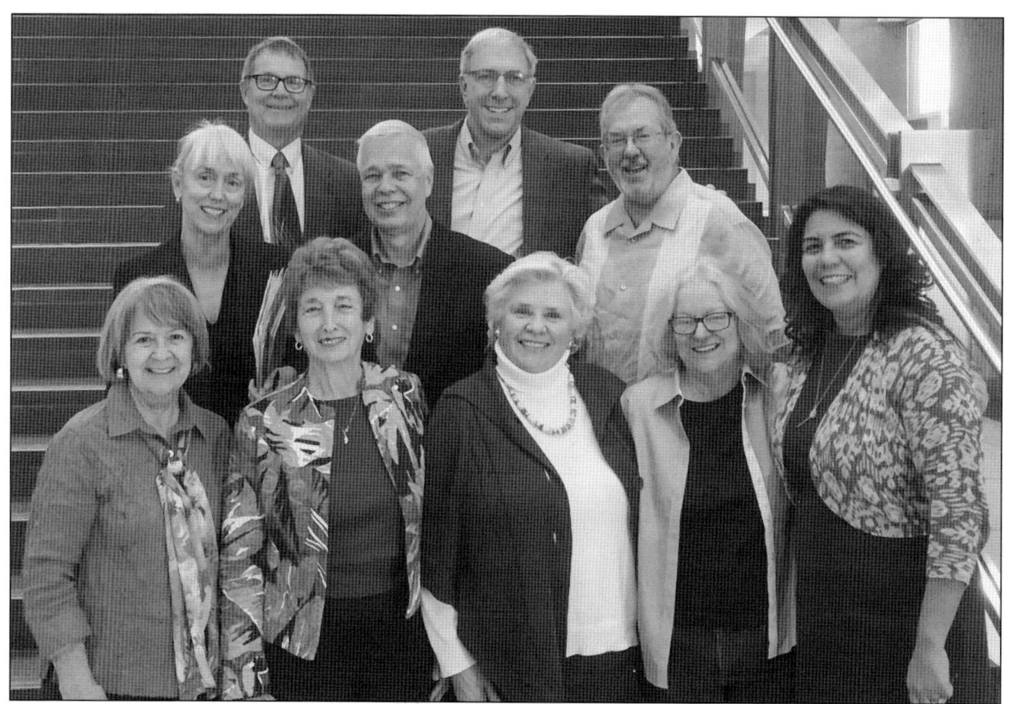

During two years of meetings, the Arizona State Fairgrounds Stakeholders Group, pictured above, generated thousands of dollars in grants (see page 51), donations, pledges, and building improvement contributions. In-kind supporters included San Tan Adobe, Swan Architects, Logan Simpson Design, MW Engineering, Viewpoint Photo, Arizona Historical Research, and volunteer cleanup groups. Members of the Arizona State Fairgrounds Stakeholders Group addressed the use of interior space in the WPA building. With support from interior designers, the stakeholders group thought the space should serve the fair by illustrating the historical nature of the building. The Arizona State Parks Historic Preservation Department was interviewed as to its space needs, and a preliminary layout was presented, seen below. (Above, courtesy of Jim McPherson, president, Arizona Preservation Foundation; below, courtesy of Debbie English, Doola Design.)

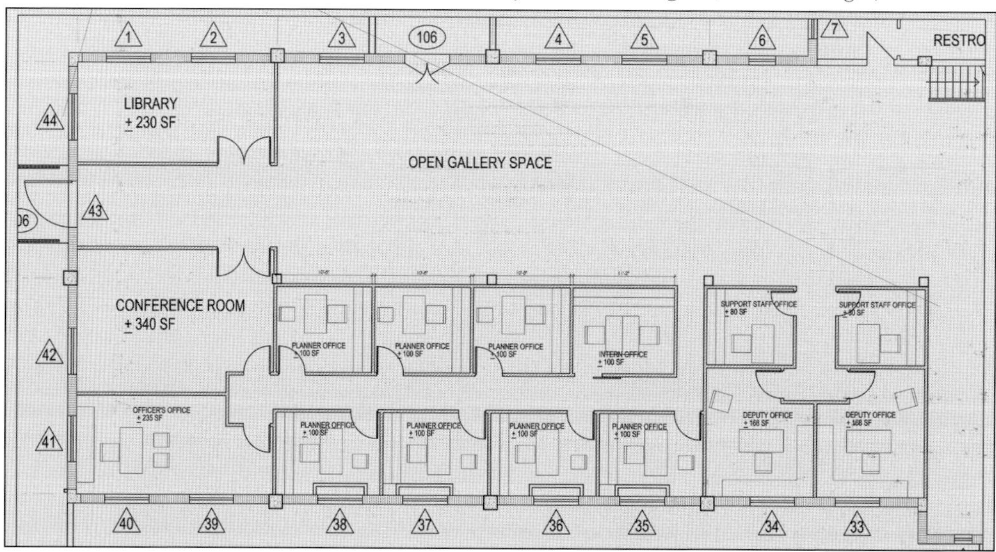

Historic Neighborhoods of Phoenix

Self-Guided Driving Tour

A Publication of the

Phoenix Historic Neighborhoods Coalition

SIXTH EDITION 2015

Printing Courtesy of PARAMOUNT PETROLEUM

Harry Hopkins once said, "Communities now find themselves in possession of improvements (resulting from the WPA) which even in 1929 they would have thought themselves presumptuous to dream of." The fair dates from 1905, but the preponderance of historic buildings on the fairgrounds are from the mid-1930s New Deal improvements. Homes in the surrounding historic districts are some of the most coveted real estate in Phoenix. Residents want to insure that the fairgrounds are returned to former glory as one of the most beautiful parks in the state. Neighborhoods want to work with the fair to add value to the physical plant. The entire property could be a testament to urban desert resiliency and sustainability while simultaneously celebrating Arizona's history and preserving the agrarian heritage of the fairgrounds. Neighbors believe that by preserving the historic buildings and adding appropriate landscaping, the fairgrounds can last another hundred years and will again be treasured as they were when first created. (Courtesy of Phoenix Historic Neighborhoods Coalition.)

Bibliography

Collins, William S. *The New Deal in Arizona*. Phoenix, AZ: Arizona State Parks Board, 1999.
———. *The Emerging Metropolis: Phoenix 1944–1973*. Phoenix, AZ: Arizona State Parks Board, 2005.
Jacobs, Henry. *The Arizona Fair*. Phoenix, AZ: Arizona State Library and Archives, 1955.
Luckingham, Bradford. *Phoenix: The History of a Southwestern Metropolis*. Tucson, AZ: University of Arizona Press, 1989.
Melikian, Robert A. *Vanishing Phoenix*. Charleston, SC: Arcadia Publishing, 2010.
Reinhold, Ruth M. *Sky Pioneering Arizona in Aviation History*. Tucson, AZ: University of Arizona Press, 1982.

About the Encanto Citizens Association

The Encanto Citizens Association was the first neighborhood association in Phoenix to preserve and protect an established geographical area. Organized in the early 1970s to defend the oldest and most picturesque neighborhoods in the city in response to the devastating threat of the Papago Freeway, the association evolved into a major force for historic preservation. After four decades of community leadership and service, the Encanto Citizens Association's signature achievements in maintaining the greater Encanto-Palmcroft neighborhood, its surroundings, and its original amenities resonate with the casual observer and with residents.

Phoenix's Greater Encanto-Palmcroft Neighborhood was named one of the ten best places to live in the United States by *Money* magazine in 2002, and this was due in part to the diligent and continuous efforts of the Encanto Citizens Association. Today, the Encanto Citizens Association continues its work on preservation of public amenities such as the southern portion of Encanto Park, the Norton House, and the Arizona State Fairgrounds.

The mission of Encanto Citizens Association is "Promoting Heritage Preservation, Education, and Contributing to the Future." More information is online at encantocitizensassociation.com.

Consistent with our mission to preserve history on a local level, this book was printed in South Carolina on American-made paper and manufactured entirely in the United States. Products carrying the accredited Forest Stewardship Council (FSC) label are printed on 100 percent FSC-certified paper.

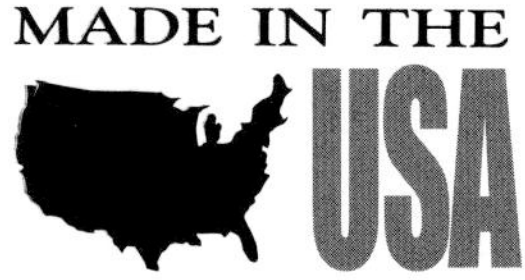